1

A
COMPANION
TO
PAUL

A COMPANION TO PAUL

Readings in Pauline Theology

MICHAEL J. TAYLOR, S.J., EDITOR

ALBA · HOUSE — NEW · YORK

SOCIETY OF ST. PAUL, 2187 VICTORY BLVD., STATEN ISLAND, NEW YORK 10314

*Library of Congress Cataloging
in Publication Data*

A Companion to Paul. Main entry under title.
Includes bibliographical references.
1. Bible. N.T. Epistles of Paul
Collected works.
I. Taylor, Michael J.
BS2651.C65   230'.08   75-19261
ISBN 0-8189-0304-X

Nihil Obstat:
James T. O'Connor, S.T.D.
Censor Librorum

Imprimatur:
+ James P. Mahoney, D.D.
Vicar General, Archdiocese of New York
July 15, 1975

*Designed, printed and bound in the United States of
America by the Fathers and Brothers of the Society of St. Paul,
2187 Victory Boulevard, Staten Island, New York, 10314,
as part of their communications apostolate.*

5 6 7 8 9 (Current Printing: first digit).

ACKNOWLEDGMENTS

Grateful acknowledgment is made to the following authors and publishers for permission to use material under their copyright:

"The Presence of God through Christ in the Church and in the World" by Jerome Murphy-O'Connor, O.P. Reprinted from *The Presence of God*, Pierre Benoit, O.P., et al, eds., Vol. 50, *Concilium* (New York: Paulist Press, 1969), pp. 107-120, with permission of the publisher.

"The Last Adam" by David M. Stanley, S.J. Reprinted from *The Way*, Vol. 6, No. 2 (April 1966), pp. 104-112, with permission of the author and the editors of *The Way* (a review of contemporary Christian spirituality) published quarterly by English Jesuits (39 Fitzjohn's Ave., London, NW 3, 5 JT, England).

"The Biblical Understanding of 'Resurrection' and 'Glorification'" by Anton Grabner-Haider. Reprinted from *The Problem of Eschatology*, E. Schillebeeckx, O.P. and B. Willems, O.P., eds., Vol. 41, *Concilium* (New York: Paulist Press, 1969), pp. 66-81, with permission of the publisher.

"The Fellowship of His Sufferings" by Barnabas Ahern, C.P. Reprinted from *New Horizons: Studies in Biblical Theology* (Notre Dame, Ind.: Fides Publishers, Inc., 1964), pp. 107-143, with permission of the publisher. This article also appeared in *Catholic Biblical Quarterly*, Vol. 22, pp. 1-32, and is reprinted with the permission of the *CBQ* publisher also.

"The Church's Assimilation of the Easter Mystery" is reprinted from *The Resurrection, a Biblical Study* by F. X. Durrwell,

INTRODUCTION

Paul is perhaps the best known of the early Christian preachers. Few doubt that after Jesus he was the most important and controversial figure in the early Church. And quite remarkably this intensely active, frequently misunderstood missionary has left us a substantial corpus of writings; his letters in fact make up about one-fourth of the New Testament. Though very personal they are not merely private letters of interest only to students and historians of religion. They are official Apostolic correspondence, directed to a variety of immediate and urgent problems confronting some of the earliest established congregations in the Christian Church. For that reason they afford a candid glimpse into the make-up of these congregations, the nature of the gospel preached to them, and the character of the man "appointed by Jesus Christ and God the Father" (Gal 1:1) to preach it. Indirectly they provide information about pre-Pauline Christianity and tell us about the shape this new faith took from the time of his conversion to his death three and a half decades after the Crucifixion.

In his writings Paul calls himself a "Hebrew of Hebrews," trained in the strict Pharisaic tradition. He is thus reminding us that along with other religious convictions he especially saw oral law as the perfect expression of God's will for men. He had done his best to destroy the new Christian sect which seemed to him to compromise many of the religious values of Judaism and to deny the importance and necessity of the Jewish legal tradition. Yet when he came to believe in Christ, he became an uncompromising adversary of those who would continue that same legal tradition in Christianity. More than any of the early Christian preachers Paul came clearly to believe that it is not legal tradition, not religious attitudes or systems that have power to save, but only Jesus. No more Christo-centric writer or documents can be found anywhere in early Christianity. No wonder the letters and history of Paul written and lived in a time when Christianity was suffering through relational changes with Judaism are often polemical and controversial.

But despite the often controversial character of Paul's works they are regarded as important source material for our knowledge of early Christianity. For long years the Pauline corpus has numbered fourteen letters, but currently his authorship of all fourteen is much disputed. *The Epistle to the Hebrews*, for example, is no longer generally considered to be Pauline, and the relatively non-Pauline vocabulary and sophisticated ecclesial structure manifest in *The Pastoral Epistles* (*I Timothy, II Timothy, Titus*) lead some scholars to doubt their authenticity as well. *Colossians* and *Ephesians* are less disputed but still questioned as authentically Pauline by many. Still most scholars, while excluding *The Epistle to the Hebrews* as a Pauline text, would include the *Colossians, Ephesians,* and *Pastoral* letters in the Pauline corpus. These latter, though possibly not Pauline in a personal sense, are seen by many to be at least reflective of the teaching of Paul, having developed from a "school" or tradition theologically rooted in his distinctive understanding of the gospel. And in view of the controversy over Pauline authenticity it should perhaps be noted that citations found in the topical essays in this volume referring to *Colossians, Ephesians,* and *The Pastorals,* should be understood in the light of this dispute and the reader is reminded that citations to these epistles could possibly be reflective of a "developed" form of Paul, if not precisely illustrating his own personal thought and writing.

This book is an anthology of topical readings providing examples of modern critical studies on questions that occur in Paul's writings. Because of the richness and complexity of his correspondence such selections could be multiplied of course. And specialists will think of other essays which, were they allowed a say in the selection, would have been included. But choices and reasonable limits had to be made and they were usually made on the grounds that the particular essay chosen, as well as addressing itself to an important Pauline question, did so in a way that joined acceptable scholarship with an easier readability and clarity of expression than is normally found in essays on the subject.[1] Paul's writings are a fund of striking formulations of Christian faith, begging for explanation and commentary; unfortunately professional biblical scholars often take up the task of explaining Paul with a scientific depth of treatment the ordinary reader finds almost impossible to follow. Looking to scholars to provide coherent commentary on a Pauline problem with some effort to relate the problem to the overall thought of Paul, one can experience more often than not disappointment and frustration. It certainly must be admitted that specific difficulties abound and each of them demands attention in scholarly detail. But a discussion of problems in some kind of perspective would also seem to merit attention. Otherwise the reader loses a sense of the whole in the study of the parts. Accordingly, this collection of essays is offered as a way a student of Paul can be given a critical *and* understandable explanation of the more important questions that come up in his correspondence, but in a manner that tries to help the reader understand a little more clearly the overall meaning of Paul for his own time as well as ours.

The authors are recognized by their colleagues to be respected interpreters of Paul; in fact their contributions have received favorable comment from many Pauline scholars. The pieces submitted here have been judged to be significant and informative steps toward the understanding of some of the big Pauline problems. No claim is made that these essays exhaust all the main Pauline topics or that the last words on the subject have been said; but it can be stated that a fair number of the difficult and recurring problems are treated here and that the words said about

---

1 It should be noted that in an effort to provide the reader with as few distractions as possible, these essays contain only the footnotes essential to an understanding of the topic under discussion. For the author's complete footnote references the original articles should be consulted.

them have proved to be helpful to many.

For the Christian reader moreover these essays provide another desirable dimension in that they are written by scholars who approach their subject as believers. The Christian biblical theologian normally is not content merely with the interpretation of individual passages in their immediate context (i.e., with exegesis). Even though he uses the same tools of interpretation that scholars of ancient literary forms and historians of religion use, he differs in that he is convinced that when he studies Paul he is confronting the inspired word of God. He forms his analysis of Pauline topics on the fundamental presupposition that the Pauline corpus is a dialogue between God and men and women of faith. His comments, therefore, seek to relate Paul's understanding of Christian faith in a way that is relevant and meaningful for the faith of Christians today.

But nothing scholars say by way of probing and clarification, analysis and attempted synthesis can substitute for reading and re-reading the words of Paul himself. Like all the biblical authors he is his own best expositor and interpreter. For those who seek an encounter with Christ analogous to that of Paul or a deeper understanding of an already experienced encounter, the final exhortation can only be to take up and read the works of Paul and see there what Christian conversion meant to this man of inspiration and faith. If the topical essays in this book help to open up some of the meaning of Paul's personal encounter with Christ and prompt the reader to return again and often to the text of Paul to examine that encounter first hand, this volume will have fulfilled its purpose as a companion to Paul.

Michael J. Taylor, S.J.

CONTENTS

PAUL'S UNDERSTANDING OF CHRIST AS THE PERSONAL PRESENCE OF GOD IN THE WORLD

Jerome Murphy-O'Connor, O.P.

The ambiguities and nuances of the concept of "presence" have been thrown into relief by contemporary concern with community and interpersonal relations. Clarity demands that we distinguish between physical and personal presence. Both are based on some form of communication, but while any direct action is sufficient to create the first type, mutual self-revelation is the indispensable and only condition of the second. Lovers are permanently present to each other in a personal way, even when separated in place and time.

The problem of God's presence, therefore, can be considered on two different levels. The traditional category of "omnipresence" is concerned with divine presence on the physical level. God is present everywhere because, as first cause, he influences all things directly. True as it is, this concept of the divine presence exercises little attraction today. In a world which is passing from the ontological to the functional period of its history the question "Does God exist?" really means: "Can God be personally present to me as a friend?" Neither the five ways of St. Thomas nor the numerous affirmations of both the Old and New Testaments concerning God's omnipresence constitute an adequate answer to this question. They do convey a valid insight, but it is on a different level to that on which the question is posed. Nor is it sufficient to try to adapt the "omnipresence" answer to the question by saying that once God's physical presence is recognized it becomes personal presence. Such an effort reveals a complete misunderstanding of the nature of personal presence in which there is much that transcends the purely intellectual dimension.

In order to appreciate the full implications of the crucial question "Can God be personally present to me?" it must be recognized that it embodies a more fundamental query: "Has God offered his friendship to men?" These two questions command the structure of this inquiry into St. Paul's understanding of God's personal presence. The first part examines the ontological possibility of this presence in terms of the apostle's view of Christ as the self-revealing invitation of the Father. For the contemporaries of Jesus, contact with him created the ontic possibility of God's personal presence, since in his person he represented God's openness even to those who had repudiated his friendship through sin. But how was this ontic possibility to be realized in the post-paschal period? Paul does not formulate this question explicitly, but the nature of his mission obliged him to give thought to the problem of communicating his faith. Hence the second part of this article endeavors to draw together those texts which suggest that the offer of God's presence only becomes an ontic possibility if Christians are, collectively and individually, other Christs. Particularly in this second part we can find, I think, some insights that will throw light on the problems presently confronting the Church.

Jesus Christ: The Invitation of the Father

The center of Paul's teaching is Christ. "Everything converges on this point; thence everything proceeds, and thither everything returns."[1] Of course, this is not to say that God is ignored. In the dogmatic part of Romans, for example, he is mentioned three times more frequently than Christ. For Paul theology and christology are one, because everything he wrote is, in one form or another, a working out of his fundamental intuition that God has revealed himself in Christ.

Personal presence is a mutual relationship based on a sign in which one person reveals himself to the other. Unless the sign (a

---

1 F. Prat, *La théologie de saint Paul II* (Paris, 1938), p. 14.

word or gesture) is given and unless the other responds with a similar openness, there may be physical presence of one to the other, but on the personal level there is nothing, an absence. In establishing this relationship one of the parties must take the initiative. Certain parts of the Old Testament seem to imply that man must take the first step in reestablishing a relationship with God that had been broken by sin, but Jeremiah and Ezekiel recognized that this was impossible (Jr: 31, 18; 31-34; Ezk 37: 14, 26). Paul shares their point of view. His conception of unredeemed man reveals the mode of being proper to the "old man" to be exclusively egocentric. If left to himself man would never open himself to God. Hence Paul continually emphasizes that the initiative is taken by the Father. It is not man who from his misery appeals to God, but God who motivated by love calls men to himself (2 Th 2:13; etc.). This love is not drawn by anything in man, because God has to make him worthy of his call (2 Th 1:11).

Paul does not speculate on how this is possible. All his attention is concentrated in the mode of God's self-revelation. In order to convince men of his openness to them, God brought himself within the orbit of their experience in such a way that this love for them became almost tangible. Hence, "God sent his Son, born of a woman" (Gal 4:4; Rm 8:3); "God shows his love for us in that while we were yet sinners Christ died for us" (Rm 5:8). No longer are God's power and wisdom revealed through an action such as the giving of the law on Sinai, but his love is made manifest in the sending of a person, Jesus Christ. The pastoral epistles may be Deutero-Pauline, but in certain instances they represent a homogeneous development of Pauline insights. This is certainly the case when Christ is presented as "the manifestation of the goodness and loving kindness of God" (Tt 3:4). Here the element of invitation implicit in Paul's formulations is brought clearly to the fore.

Jesus is not called "God" in the more primitive strata of the New Testament. Only toward the end of the first century did the title come into frequent usage. The earliest probable instance occurs in the Pauline epistles: "Of their race [i.e., the Israelites] is the Christ according to the flesh, who is over all, God blessed forever" (Rm 9:5).[2] R. Brown has suggested that two closely related factors contributed to this development.[3] The majority of the texts which call Jesus "God" originally had a liturgical *Sitz im Leben;* praise of Jesus in a context dedicated to the praise of God tended to narrow the gap between the two. Moreover, as the first Christians penetrated the mystery of Jesus they gradually realized how much of himself God had revealed in his Son, and this led to a broadening of the title "God" to include Father and Son.

This awareness of Christ's unique relationship to the Father is particularly marked in the christological hymn of Colossians 1:15-20. For our purpose it is irrelevant whether the hymn is Pauline or not; its use by the apostle is sufficient evidence that the ideas it embodies harmonized with his own patterns of thought. The key insight of the hymn is the identification of Christ with Wisdom. Paul had already applied sapiential categories to Christ, but had not fully exploited their possibilities. The sapiential texts which speak of the creative wisdom of God are best understood as expressions of awe at the thought of the unique creator of so many marvels. This view of reality is essentially optimistic. The world is not a frightening place into which man is thrown as into a sea of alien being. It is a place of wonder and beauty, because it is viewed in a perspective that gives it unity, meaning and purpose. For the sapiential writers this perspective was given by Wisdom; for the author of the hymn it is provided by Christ.

However, there is no parallel in the sapiential literature to the assertion of the hymn that Christ embodies the finality of the cosmos ("All things ... to him have been created"—Col 1:17). Acceptance of this formulation marks an evolution in Paul's thought, which becomes evident if we compare 1 Corinthians

---

2 This text is a famous crux, and there is no unanimity on its interpretation. At most it can be said that the punctuation adopted here does the least violence to grammar and New Testament usage.

3 R. Brown, "Does the New Testament Call Jesus God?" in *Theol. Studies* 26 (1965), pp. 545-73.

8:6: "For us [there is but] one God, the Father, from whom [come] all things, and to whom we [go]; and one Lord, Jesus Christ, through whom [come] all things, and through whom we [go]." Here *God* is the Alpha and Omega of everything that exists (cf. Is 44:6)—a commonplace in any theistic understanding of the world.

How is this to be reconciled with the role attributed to Christ by the hymn? One possibility is to see the hymn as an implicit affirmation of the divinity of Christ. This approach would give full value to the assertion that Christ is "the image of the invisible God" (Col 1:15). A second possibility which does not exclude the first, and which may be more probable if the hymn is pre-Pauline, is to see Christ as the perfect fulfillment of God's design for his creation, because in him God and man are joined in total harmony. This second interpretation would seem to be confirmed by the second strophe where Stoic and sapiential categories are combined, because there we see that it is by reconciling a sin-divided cosmos through his Son that God causes it to dwell in Christ (Col 1:19-20). Thus, in addition to being God's invitation to the world, Christ also manifests the result of the acceptance of that invitation; the pristine harmony of the cosmos is restored.

In thus describing the reconciliation of all things as an already accomplished fact, Paul speaks with the certitude of optimism (compare the more realistic view of Rom 8:20-21). The idea of material realities as being in need of reconciliation is totally foreign to us, but Paul in harmony with the Old Testament writers viewed all created reality in a single perspective. In sinning, man upsets the delicate balance of the whole, and in certain cases he distorts the intrinsic finality of material entities (cf. Lv 26:33-35). It is he who creates the need for reconciliation, and the work of reconciliation is focused in and through him. By responding to God's invitation in Christ, man contributes to the restoration of the whole. In a sense he re-creates material reality. He draws everything he touches into his own theocentric finality. This insight into man's role as a prolongation of that of Christ leads naturally into the second part of this study.

The Whole Christ

For all the clarity of his awareness of Christ as the self-revealing invitation of the Father, Paul never calls him the Word, as does St. John. Christ is the Word for those who experience him, who are fully conscious of who he is and what he means. But Paul's life was dedicated to those who did not know Christ, and his mission was to ensure the presence of Christ among them. Genuine confrontation with Christ is the only road to faith and thus to the presence of God. Faith, however, involves a literally appalling decision. The demand implicit in the preaching is that one accept Jesus Christ as totally similar to us (Jesus the man) and at the same time as totally "other" (the risen Christ, the Savior). There is no security here, nothing the intellect can firmly grasp. From any purely human point of view it is simply "a stumbling block to Jews and folly to Gentiles" (1 Cor 1:23). One cannot even attach oneself to Jesus, because the climax of the decision is baptism into his *death* (Rm 6:3). Nothing human can adequately motivate this decision. Preaching can only bring man to the threshold. Its function is limited to clarifying the confrontation, but this confrontation with Christ can only take place when the Word is proposed in such a way as to force man to consider two radically different planes of experience ("Jesus" and "Christ") *together*. "Plausible words of wisdom" (1 Cor 2:4) —i.e. persuasive arguments—are totally inadequate because they eradicate the element of "otherness" that is of the very nature of this confrontation. Simple affirmation is no better: "The kingdom of God does not come to be through words, but through power" (1 Cor 4:20). Genuine faith "does not rest in the wisdom of men but in the power of God" (1 Cor 2:5). This power is released by the context in or from which the Word is spoken, and which makes the element of "otherness" inescapable. Paul never formally defines this context, but various indications scattered throughout his letters suggest that it is the believing community.

Of the community at Corinth Paul says, "You yourselves are our letter of recommendation written on your hearts to be read and known by all men; and you show that you are a letter of

Christ delivered by us, written not with ink but with the spirit
of the living God, not on tablets of stone but on tablets of human
hearts" (2 Cor 3:2-3). Knowing the unhappy situation of the
church at Corinth, one might suspect a touch of irony here, but
even if Paul is speaking on the level of possibility, we have here
an important insight into the role of the Christian community.
Its way of life should be an extension of the invitation embodied
in Christ. In Philippians this is defined as "a holding forth of the
Word of life" (Ph 2:16). It is clear from the context that it is
not a question of verbal proclamation. The influence of the
believers, that which makes them "shine as lights in the world",
is the quality of their lives. It would be an oversimplification to
say that their obedience enhances the credibility of the Word,
and that this credibility is its power. The Christian life lived in
its fullness produces an emotional shock on the uncommitted
observer similar to that produced by the resurrection on the first
disciples. It attests that the believers are no longer enmeshed in
the limitations that weigh upon him, that they have found a
source of life and strength whose need he now experiences
more keenly than ever before. Thus a receptivity to the Word
is generated because it is demanded as an explanation. Hence it is
natural to find Paul thanking the Philippians for their "partner-
ship (*koinonia*) in the spreading of the Gospel" (Ph 1:5).

The apostle never said anything like this to the Corinthians.
On the contrary he had to admonish them: "Strive not to be an
obstacle either to Jews or to Greeks or to the Church of God,
just as I, for my part, render service to all in everything. I seek
not what benefits myself but what benefits everyone else, so that
they may be saved. Become imitators of me, just as I am an
imitator of Christ" (1 Cor 10:31-11:1). This text is important
because it introduces the themes of "obstacle" and "imitation".
We see here that a community can be a barrier to faith. Most
frequently this theme is referred to the person of Paul. When
he speaks of the possibility of his being an obstacle to the Word
(1 Cor 9:12; 2 Cor 6:3; 11:7), what is uppermost in his mind is
the question of his motivation. The impact of his words would be
greatly diminished were there reason to suspect that he was

acting from any motive other than the need to communicate the tremendous experience he has undergone in his encounter with Christ (2 Cor 5:14). Impeccable behavior stemming from a lesser motive would not ring true. His sensitivity on this point is so delicate that he has no need to speak of the adverse impact of un-Christian behavior. Despite its seeming arrogance, the exhortation "Become imitators of me" is only the other side of the same coin. Unless the apostle has truly "put on Christ" (Gal 3:7), unless he speaks as another Christ, he is incapable of confronting his hearers with Christ.

In Paul's theology the factor that enables the believer and the community to re-present Christ is the presence of the Spirit; both are temples in which the Spirit dwells (1 Cor 3:16-17; 6:19). This is not a personal presence. Through the action of the Spirit God empowers man to realize the possibilities opened to humanity by Christ. This is the ultimate source of the quality of "otherness" that should distinguish Christians both collectively and individually. This quality of "otherness" is sanctity, or transcendence made manifest. It is impossible to define its component elements adequately, but Paul touches on one aspect of the problem when he speaks of the eucharist at Corinth.

Ideally the eucharistic assembly should be a proclamation of the Lord's death (1 Cor 11:26). It should be a visible sign that God "loved us and sent his Son to be the expiation for our sins" (1 Jn 4:10). Paul's attention is focused primarily on the liturgical assembly as realizing the Father's invitation to personal presence, not on the presence of Christ in the eucharist. The two aspects are intimately related, but the latter does not automatically imply the former, as Paul emphasizes: "When you meet together, it is not the Lord's supper that you eat, for in eating each one goes ahead with his own meal, and one is hungry and another is drunk" (1 Cor 11:20-21). The behavior of the Corinthians had nullified the revelatory character of the meal, so that Paul could say without equivocation that the meal the Corinthians ate subjectively was not the Lord's supper. Many unsuccessful attempts have been made to diminish the impact of this statement, but it is clear that for the apostle external appearances affect an essential dimension of the liturgical celebration, although not, of course, affecting the reality of the Lord's sacramental Presence. In order to understand this we must recollect that the reconciliation effected by the death of Christ has both a vertical and a horizontal dimension: man is reconciled with God and with his fellow men. These cannot be separated because one is the condition of the other. Man's being is essentially social. His need for others and his dependence on them are so much a part of the structure of his being that he cannot develop normally as a person without them. Yet aggressiveness is equally a feature of human nature. Man feels threatened by the other and instinctively builds psychic, and even physical, defenses against intimacy. This tension—man needs to trust and yet he cannot—is perhaps the most painful evidence of his fallen state.

It is against this background that Paul's statement stands out in clearest relief. The eucharist is the sacrament of the reconciliation effected by Christ and those who participate in it should manifest that this tension has *in fact* been resolved. A community in which complete peace and mutual confidence reign contrasts vividly with its environment; it has the quality of "otherness" that is the only appropriate setting for the Word. The eucharistic assembly is a contradiction in terms unless the participants are in fact reconciled with each other. Yet it should not be overlooked that at the same time the eucharist has a role to play in the creation of that union, since it includes both the vertical and horizontal dimensions: "The bread which we break, is it not communion (*koinonia*) in the body of Christ?" (1 Cor 10:26). It prolongs and intensifies the effects of baptism, whose social dimension is also strongly marked in the epistles: "You have put on the new man ... *where* there can be no distinction between Greek and Jew, circumcised and uncircumcised, barbarian, Scythian, slave, freeman, but Christ is all, and in all" (Col 3:10-11). The "new man" is the whole Christ, head and members.

In the texts discussed above, Paul gives equal emphasis to the community and to the individual. Both can be signs or anti-signs. As signs they are christological. If the Word spoken by the individual effects a real confrontation with Christ, it is because he is another Christ. If the community projects the Word of life, it is because it truly is the body of Christ. In both cases Paul's thought moves on the phenomenological level. He has in mind a perceptible quality that has the effect of transforming the causal presence of God in preaching and the liturgy into the ontic possibility of his personal presence. If, as we have seen, Christ is *the* invitation to this presence, he is also the paradigm of man's response. This appears most clearly in the "new Adam" texts where the obedience of the last Adam is contrasted with the disobedience of the first Adam (Rm 5:12-21).

These two figures represent the two strains of man's collective and individual heritage. In the present they are in tension, and the reality of the ontic possibility of God's presence is conditioned by the extent to which the influence of Christ prevails over that of Adam. Thus the image of Christ in the individual or the community is never perfect. A more perfect representation is always possible. "We all, with unveiled face reflecting the glory of the Lord, are being changed from glory to glory" (2 Cor 3:18). After his experience of God on Sinai, Moses' face was so radiant with reflected glory that he had to keep it veiled from his fellow Israelites. But this brightness, like the covenant it symbolized, was only transitory. The new covenant, however, is symbolized by the glory of Christ. Because believers are formed in the image of Christ (Rm 8:29) they are his glory. In both the Old and New Testaments, "glory" denotes a visible, effective manifestation of God. Just as Christ mediated the Father to men, so do the believers mediate Christ to a generation that never knew him in the flesh. By "from glory to glory" Paul simply means that the image of Christ in the believer should become progressively more manifest. It would be false to the apostle's essential realism to understand the image of Christ in a mystical or static sense. To be transformed means to have "the mind of Christ" (1 Cor 2:16; Ph 2:5; Rm 15:5), and, as Bultmann has pointed out, "mind" in these contexts might almost be rendered by "character"—which is formed and made manifest in one's way of being.

This dynamic element is more evident in a second text: "And

his gifts were that some should be apostles, some prophets, some evangelists . . . for the building up of the body of Christ, until we all, together, come to unity in faith and knowledge of the Son of God, and constitute the perfect man, fully mature, who realizes the plenitude of Christ" (Ep 4:11-13). The conciseness and the profundity of this text make it difficult to translate, and although another hand played a major role in the formulation of Ephesians, the thought is fundamentally that of Paul. As in 2 Corinthians, we are concerned with a process of becoming. Until the end of time the body of Christ can be built up both intensively and extensively. By striving together toward ever more perfect unity in commitment and action, the believers ("the new man") progressively bring into being "the perfect man", who is the whole Christ in his plenitude.

Until this final moment the life of the Church is shrouded in the same ambiguity that characterized the earthly life of Jesus. In neither case is God's invitation so clear and forceful as to *demand* acceptance. This would be contrary to the concept of personal presence. Friendship is not demanded. The self is revealed in hope and never all at once. Even on the human level, mystery surrounds the reaction to the initial sign. One may rationalize it to a certain extent but the ultimate answer always escapes us. There is inevitably an element of blind trust, or faith. We should expect, therefore, to discover the same basic structure in the creator's dealings with his creatures. In this case, however, the problem is complicated by the fact that the offer of friendship is made indirectly. Everything hinges on the credibility of the intermediary. Paul was intensely conscious of this, and one has the strong impression that he would agree with those who blame Christians for the death or absence of God. It is not so much that Christians, through an exaggerated interest in conceptualization, have created a false image of God, but that they have imagined they could convey God's invitation to personal presence by words alone.

For Paul the reiteration of the invitation must take the form of a re-presentation. As the original invitation (Christ) was living and personal, so must be its repetition. Words are indispensable, but their sole function is clarification. They are meaningless unless they are in response to the questions generated by the contact of two personalities. Divorced from the context of the whole Christ, they only serve to mystify. The true sense of mystery can only be engendered by an element of transcendence in the believing community, an "otherness" in the bearing of its members. Unless believers are so transformed by the Spirit of Christ (Rm 8:9-10) that the word "Father" comes naturally to their lips from something deep within them, and that they in consequence live as other Christs and so constitute the whole Christ, God's invitation to friendship is not a credible option. The offer can be nullified by those who pride themselves on having accepted it. In a word, the personal presence of God in the world depends on the fragile ambiguous sign he has chosen, the Church. When men respond to this sign they can see the hand of God in events and in material reality, and in their response the word is transformed.

CHRIST, THE LAST ADAM

David Stanley, S.J.

The Christian message of salvation acquired its character as "good news" from the experience of the risen Christ, as the "original eyewitnesses" (Lk 1:2) were privileged to enjoy. This experience, to which the first disciples responded by the commitment of Christian faith, resulted in the acquisition of a totally new knowledge of Jesus Christ, the significance of his earthly life, and above all, of his death. To interpret and articulate their new found belief, the apostolic college under the guidance of Peter had recourse to the Scriptures, the sacred literature of Israel, finding there certain images and themes, through which God's gracious, saving acts performed for the chosen people had been expressed.

Accordingly, in the summaries of the primitive preaching recorded in the Acts of the Apostles, we find various historical figures from Israel's past, and certain key events in her experience of God's activity on her behalf, employed by the earlier Christian evangelists in order to set forth the significance of Jesus' redemptive work. He is depicted as the answer to the divine promise made of old to Abraham (Ac 3:25-26). His exaltation at God's right hand is proclaimed as the accomplishment of the dynastic oracle, given by Nathan the prophet in God's name to David, (Ac 2:30-31; 13:23) that a son of his royal line should inherit his throne forever. In his speech before the Sanhedrin, Stephen the proto-martyr interprets Old Testament history in the light of the death and resurrection of Christ, and thereby discovers a series of famous Israelites, who may serve as types of the crucified and risen Lord Jesus. In addition to

Abraham, there is Joseph, Moses, and especially the prophets (Ac 7:2-8, 9-16, 17-40, 52).

One of the most prominent themes in the christology of the apostolic age was that of the suffering and glorified Servant of God, of whom the second Isaiah had sung so poignantly and mysteriously. The kerygma of the Jerusalem community had first applied this motif to Jesus as the Servant glorified (Is 52: 13) by the God of the patriarchs (Ac 3:13) through his resurrection and ascension (Ac 3:26). Jesus was regarded as the Servant against whom Herod and Pilate had, with the collaboration of Jews and Romans, conspired and contrived to execute (Ac 4:27-28). The earliest inspired authors of the gospels, in their turn, expressed Jesus' prediction of his sufferings and death in terms of the Isaian suffering Servant (cf. Mk 8:31; 9:31; 10: 33-34).

Paul and the Themes of Creation

When we turn to the writings of Paul, whose initial experience of the risen Christ differed notably from that of the twelve, who had been favored with a close association with Jesus during his public ministry, we soon discover that his approach to the Christian mystery is unique. Paul's conversion by the Damascus road had brought him face to face with the exalted Lord, who stood revealed to him as Son of God (Gal 1:16). It was only in response to his query of amazement, "Who are you, Lord?", that Paul learned to identify this celestial, divine person with the humble, despised rabbi Jesus of Nazareth (Ac 9:5). From his reminiscences of this extraordinary event, we see Paul attempting to describe its wholly unprecedented character by comparing it with God's creation of light (Gn 1:3) 'because the God who said, Let light shine out of darkness (is he) who caused light to shine in our innermost self to impart the illuminating knowledge of the divine glory in the face of Christ' (2 Cor 4:6).

Indeed, Paul appears to have been the first Christian theologian to make use of the early chapters of Genesis to body forth his very personal insight into the mystery of Christ. The teaching of our Lord himself, reported in the gospels, provides little precedent for the use of these images and motifs. Jesus' unequivocal prohibition of divorce (Mk 10:6-7; Mt 19:4-5) constitutes his single recorded reference to the opening chapters of Genesis. Only rarely too do the prophetic writings of the Old Testament allude to the creation in presenting Israel's hopes of the eschatological salvation. The final conversion of God's people was thought of as demanding a creative act of God (Jr 31:22). The second Isaiah depicted the hoped-for return from the Babylonian exile as a new creation (Is 43:17-18). The third Isaiah at a later date poetically described God's definitive saving action as the creation of a new sky and a new earth (Is 65:17; 66:22-23). It is only in late Judaism that the figure of Adam is used as a vehicle of theological teaching by certain of the sapiential writers (Si 17:1ff; 49:16; Ws 2:23-24; 9:2-3; 10:1).

We obtain a hint from the resumes of Paul's preaching to pagans in Acts, which may partly explain his highly original preference for these themes of creation. When Paul preached to Jewish audiences, he was accustomed to introduce his version of the gospel with a review of Israel's history (Ac 13:16-25). In addressing gentiles, however, he had to begin with the doctrine of the one true God. Thus at Lystra Paul asserts that the God of Israel is the sole source of all creation, the one "who made sky and earth and sea and everything in them." He alone regulates, by his loving providence over mankind, the natural cycle of the seasons, as he also directs human history in accordance with his own designs (Ac 14:15-17). At Athens Paul repeats the truth that Yahweh is "the God who made the earth and everything in it," "the one who gives to all life and breath and everything," who "made from a single common origin the whole race of mankind . . ." (Ac 17:24-26). The latter part of this citation probably contains an illusion to Adam, who as common parent gave to the human race its basic unity.

The antithesis Adam-Christ

The first appearance of what has come to be regarded as Paul's characteristic presentation of Christ's redemptive work appears in 1 Corinthians, a letter from the middle years of his literary activity. Of the several pastoral problems to which Paul addresses himself here, the most important undoubtedly was the hesitation, on the part of certain members of the Corinthian community, in accepting the crucial doctrine of the eschatological resurrection of the just. This doubt the Corinthians appeared to have combined, inconsistently enough, with an orthodox faith in the resurrection of Christ himself; and Paul was quick to point out that a denial of the resurrection of those "who have died in Christ" was tantamount to a denial of one of the central events announced by the traditional Christian gospel (1 Cor 15:3-4). What these wavering Corinthian converts did not grasp, it appears, was the social character of our Lord's death and resurrection. Jesus did not die as an isolated individual: he involved mankind in his death; or rather, he created the possibility of our involvement in his death. As Paul would later write to Corinth, "One died for all; therefore all have died" (2 Cor 5:4).

To counter the doubts in the Corinthian Christians concerning their personal involvement in Christ's resurrection, Paul first declares that "Christ has been raised from death as the first fruits of those who have fallen asleep" (1 Cor 15:20). His reference is to the ancient ceremonial dedication of the first fruits prescribed in the Mosaic Law (Lv 23:10-14). This act constituted a solemn obligation for Israel, since it was an acknowledgement of God's exclusive ownership of the land and its produce. At the same time, this oblation of the first fruits was in effect the consecration of the whole harvest to Yahweh. Paul was aware that this significant ritual had been carried out in the Temple on the very day when Jesus rose from death. The risen Lord is rightly called "first fruits of those who have fallen asleep," not merely because he has initiated the universal resurrection of the just, but also because his own glorified humanity will one day effectively realize in us the final object of Christian faith and hope.

At this stage of his argument Paul introduces Adam for the first time in his letters. "For since through a man (came) death, so also through a man (will come) resurrection of the dead. For just as in Adam all die, so also in Christ all will be brought to life" (1 Cor 15:21-22).

To appreciate the scope of the antithesis which Paul here sets up between Adam, the sinful parent of the human race, and Jesus Christ, "who was handed over for our sins and raised for our justification" (Rm 4:25), we must recall the comprehensive or global character of the biblical concept of death. When, as here, Paul speaks of death in the context of sin, the term does not connote merely physical death. It includes also what we seek to express by the phrases spiritual death (grave sin), and eschatological death (eternal punishment). The total reality of death for the Old Testament writers comprised in fact complete and final separation from the living God of Israel. Such indeed was the destructive effect of Adam's sin upon the entire human family, as Paul will declare in a later letter (Rm 5:12ff). The purpose of Christ's resurrection then was to undo the baleful influence of Adam upon mankind. The life which he wills to bestow upon all, who are to be united with him by their own glorious resurrection, is life in the fullest sense. It is eternal life, indeed, and its communication will affect the Christian even on the material side of his person. To assert in its fulness the Christian belief in the efficacy of Jesus' redemptive resurrection, Paul says equivalently, it is not sufficient merely to accept the greek philosophical argument for the soul's immortality.

Paul returns to the contrast between Adam and Christ somewhat later in this same chapter, in order to expand upon this truth. Thus scripture also states, "the first man, Adam, became a living being; the last Adam became a life-giving Spirit" (1 Cor 15:45). Paul cites the second creation-account given in Genesis (Gn 2:7), in order to recall the origins of Adam from the earth, and to remind the Corinthians that Adam's origins have left their mark upon all his children. "The first man was from the soil of the earth ... those made from the earth are of the same nature as the earthly man..." (1 Cor 15:47-49). Paul is leading up to his final point: "I tell you this, brothers: flesh and blood cannot inherit the kingdom of God" (Ibid 15:50). The human nature which we have all received from Adam is powerless to attain the fulness of that divine life which communion with God demands. Human nature must somehow be empowered to transcend its earthly limitations no less than its sinfulness.

It is precisely as risen that Christ possesses this power to enable man to qualify for the kingdom of God. He has, through his own resurrection, achieved the definitive status to which all men are destined. Hence, he is "the last Adam," the eschatological man, in whom the total effect of his own redemptive work is forever incarnated. Paul denominates the glorified Lord as "life-giving Spirit", in contrast with Adam, who at his creation from the earth "became a living being." In so describing Christ, Paul does not intend to imply that this transformation of his humanity has made it immaterial. By calling Christ "life-giving Spirit," Paul asserts that the Lord is, in his risen state, the source of the Spirit, whose operations in us are henceforth identified with his own (2 Cor 3:17-18). There is a very real sense in which "the Lord is the Spirit." In the Nicene Creed, the Church means to underscore this same truth when she applies the two characteristically Pauline epithets for the risen Christ, "the Lord and the life-giver," to the Holy Spirit.

Christ's function as "life-giving Spirit" is defined by Paul in the passage we have been considering with the help of another idea, which he took from the first account of creation in Genesis: man's fashioning in the image and likeness of God. "Just as surely as we have borne the image of the earthly man, so too we shall bear the image of the heavenly man" (1 Cor 15:49). The risen Christ, who has assumed the office of the creative Spirit of God (Gn 1:2) will work the transformation of the Christian in his own image by effecting the resurrection of the just, through which the ultimate state of man's glory is to be realized even in man's bodily parts.

Paul continues to fill out the details of this picture of Christ as the "last Adam" in the celebrated section of Romans, where he treats the problem of the origins of human sinfulness (Rm 5:12ff). He institutes the contrast between the first parent of mankind and the risen Lord by calling Adam "the type of him who was to come" (Rm 5:14). Adam's personal act of disobedience led, in some mysterious way which Paul himself does not make altogether clear, to the sinfulness found in his descendants (Rm 5:12-15). This evil inflicted upon humanity by the transgression of Adam was to be remedied by the saving obedience of Jesus Christ (Rm 5:19). This life-giving obedience was actualized in Paul's view (although he does not expressly say so here) by Jesus' acceptance in all their concrete circumstances of the two greatest events in his earthly career, his death and resurrection, through which he has been constituted "the last Adam."

The Pauline View of the Redemption

We may at this point present a synthesis of the principal features of Paul's personal thought concerning man's redemption. He fixes his attention almost exclusively upon the two-faceted event, which forms the heart of the gospel: Christ's death and resurrection. Paul does not include the incarnation, as John was to do in the fourth gospel, as a part of the redemptive event. For Paul, the coming of God's Son into the world is considered simply as his entry, so far as that was possible for one who was sinless, into the sinful family of the first Adam. It was a necessary presupposition to his labor of redemption. He had to associate himself intimately with sinful mankind, if he were to give the Father what rebellious man was incapable of rendering to him: one act of filial, obediential love. Hence for Paul, the Son of God came "in the likeness of sinful flesh" (Rm 8:3); he was "born of a woman, born under the Law" (Gal 4:4).

By accepting his death in all its concrete reality from the hand of his Father, Jesus Christ destroyed forever the sinful solidarity which had bound humanity to the first Adam. For he freely "became obedient even to death, yes, death upon the cross" (Ph 2:8), as the one effective, redeeming representative of the whole race. By his resurrection, Christ created a new supernatural solidarity of grace, thereby creating the possibility of an entirely new relationship for man towards God as his Father, through his union with the unique Son of God. "And he died for all in order that the living might no longer live for themselves, but for him who died and was raised for them" (Cor 5:15).

Yet in order that man personally might attain this salvation, he must pass through the ultimate redemptive experience, Christian death, the "new creation" that became a reality in Jesus' own death. The possibility of attaining this crucially necessary experience, Paul teaches, is initially opened to the individual through Baptism, the sacramental participation in Jesus' redeeming death (Rm 6:3-4). Yet another experience, participation in Jesus' resurrection, which his Baptism also makes possible, is also needed for the completion of man's salvation: and it is to occur at the parousia (1 Cor 15:23ff).

Thus the emphasis in Paul's thought is not upon the vicarious nature of Jesus' redemptive work, although that element is not absent, but rather upon the efficacy of Christ's death and resurrection in involving man in a totally new human experience. For this he is prepared here below by the Christian sacraments, principally by Baptism and the Eucharist. Ultimately, however, he is saved by being totally conformed through death in Christ and resurrection to Christ, who exhibits in himself the definitive form of redeemed human nature as "the last Adam."

The image motif in Pauline Soteriology

Closely connected with the theme of the last Adam is another motif, which has a significant role in the soteriological thought of Paul. It too comes from the creation stories of Genesis, where man is described as being created in the image and likeness of God, inasmuch as he is destined to "have dominion... over ... all living things" (Gn 1:26-28). God, supreme Lord of creation, graciously bestows upon man a share in his universal dominion of his creatures; and hence man can be said to be made in the divine image. That Paul is indebted to the passage in Genesis for the theological theme of the image is clear from its first appearance in his writings (1 Cor 11:7-8), where the context contains several allusions to God's creation of man. Here the Christian is denominated "the image and glory of God," a conception whose potentialities will continue to be exploited by Paul in subsequent letters.

The risen Christ, the last Adam, is proclaimed in Paul's gospel as the image of God (2 Cor 4:4), for Paul views the Christian existence in this world as a continuous process of transformation into this aspect of Christ. "All of us, while with unveiled face we reflect, as in a mirror, the glory of the Lord, are being transformed into the same image with ever-increasing glory, as by the Lord (who is) Spirit" (2 Cor 3:18). Later, in writing to Rome, Paul sets forth God's plan for man's salvation in terms of this same theme. "Those whom he (God) had known from the beginning, he also predestined to be shaped in the image of his Son, that he might be the first-born among many brothers" (Rm 8:29). To attain salvation, for Paul, is to enjoy "the glory of the freedom of the children of God" (Rm 8:21), which involves "the redemption of our bodies" (Rm 8:23). Man is saved by being molded "in the image of his Son," who as risen is himself "the image of the invisible God" (Col 1:13). It is only through being raised from death to glory in his total personality, with and through Christ, that man arrives at the goal for which he was created: true sonship with the Father. Thus, by means of this image theme, Paul is enabled to present the redemption, not as an impersonal or magical process, but as a progressive growing into a very real interpersonal relationship, that of son to father, with God in Christ.

In Paul's letters, Christ appears as the new man, a phrase synonymous with that of the last Adam; and here again the image motif recurs in combination with this conception. Through his baptismal experience and by the baptismal grace, the Christian "has put off the old man with his conduct, and has put on the new Man, who is continually being renewed in the image of the Creator in order to know him more fully" (Col 3:9-10). It is, as we have just seen, only by knowing God as his Father that this fulness of knowledge is arrived at. Thus Paul exhorts the Ephesians to strive for "the Knowledge of the Son of God," which for him is "mature manhood, that full measure of development found in Christ" (Ep 4:15). Christian spirituality is simply the unfolding of an ever-increasing consciousness of our relationship as sons and daughters to the Father. And the pattern which

must be followed is that of the risen Christ as the last Adam, as
Paul adds a few lines further on in this same letter: "You must
put aside your old way of living, the old man, who is constantly
being corrupted by deceptive desires . . . and put on the new Man,
created by God in justice and holiness and truth" (Ep 4:22-24).

Conclusion

It is an unwritten axiom of the biblical view of sacred history
that "the end must correspond to the beginning." We see this
viewpoint functioning in the attempts by so many New Testament writers to return to the origins of Israel's history. They do
not however go back beyond Abraham or Moses. It is the religious genius of Paul which exhibits an unprecedented originality
of thought, by returning to the very beginnings of the cosmos to
seek inspiration in the creation stories of the opening chapters
of Genesis. His presentation of Christ as the last Adam epitomizes
his view of Christian eschatology. In the exalted Christ, our human
nature has, for Paul, attained its definitive perfection; and it is
through the power unleashed in history by God's raising of
Jesus that our own future redemption is to be accomplished at
the parousia. Yet the process is not a mechanical one: it involves
the Christian in a most personal experience, his individual participation in the "new creation," which is Christian death. This
death in Christ becomes in Pauline spirituality the most crucial
event of our earthly existence. It is by saying Amen to the
Father as our Father that our final access to God is opened up for
us. This union will be completed ultimately only with one further
act of filial obedience, our bodily resurrection, by which we
are made eternally conformable to the last Adam, Christ our
brother, "the image of the invisible God." "The Son of God,
Christ Jesus, whom we have announced among you, you did not
find wavering between Yes and No . . . for to all God's promises
he supplies the Yes which confirms them. That is why we voice
the Amen through him, when we give glory to God" (2 Cor
1:19-20).

THE PAULINE MEANING OF
"RESURRECTION" AND "GLORIFICATION"

Anton Grabner-Haider

If the Christian message is to be proclaimed to modern man as a life-giving force, its central precepts will have to be continually re-examined. This process emerges as one of dialogue between the message that is being passed on and those who hear it, a dialogue that explains the Gospel's content while also promoting further discussion of it. Furthermore, it is not simply the hearers who question the Gospel but also vice versa. The Christian message must be open to such encounters and to constant reclarification. Moreover, these encounters should take place in such a way that historically-conditioned man can discover himself in Jesus Christ's historically-conditioned witness of faith. The constant factor in this process of understanding, reapplying and handing on ("tradition") is man, living in history, acting in freedom and personal responsibility, and constituted as a physical and social being.

What then does Christ mean for us today? More precisely, what are we to make of the biblical belief in "resurrection" and "glorification"? What did the biblical writers mean us to understand by these two concepts, and what is their significance for us today? How do we proclaim them now in a meaningful way, and what place do they have in our lives? These are the questions I would like to examine briefly in this article in the light of the biblical—particularly the Pauline—understanding of these two concepts. Raising such questions at all presupposes that what the biblical writers intended us to understand by these concepts is by no means self-evident.

New Testament Eschatology

Belief in resurrection and glorification belongs in the larger area of biblical—more specifically New Testament—eschatology. First, therefore, we have to have at least a basic idea of what New Testament eschatology involves. At this stage in the Church's history it was believed that the world and mankind were heading for a new and imminent future, a future that breaks into the temporal order of world and man. With it will come what is perfect, and it will drive out what is imperfect (1 Cor 13:10). This future, which is also the end, is the Lord Jesus Christ (Ph 4:5) who, through his resurrection, has become the Lord of all creation. It is he who is awaited and it is he who encompasses the world's duration. Mankind's expectations are centered on him (cf. 1 Th 1:10; 1 Cor 1:7; Ph 3:20). But the "day" of his coming has already started. Already it has cast its light over God's creation. Even now the "Day of the Lord" is approaching this world, and its proximity makes itself felt. Creation lies in its shadow, and men are already a part of it (1 Th 5:8).

The New Testament sees Christ as the future of the world and of man. What is this future? It is both with us now and yet still removed from us. New Testament eschatology as a whole, though this is clearest in St. Paul's writings, is stamped by (a) a present mode of expression and (b) a futuristic one. To mention just a few characteristic occurrences of each: (a) God sent his Son as the old world order reached its completion (Gal 4:4); Christ brought us redemption while we were still sinners (Rm 5: 8); now is the decisive moment, now is the day of salvation (2 Cor 6:2); (b) but the return of the Lord of this world, and his judgment, are not yet (1 Cor 1:7; 2 Cor 1:4; Ph 3:20f; Th 2:19, etc.); mankind and all creation awaits, groaning in their hearts, the glorious freedom of God's sons (Rm 8:22ff); Paul says he has not yet won the prize, not yet reached fulfillment (Ph 3, 12ff.); Christ has yet to set the world free so as to bring it under his Father's rule (1 Cor: 15, 20-28).

This tight mixture of present and future is New Testament eschatology's most obvious characteristic. Christ is the world's future in that he is himself approaching it in ever greater fullness. As it is in Christ that God approaches his creation, to that extent Christ is God's future (in Christ is all that is involved in God's future). Christ's death and resurrection herald the onset of God's rule over his creation. Through his Son, his final emissary, the creator initiates the process of giving true and eternal life to his creation. He is establishing his "new creation" (2 Cor 5:17). In Christ's resurrection from the dead God launched the new and ultimate creation, and to that extent his future is already present among us now (the present-orientated aspect of New Testament eschatology). But what has been begun still remains to be fulfilled in all things, is therefore in process and will one day embrace all creation (future-orientated aspect).

God himself is the future of man and of the world. Through Christ he approaches creation. The Christ-event as a whole (death and resurrection) is a proleptic event: it has initiated and empowered a new and enduring order which it has situated within the temporal span. It is now growing to maturity and Christ is its driving force. What Christ has begun now develops in human history and reaches fulfillment in God, its future.

The Meaning of Resurrection

The resurrection and glorification themes hold pride of place within the New Testament eschatological proclamation of faith. In the first place, both refer to Christ: God has raised him up from the dead and he is Lord (Rm 10:9); God has raised him up among the people and has given him a name which is above every name (Ph 2:8ff). In the order of that which is promised, however, both experiences are also applied to mankind: mortal and corporal though we are, God will also raise us to new life through his Spirit who is in us (Rm 8:11); our bodies will be fashioned like his glorious body (Ph 3:2).

But what, in biblical terms, does resurrection mean? From what world of experience does the belief emerge? In what form did it originally arise and what was its ultimate development?

The cry "God is dead" rings passionately through the cultic

myths of the ancient East. Baal, the god of growth and fertility, sleeps the sleep of the dead during the summer dry season. Mot, the god of death, rules the people. With the onset of the rainy season, Baal rouses himself after a fierce struggle with Mot. A natural process is thereby made into a divine myth. But as the Old Testament shows us, Yahweh did not die. "Behold, he that keepeth Israel shall neither slumber nor sleep" (Ps 121:4), the psalmist sings, mocking the followers of Baal. Yahweh is a living God (Jr 10:10). The people of Israel are "sons of the living God".

In the earliest Old Testament books the underworld is the world of the dead, a land of no return that knows no human voice, only squekings and murmurings, signs of a greatly diluted but continuing existence. The underworld implies permanent removal from Yahweh's face.

But gradually the belief arises that Yahweh is also Lord of the underworld. This is clearly the beginning of the biblical hope in resurrection. It takes on a more definite shape in post-exilic apocalyptic-eschatological literature and is in fact a response to Wisdom literature's despair in the face of death. "He [Yahweh] will swallow up death in victory; and the Lord will wipe away tears from off all faces; and the rebuke of his people shall be taken away from off all the earth" (Is 25:8). "Thy dead men shall live, together with my dead body shall they arise. Awake and sing, ye that dwell in the dust" (Is 26:19). Isaiah here is applying this hope only to the people of Israel: even their dead will be delivered from the shame of exile.

In Daniel 12:2, this hope is expressed differently: "And many of them that sleep in the dust of the earth shall awake, some to everlasting life, and some to shame and everlasting contempt." This text represents a similar position to that held by the Hasidaeans. Though it offers hope in resurrection even to the wicked, there is still no mention of resurrection for all. This extension, however, arises and becomes ever more strongly emphasized in the period immediately following the writings mentioned above. The history of religion shows that both in and outside the Bible, Jewish apocalypticism is the champion of hope in universal resurrection. Its basic testimony is: God is the Lord of the living *and* the dead.

And that is precisely what the New Testament proclamation says of Christ Jesus: Jesus is the Lord and God raised him from the dead (Rm 10:9). "For this reason Christ both died and rose again, that he might be the Lord of the living and the dead" (Rm 14:9). At first, Jesus' resurrection was proclaimed with almost unbridled enthusiasm until eventually there emerged from this exomologesis a formula that combined resurrection and death in the one proclamation: "Jesus is dead and is risen again" (1 Th 4:14). The point is that it was the resurrection that so stimulated early Christian fervor, was seen as challenge and acclamation, and was then crystallized into a datum of belief.

Another presentation of this theme, and the most immediate accounts of Jesus' resurrection, are contained in the gospels. They witness to the inexplicable nature of the resurrection event, though what they express is not as neatly done as in the formulas mentioned above. In both, however, Christ's resurrection is seen as an event, even if only in its biblical meaning of *dabar*. Just as the world is created through God's word (*dabar*), or just as what God said to his prophets and his people actually came about, so also did Jesus' resurrection take place. It is God's deed, an event that is open to human experience and takes possession of its language. The event is the creative action of God's power and Spirit and it is formulated in terms of the two metaphorical expressions "awaken" and "cause to arise". The dead Jesus is assumed into the life-power (Spirit) of God.

The biblical witnesses go on to speak of "appearances" made by the risen Lord. "Appearances" (*ophthenai*) means on the one hand disclosure of a totally hidden mystery (*apokalypsis*), and on the other a human encounter and experience. He who is risen encounters a person in the act of retiring from his view; he is experienced as one who is on his way elsewhere, as a wholly autonomous being. He discloses himself in language and in human life. The resurrection of Jesus occurred in the form of the risen Lord's testimony to himself, within human history and experience, just as *dabar* issues from God and happens in a human context. The crucified Jesus is encountered as the risen Lord. In this experience and encounter the crucified Lord discloses himself in the risen Lord and thereupon he withdraws once again; through the encounter we are permitted lasting awareness of his self-giving and his continuing existence for others.

For the world as a whole, Jesus' resurrection signifies a turning point, the beginning of something totally new that possesses ultimate validity. A new era has begun in which man is enabled to reach his full human potential. "New life" (Rm 6:10f.), as reality and possibility, is now open to all men equally. In his resurrection, Jesus' death, which is for us all, turns into life for God and from God. Jesus' cross is now the way to life, a door that will never be closed. The resurrection discloses the cross' hitherto veiled life-force, existence for others and love. The world is put on a completely different basis and human life is transformed: Jesus' resurrection is the beginning of the general awakening from the dead, the onset of life's total victory. "Just as all mankind died in Adam, so in Christ all are given new life" (Cor 15:22). Christ is "the author of life" (Ac 3:15), the "first-born from the dead" (Col 1:18). All creation is taken up into the new life of Jesus Christ (Rm 8:20ff.). Jesus died for all, representing us all; in his resurrection he conquers for all, representing us all. To each of us has been given equal opportunity for true life. Jesus' death for us is the conquest of death, and through his life, offered for us, he has become love itself. The culmination of God's kingdom is the acceptance by all men of this new life. God's future is attained through the universal attainment of the reality of the resurrection.

Glorification

In view of his resurrection, Christ is already and essentially "he who is raised up," which is to say he is already glorified. His resurrection was part of the process by which God took him to himself. This becomes clear in the hymn to Christ in Philippians where mention of Jesus' death leads immediately and exclusively to the mention of his exaltation: "He humbled himself and became obedient unto death, even death on a cross. Therefore God has highly exalted him and bestowed on him the name which is above every name" (Ph 2:8f). The situation is similar in Luke: "Was it not necessary that the Christ should suffer these things and enter into his glory?" (Lk 24:26). From this we can conclude that originally resurrection and exaltation were independent interpretations of the same event. Jesus' entry into the life of the Father is seen in two different traditions: in the one case as resurrection and in the other as exaltation—that is, glorification. In the passages just mentioned, Jesus' new life is interpreted in accordance with the structure of the Old Testament enthronement formula.

However, according to another tradition, resurrection and exaltation are regarded as correlative. Here the resurrection is the origin of exaltation; glorification and enthronement are the continuation and consequence of awakening. The epistle to the Romans would appear to confirm this: "It is Christ Jesus, who died, yes, who was raised from the dead, who is at the right hand of God, who indeed intercedes for us" (Rm 8:34); and elsewhere the same epistle says that Christ Jesus was designated Son of God in power according to the Spirit of holiness by his resurrection from the dead" (Rm 1:2f.). Exaltation and glorification are therefore the object and consequence of the resurrection; the ultimate glorification of the Father occurs through the glorification of the risen Lord; this marks the fulfillment of his rule and dominion as creator of all (1 Cor 15:28). The theme of the glorification of God is central to and ultimate in Pauline theology.

What, in greater detail, does "glorification" mean in its biblical usage? The Hebrew Old Testament uses the word *kabod*, meaning that which invests man with value and substance. In Sinai, Yahweh's *kabod* appears as fire (Ex 24:17); it shows itself to be terrible in punishment and indispensable in time of trouble (Lv 9:6. 23f.). *Kabod* is the "weight" (*gravitas*) of Yahweh, though it can also be interpreted as his power over the world which he wields as its Lord and creator. This dominion is expressed and exercised in human history (Ezk 3:23; 8:4; and elsewhere), but only at the end of time will it become visible as something bathed in glory (Ex. 43:3ff.).

In the Septuagint, Greek-speaking Jewry translated *kabod* by *doxa*, whose primary meaning is the glory and power of God, his splendor and beauty. Greek papyri and astrology give this word the additional meaning of dazzling brightness (brilliance) and also use it to mean the magical power of the Godhead. For those who came directly under the influence of Hellenism, the word *doxa* could mean all these things.

By the time the New Testament came to adopt the notion of God's *doxa*, it had been fundamentally influenced by Jewish apocalypticism. Here the divine *doxa* is seen as a specifically eschatological event: God will establish his dominion over all history (Eth. En. 25:7); his will be a heavenly throne encircled by sparkling stars, cherubs and rivers of fire (Eth. En. 14:8ff.); evil will melt before his face and the angelic powers will bend the knee in worship. But the just and the saints will also be clothed in God's *doxa* and their faces will reflect the brilliance of its light (4 Esr. 7:97). Almost invariably, God's *doxa* is mentioned in connection with his dominion over all creation.

The New Testament shows that through his resurrection Christ received a share in God's glory. He is charged with the task of establishing God's dominion over all creation and for this reason is endowed with the power and the brilliance that belong to God in his glory. Through his resurrection he has become "the Lord of glory" (1 Cor 2:8); the Gospel as a whole proclaims the glory of God, emphasizes and highlights it (2 Cor. 4:4). But Christ does nothing for his own glorification: the power he possesses is exercised solely to the glorification of the creator ("Jesus Christ is Lord to the glory of God the Father"— Ph 2:11). The Christ-event was the beginning of the glorification of God (Rm 15:7), and what Christ began must come to fruition in human history. Just as he was the first to share in the glory of the Father, so through him are all men to share in the same glory. Whoever, through Christ, obtains access to the Father may hope for a share in God's glory: "We rejoice in our hope of sharing the glory of God' (Rm 5:1-2). Whoever is willing to suffer with Christ and to further his life-purpose may hope to come into

God's glory with Christ (Rm 8:18). Whoever, whether knowingly or unknowingly, has yielded to Christ and has confessed to faith in his life-giving cross, freedom and love, may hope for ultimate union with Christ in glory (Ph 3:20). By dying for mankind Christ became the first to enter into God's glory, and this possibility is now extended to all mankind. Christ is charged and empowered with the task of continuing in history what was begun through his death and resurrection—the establishing of the kingdom. Where Christ is, and where in us he comes to new life, the world is progressing into God's future.

The Resurrection and Glorification of The Body

When the New Testament speaks of resurrection and glorification it is referring to the body. Christ's new life is a new life in the body and he lives on in those who confess his name ("the body of Christ"); he is glorified bodily (Ph 3:21). We, too, can look forward to the resurrection of the body in which our bodily form will be a permanent one determined by the life-giving power of God (1 Cor 15:44); man's physical body will be glorified and will share in Christ's bodily glory.

But what does the Bible mean by body, and in what actual context did it attain the meaning given it there? In Old Testament Semitic thought, man is an indivisible unity, and this unity is given him by the creator. Unlike hellenistic dualism, they did not see themselves as body and soul but simply as God-given life (*nepes*). The same unity characterizes New Testament anthropology. Here, especially in the Pauline writings, man is designated either as *sarx* or as *soma*. *Soma* is used in the context of resurrection and glorification, and it is an expression that in the Septuagint has no Hebraic equivalent to preserve the unity the New Testament writers intended to convey. Apocalyptic Jewish literature enriched the meaning of the expression by investing it with a significance peculiar to that genre. *Soma* was the whole man, formed by the creator, struggling between the forces of good and evil, a man of action and a social being and above all one who had to commit himself personally.

Thus for St. Paul, man, in his "body" and in his "members",
is the battleground on which is fought the struggle between sin,
which leads to death, and righteousness, the new life to which
God calls us (Rm 6:12f). It is as physical beings that we embrace
either the rule of Christ or the rule of sin (Rm 6:6; 7:14; Gal
6:17). We encounter the world through our bodies, and the
impact it makes on us occurs through our bodies. Existence in the
world means existence in the body. As a physical creature of this
world, a man's being is orientated toward that of others. Only
through the body do we communicate with our fellow men. As
a physical being, man always has two possibilities: he can either
shut himself off from his fellow men, which will mean wedding
himself to selfishness, or he can identify with them, which will
mean realizing his dependent co-existence in the form of active
love. The body is the whole man, who as such faces the necessity
of deciding for or against God, of identifying with his brothers
or rejecting them. The Bible does not regard man's physical
existence as a passive condition but as one in which he experiences
himself as man in an historical context and on the basis of his
actions. In the permanent facing of his decision for or against
God he stands permanently open to the choice of new life, or
death through sin. Christ's resurrection enables creation to reach
its full potential. It was not just any death that led to resurrection,
but only Jesus' death, for all mankind. Jesus' selfless existence led
to new life. The resurrected Lord is new life to those who join
themselves to him. He lives on bodily in those who choose to
follow him in his freedom, obedience and love. Men who await
bodily resurrection await, in effect, participation in the infinity,
glory, power and life of God (1 Cor 15:42f.). The New Testament goal is to see all men developing fully as such: they must
not refuse new life but should embrace it. The hope expressed
in the New Testament is that men will learn to live with and
for one another, that God's love, revealed in Jesus, will come to
fruition, and that the human race will be lifted up into the divine
mystery.

Prolepsis and Anticipation of the Future

With Christ's resurrection and glorification the anticipation of the future has begun. Not only are bodily glory and resurrection now possibilities open to all men but, more important, they are already in process. Resurrection as physical reality has been set in train, for the Spirit of God, who activates the process, is already active among us. He is given to those whose lives witness to God's love (cf. Rm 5:5; 8:11). The Spirit, if one cares to look at it this way, is given to us as an advance payment against a binding contract. He who has received the Spirit may hope that what is begun in him will achieve fruition. The gift of the Spirit is the beginning of the redemption of the body (Rm 8:23). He who follows God in Christ is approaching resurrection. God's Spirit is the anticipation of the new life, of God's future for us, and he makes the bodily resurrection possible. Resurrection and the new, glorified body are primary features of a process of maturation that participates in the development of God's new creation. Where men through love open themselves to the Spirit, Christ incorporates them in his resurrected body.

In the same way, the glorification of the body is also anticipated, though the climax of God's glorification lies in the future (Rm 5:2; 8:18). In Romans 8:30, and nowhere else in his letters, Paul tells us that God has already glorified those whom he has justified. Here Paul is quoting from an early baptismal tradition which he has built into his own eschatology. Those who follow the creator's call are already endowed with his glory and so already reflect the glory of the Lord "with unveiled face" (2 Cor 3:18). Through Christ's saving action the world is clothed in God's glory, with the result that "we all, with unveiled face, beholding the glory of the Lord, are being changed into his likeness from one degree of glory to another" (2 Cor 3:18).

Like resurrection, glorification is something already in process throughout the world. It began with Christ and will one day embrace all men. It does not continue of itself but only through us. We have to be open to the future so that we thereby become "fellow workers for God" (1 Cor. 3:9; 15:58). The future, as God's future, is a challenge to world and man: it is the challenge of the creator to his creation.

Growth in God's new creation is impossible without our continuing collaboration. If man refuses to realize himself as a dependent social being, then bodily resurrection and glory are not anticipated. Thus we are urged to "glorify God in your body" (1 Cor 6:20). God's kingdom will be realized in this world and his glory will reside in our bodies and in our realized potential. For this reason the highest spiritual worship open to us is within the context of our bodily existence (Rm 12:1). There is, in fact, no other possible context. It is here, in this present form of existence, that the creator comes into his own and completes what he has begun. St. Paul sees our present mode of existence in terms of approaching resurrection and glory. Our bodily existence is orientated toward the new life of Christ, and so St. Paul perpetually urges us to cooperate in the work of the risen Lord (1 Cor 15:58). We are called to share in God's future, and in following this call it will be the extent of our commitment to our fellow men, to our own self-realization and to the renewal of the earth, that counts. On account of Christ's resurrection, human history has been given enduring value: bodily existence now implies potential and task, the anticipation of future resurrection and glory, openness to the future.

Summary

Central to the Gospel is the proclamation of Christ's resurrection and glory and the participation in these events that we may hope for. The proclamation of this theme has three basic component parts: message, challenge and promise. In the first place, resurrection and glory are beliefs proclaimed: Jesus is risen from the dead and has entered into the life of the Father so that he now rules with him. What has thereby been begun continues in human history, in that resurrection and glory are now open to all men. This message is also a challenge in that it demands a response from those who hear it. Because Christ is now at work in the world, suiting it to a new life, man is challenged to participate in this the Lord's work (1 Cor 15:58). This means that man has to be open to the new life God offers, submit himself to God's rule and witness to Christ's love.

Third, the message is a promise opening up for us undreamed of possibilities, the sole hope of true life and true self-realization. A new creation is developing which, though not made by man, cannot be made without him. All men are to be included in the resurrection of Christ and so all men are to come face to face with their creator.

Jesus' death on the cross, his death in obedient love, became the death of death, and so a new life. The world is therefore still evolving, and God has blessed it. Jesus' life and death for us became his resurrection. In the New Testament understanding, Jesus' resurrection took place in human history through his appearance before witnesses, in that through his encounters with them he finds new life in them. The same thing happens now, to the glory of the Father, wherever men express in their own lives the love and selflessness he showed, wherever his love is active in society.

Through Jesus Christ, resurrection and glory take place in human history because since the incarnation human history has been the sole context of God's self-revelation in Christ. But God is not absorbed by history: he confronts it; we encounter the resurrected Lord precisely in the act of his withdrawal from us. The world is permanently challenged by the as yet incompletely realized achievement of the resurrection. This is not to say that Christ and world are alienated: on the contrary, he is situated firmly in our midst, for we and our world are destined to become God's new creation.

Thus Christ is God's future and therefore our future. Through Christ God approaches us and through Christ we discover ourselves. Christ is the attainable future.

THE FELLOWSHIP OF HIS SUFFERINGS

Barnabas Ahern, C.P.

Through conversion St. Paul gained a new spiritual life. On the road to Damascus he received from the risen Christ the messianic gift of the Holy Spirit who ever after inspired and ruled his activity as that of a true son of God. For the Apostle this meant, in the expressive phrase of Philippians 3:10, that he had come to know Christ, "in the power of his resurrection." But that was not all. He affirms in the same breath that, through conversion, he came to know also "the fellowship of his sufferings." This significant addition is in accord with the polarity of all Pauline thought which joins death and resurrection as two inseparable aspects of the same salvific mystery, whether in the life of Christ or in the lives of Christians.

It is not easy, however, to determine the precise application of this death theme to the enigmatic phrase, "the fellowship of his sufferings," for the context does not define or explain its authentic meaning. Paul, moreover, has spoken so rarely of the historical details of the Passion that the expression, "sufferings of Christ," fails to command the unanimous interpretation accorded to words of obvious meaning.

Due to this uncertainty, the controverted phrase needs to be studied in the light of Paul's general doctrine, especially as it is found in the great epistles of Corinthians, Galatians and Romans. For when he wrote Philippians, Paul had already advanced beyond the limitations of the early kerygma—the apostolic preaching in the first year after Pentecost—and even beyond the limitations of his own doctrine in his first epistles, those to the Thessalonians. During the first months at Corinth, he went through a maturing process which virtually developed his thought and significantly influenced his preaching. This enrichment is reflected in the epistles which followed. Their fullness constitutes the background of his words in Philippians. Hence a review and examination of relevant themes in the Pauline corpus will help greatly to explain his affirmation that conversion brought him to know Christ and "the fellowship of his sufferings."

The doctrines on suffering in First and Second Thessalonians reflect the teaching of the primitive church as enunciated in Acts 14:21: "Through many tribulations must we enter the kingdom of God." In accord with this truth, Paul takes it for granted that the Christian lives in a climate of suffering. He insinuates this in an opening phrase of his first letters to the Thessalonians and frequently alludes in both letters to the sufferings borne by himself and his Thessalonian converts. Thus he employs many forms of *thlipsis,* a Greek word more and more frequently used for those tribulations which usher in the glorious Risen Christ.

Such suffering is not a mere accident; rather, it is a necessity imposed by divine decree, for in First Thessalonians Paul parallels his earlier statement in Acts with the equivalent phrase, "we are *bound* to suffer." Even though the struggle between good and evil will break out in titanic fury at the end of time, still it has already begun: the "Tempter" is active; the "mystery of iniquity" is at work (*cf.,* 2 Th 2:1ff.). Hence, for Paul, there is no break in continuity between the sufferings of the present moment and the eschatological crisis of the final age of the world.

This explains the rich joy which the Thessalonians and Paul himself experienced in their trials. Looking forward eagerly to the imminent coming of Christ, they were able to identify their trials as a share in the tribulations of the "last age." Hence, their hope was something more than ordinary hope; it was an attitude of patient and perservering waiting in the midst of trials. In the New Testament this virtue is always, at least implicitly, connected with messianic salvation, for it represents the power of hope to endure in the midst of sufferings which lead to final reward. The patient endurance of trials, therefore, fills the Christian with joy, for it brings the conviction that such fidelity in the midst of messianic tribulations provides a pledge of salvation at the time of the *Parousia* or the second coming of the Risen Lord.

This doctrine of the Epistles to the Thessalonians might lead one to conclude that Paul's teaching on suffering is identical with that of contemporary Judaism: i.e., the patient endurance of trial is really a blessing, for it is only by passing righteously through the messianic throes that one will enter the messianic kingdom. Fragmentary references in these letters show, however, that Paul thinks of suffering in a *Christian* light: trials are the continuation of the tribulations which Christ himself inaugurated. What is more, these references when coupled with other doctrinal elements in these epistles, suggest a concept which Paul will develop later. The bond between the sufferings of the Christian and Christ is based on intimate union.

In Thessalonians Paul speaks of the suffering Christians as "imitators" of the suffering Christ. As St. John Chrysostom points out, the term of comparison in First Thessalonians 1:6 is suffering with joy: "You became imitators of us and of the Lord, receiving the word in great tribulation, with joy of the Holy Spirit." A second text which is more casual in its reference to Christ, centers the comparison in suffering alone: "For you have become imitators of the churches of God which are in Judea in Christ Jesus, in that you also have suffered the same things from your own countrymen as they have . . ." (1 Th 2:14). To explain this bond it would suffice to invoke the dominant theme of these letters with regard to suffering and to conclude that the conformity between the suffering Christ and the suffering Christian arises from their common adherence to the design of God that all who attain messianic glory must pass through messianic trial. There are indications, however, that Paul's concept of imitating Christ involves a more intimate bond.

It is significant that the word "imitator" always denotes moral effort in the New Testament. It reflects the saying of Jesus: "If anyone wishes to come after me, let him deny himself, and take up his cross, and follow me" (Mk 8:34). We see a close connection with the concept of a disciple following his master. This theme of master-disciple is actually found in First Thessalonians, where Paul makes clear that the precepts governing Christian life have come from God through and in Christ Jesus (4:2f.: 5: 18). He is, therefore, the mediator of God's will and the master of all who are subject to it. It is noteworthy that, to express this role of Christ, Paul uses the phrase "in Christ Jesus" which recurs through two letters and which, at least in the following epistles, frequently refers to an intrinsic bond.

Even in the present epistles, moreover, Paul shows Christ forming his disciples by actual influence from within. He writes in First Thessalonians: "May the Lord make you to increase and abound in charity . . . that he may strengthen your hearts, blameless in holiness before God our Father, at the coming of our Lord Jesus Christ" (1 Th 3:12f.). In his first epistles, therefore, Paul's concept of imitating Christ in suffering may be based not only on the duty of the Christian to follow the same divine will that imposed messianic suffering on the Savior, but also on the intrinsic necessity of living the pattern of life that flows inevitably from inward communion with him who, while on earth, suffered the trials of the Messiah.

There is also another suggestive element in these early letters. Paul asserts that the joy of suffering with which the Christian imitates Christ is a gift of the Holy Spirit. "You have become imitators of us and of the Lord . . . with joy of the Holy Spirit" (1 Th 1:6). This is significant, for the Holy Spirit is present in the Christian as God's permanent gift (*cf.*, 1 Th 4:8). The way is thus prepared for the subsequent Epistle to the Romans, wherein Paul teaches that the Christian has reason to rejoice in trial since he can rely on the ever-present Spirit to strengthen his resistance and to fulfill his hope (Rm 5:3-5).

There is yet a last phrase to suggest that, even in Thessalonians, Paul anticipated his later doctrine on the profound influence of Christ in all Christian suffering. He writes: "May the Lord direct your hearts into the love of God and the patience of Christ" (2 Th 3:5). As it stands, the phrase is open to several interpretations.

J.E. Frame (*Epistles of St. Paul to the Thessalonians*, p. 296) suggests that it refers to Christ not only as the supreme model but also as the efficient cause of the Christian's patience. Paul, therefore, asks here that his converts may be strengthened with a patience that is both inspired by the example of Christ and actually bestowed by him.

B. Rigaux (*Les Epîtres aux Thes.*, 700) and M. Zerwick (*Graecitas Biblica*, 12), while accepting this explanation of Frame, enrich it by interpreting the phrase in the light of Paul's doctrine on the union of Christ with his members. Seen in this light, the patience which Paul requests for his converts is truly "Christ's patience," not only because he bestows it but also because he, as the "Body," must claim whatever belongs to his members. There is much to recommend this thoroughly Pauline interpretation. Not only is it warranted by Paul's allusions in Thessalonians to the bond between Christ and his followers, it is also a corollary of the words spoken to Paul in his inaugural vision: "Saul, Saul, why dost thou persecute me? . . . I am Jesus whom thou are persecuting" (Ac 9:4-5).

Such allusions to a distinctly Pauline explanation of suffering, though precious, are only fragmentary and incidental; as such, they leave much room for discussion. The fact is that in these first two epistles Paul does not emphasize the role of Christ in *present* life and suffering. His attention is fastened on the Parousia or final coming, and his thought is strongly colored by the eschatological outlook of late Judaism and early Christianity. Hence it may be that in Thessalonians he is content to emphasize only that aspect of the bond between Christ and the Christian which is based on God's will ordaining trial both for the messiah and his followers as the necessary means for entering the kingdom.

Passing now to the period of the great Epistles of First and Second Corinthians, Galatians, and Romans, we notice a marked shift of emphasis from the outlook and teaching of Thessalonians. Paul's own experience offers the probable reason for this new development. Leaving Thessalonica, he went to Athens where, in his address at the Areopagus, he followed the pattern of his earlier preaching (Ac 17:16-31). Not only did he develop the theme of resurrection-parousia, but he also embellished his words

with oratorical devices. This method of preaching met with
signal failure so that, coming to Corinth immediately afterwards,
he feared even worse (1 Cor 2:1-3). But now he deliberately
altered the theme of his discourse to emphasize the role of the
death of Christ in God's plan for salvation. He also changed to a
simple style of preaching and addressed especially the less promising elements of the population.

As the months passed, Paul witnessed a phenomenon which
made a deep impression upon him. He had already seen at Thessalonica that spiritual fruitfulness was possible even under a storm
of suffering. Now at Corinth he came to see that suffering and
human weakness provide the climate that is most conducive to
the activity of God's saving power. He was not slow to grasp the
implications of this experience. It squared perfectly with the
Isaian picture of Redemption. Salvation did not depend upon human strength but only upon God, so that all glory belongs to him
alone:

> The haughty eyes of man will be lowered,
> the arrogance of men will be abased,
> and the Lord alone will be exalted on that day.
> By waiting and by calm you shall be saved,
> in quiet and in trust your strength lies.
> (Is 2:11; 30:15)

This principle of "salvation through God alone" pervades
biblical thought, appears frequently in non-biblical Jewish literature, and finds some of its most beautiful expressions in the
hymns of Qumran. In one of these hymns, as translated by
Menahem Mansoor, we read:

> For I know that truth are the words of thy mouth
> and in Thy hand is righteousness, and in Thy thought is
> All knowledge; and in Thy power is all might and all
> glory is with Thee. In Thy wrath are all judgments of
> affliction,
> But in Thy goodness there is abundance of forgive-
> ness, and Thy mercies are on all Thy favored sons. For
> Thou hast made known to them Thy true counsel,
> And through Thy marvelous mysteries Thou hast
> enlightened them. And for the sake of Thy glory, Thou

hast cleansed man from transgression so that he may consecrate himself
For Thee...   (IQH 11:7-11)

Paul himself recognized this principle at work in the unfolding
of the divine plan at Corinth. Human weakness and human
contradiction provided the ambient for fruitful divine activity,
that all might recognize and give glory to the true author of
salvation. At Corinth the Apostle came to see in a new way that
men must become aware of their own human powerlessness if
they are to make room for the power of God. Trial and weakness,
therefore, because they lead to such awareness, are both a preparation for and a sign of God's work.

Paul returns to this theme time and again in the first three
chapters of First Corinthians. He identifies it as the governing
principle in the divine choice of the crucifixion of Christ for the
work of salvation; God has chosen what is humanly "weak" and
"foolish" to accomplish His greatest mercy, that men might see
clearly how fully the power and wisdom of salvific activity is all
His. In this new emphasis on the death of Christ as interpretative
of the nature of the salvific plan, Paul delivered the very "testimony of God" (1 Cor 2:1). He focussed attention on the human
"weakness" of the way in which Christ attained messianic glory
and so demonstrated that salvation is wholly God's work and
wholly a work of love.

The Apostle saw the principle of power-in-weakness directing
also the extension of salvific activity through his own preaching:
"It pleased God, by the foolishness of our preaching, to save
those who believe" (1 Cor 1:21). The same principle was at work
in the selection of the first converts: "The foolish things of the
world has God chosen to put to shame the 'wise,' and the weak
things... and the despised... and the things that are not" (1
Cor 1:27-29). Moreover, to counter the arrogance of the Corinthians who were preening themselves as though they had attained
the fullness of salvation, Paul emphasized the fact that the apostles
in whom God's power is most active experience an acute feeling
of human insufficiency and suffer great trials constantly.

Nowhere, perhaps, does Paul express this reaction so poignantly than in Second Corinthians: "We carry this treasure in vessels of clay, to show that the abundance of the power is God's and not ours. In all things we suffer tribulation, but we are not distressed; we are sore pressed, but we are not destitute; we endure persecution, but we are not forsaken; we are cast down, but we do not perish; always bearing about in our body the dying of Jesus, so that the life also of Jesus may be made manifest in our body. For we the living are constantly being handed over to death for Jesus' sake, that the life also of Jesus may be made manifest in our mortal flesh" (2 Cor 4:7-11).

Thus, always and everywhere, God manifests his power in a context of human weakness. The reason remains ever the same: Men must learn that all spiritual strength comes from God alone and can be used only with His help, "so that, just as it is written, 'let him who takes pride, take pride in the Lord' " (1 Cor 1:31).

The shift of emphasis in First Corinthians from resurrection-parousia to death-resurrection is accompanied by new attention to the riches and requirements of Christian life *here on earth*. Succeeding epistles will concentrate more and more on this, until, in the later captivity epistles, Paul's attention rests almost entirely on the anticipated resurrection which union with Christ brings even in this life. But these subsequent developments are already contained substantially in the teaching of First Corinthians. There he writes of the Christian's present union with Christ and of the dynamic activity of the Spirit whom he bestows. "Flee immorality," he demands. "Every sin that a man commits is outside the body, but the immoral man sins against his own body. Or do you not know that your body is the temple of the Holy Spirit, who is in you, whom you have from God, and that you are not your own? For you have been bought at a great price. Glorify God in your body" (1 Cor 6:18-20).

This doctrine of First Corinthians, however, is not complete; it must be complemented by the teaching of Romans and Galatians. For in these two letters Paul penetrates the involvements and applications of union with Christ which comes to the Christian through the Spirit at the moment of Baptism.

To appreciate the doctrine of these epistles one must keep in mind that Paul is the "witness of the Resurrection" par excellence. In his account before King Agrippa of the miraculous event on the day of his conversion, he recalls Christ's words, "I have appeared to thee for this purpose, to appoint thee to be a minister and a witness to what thou hast seen, and to the visions that thou shalt have of me" (Ac 26:16). Paul remained true to this awareness of the Savior. Christ was always, for him, someone present and living. His constant allusion to Christian life as life "in Christ" serves as the classic emblem of his own conviction that Christians have been incorporated by Baptism into the body of the risen Christ.

Equally fundamental in his thought is the truth that Christ died and rose again, not merely as an individual but as the embodiment and representative of all men. The Hebrew conception of "corporate personality," essential for understanding Old Testament messianic prophecies, is essential also to Paul's concept of the role of Christ. Like Adam he, too, is a "corporate personality," a new Adam. Paul writes: "For as in Adam all die, so in Christ all will be made to live.... Even as we have borne the likeness of the earthly [man], let us bear also the likeness of the heavenly [man]" (1 Cor 15:22, 49). Through the law of solidarity his death and resurrection are efficacious for all: "We have come to the conclusion that, since one died for all, therefore all died" (2 Cor 5:14).

The efficacy of Christ's redemptive act takes effect in the individual through the rite of Baptism which is at once "a tomb and a womb." At Baptism, according to Paul's thought, the body-person of the Christian is united to the body-person of Christ. Here we sense the physical realism of Old Testament thought which always considered the "body" not a part of man in contrast to the soul but the whole man as a concrete reality. The body, consequently, has an important role in the Old Testament prophecies of the final salvation. In Paul's thought, therefore, baptismal union takes place between two real, physical persons, the individual Christian and the individual glorified Christ.

These factors serve to explain the Apostle's words on the union of the baptized with the death of Christ: "Do you not know that all we who have been baptized into Christ Jesus have been baptized into his death?" (Rm 6:3). In the simple realism of Paul's thought, Baptism so unites the body-person of the Christian to the body-person of the glorious Christ that he, who died and rose again as a corporate personality, is able to share with his members the salvific effects of his death and resurrection.

For Paul, as C.H. Dodd expresses it, "the whole sacrament is an act by which the believer enters into all that Christ did as his representative in that he was delivered up for our sins, and rose again for our justification" (*The Epistle to the Romans*, p. 87). Paul explained what it meant to share through Baptism in the effects of Calvary. The Christian is freed from subjection to the law, from the shackles of the "body of sin," from servile obedience to the world, from the death of sin. In a word, he is liberated with the "freedom wherewith Christ has made us free" (Gal. 4: 31).

In order to understand Paul's conception of this truth and its application to Christian life, it is necessary to keep in mind an essential doctrine—that the death of Christ was a death of obedience and love. It brought an end to his bondage "in sinful flesh. . . under the law" (Rm 8:3). His death, however, was not merely a negation of contact with the world; it was prompted and accompanied by an interior act of consummate obedience to the Father and of ardent love for men inspired by the Holy Spirit. His death was, above all else, a visible expression of the surrender of his whole humanity to the will of the Father who sent him to die out of love for men (Rm 5:6-8). The dynamism of such a death, vital with love and obedience, could never die. Once he had passed through death and escaped the limitations of life on earth, this abiding spirit found full and necessary expression in the messianic glorification of the Savior rising from the dead. Far from being a mere extrinsic reward, his glorious resurrection and salvific activity as messianic Son of God are the vital products and full flowering of the love and obedience which filled his soul in its passage through death.

This aspect of Christ's death-resurrection helps to explain a striking feature of St. Paul's doctrine on Baptism. For him sacramental death marks the point of departure for an altogether new life, in which the Christian ever remains "dead to sin, but alive to God" (Rm 6:11). This is possible only because, in Baptism, the Christian shares the very Spirit of Christ which endures forever in the body-person to which the new member is united. If, therefore, baptismal incorporation brings death to the old life through the power of Christ's death, it is because the Spirit who prompted the loving obedience of his death now becomes active in the new member, transforming him radically from the carnal state of egoism to the spiritual state of God-mindedness. "It is now no longer I that live, but Christ lives in me. And the life that I now live in the flesh, I live in the faith of the Son of God, who loved me and gave himself up for me" (Gal 2:20).

This concept of Baptism influences the whole Pauline program of Christian life. Because the baptized always remain members of the body of Christ, the power of his Spirit is ever present to keep them centered in God and dead to sin and to self. Life in Christ requires this: "Thus do you consider yourselves as dead to sin, but alive to God in Christ Jesus" (Rm 6:11).

It is in chapter eight of Romans that Paul penetrates deeply into the workings of this death principle. He makes clear that the Holy Spirit, received in Baptism, is always active in the Christian, guiding him with vital inspirations that deliver him from the tyranny of sin and death; for "the inclination of the Spirit is life and peace." Because he is the "Spirit of Christ," his every gift conforms the baptized to the image of the Son. This means that "they who are led by the Spirit are sons of God"; for the Spirit infuses into them the Son's love for the Father. This love always inclines to the Father's will; and so, by its very nature, it is a principle of opposition to the "flesh." "The wisdom of the flesh is hostile to God, for it is not subject to the law of God, nor can it be." "Flesh," in Paul's language, includes everything in man hostile to God.

Flesh turns man away from God, and leads to sin and death. But by conserving and stengthening in the baptized the Son's love for His Father, the Spirit leads man to wage ceaseless war on the deeds of the flesh. In every conscious act the Christian must continue, through the power of the Spirit, to sacrifice all resistance which still remains in the flesh. Hence Paul writes, "Brethren, we are debtors, not to the flesh, that we should live according to the flesh, for if you live according to the flesh, you will die; but if by the Spirit you put to death the deeds of the flesh, you will live" (Rm 8:12-13). It is this principle which gives originality to the moral and ascetical doctrine of St. Paul.

The Apostle treats the same theme in Galatians, where he clearly attributes to the activity of the Holy Spirit the elimination of all that is evil in Christ's members: "Walk in the Spirit, and you will not fulfill the lusts of the flesh.... They who belong to Christ have crucified their flesh with its passions and desires. If we live by the Spirit, by the Spirit let us also walk" (Gal 5:16, 24f.). The word "crucified" is not a mere figure. Baptism gives a share in the death which loving fidelity to God's will produced in Christ, so that Paul could write, "With Christ I have been nailed to the cross" (Gal 2:19). The continuance of the baptismal contact with the risen Savior fills the members of his body with the strong love that crucifies whatever is hostile to the will of God. "They who belong to Christ have crucified their flesh with its passions and desires" (Gal 5:24).

Christian life, therefore, involves an enduring paradox. The Christian, on the one hand, lives on an eschatological plane, sharing the risen life of the Savior and his love for the Father. Paul writes in the name of every Christian, "I live, now not I, but Christ lives in me" (Gal 2:20). On the other hand, the activity of the Holy Spirit has not yet transformed the whole of man, or the whole of the world around him. Therefore, the "now' of life upon earth combines the present temporal level with the final eschatological moment. As long as the Christian is in the world he must carry a "body of death"; he is always able to "yield his members to sin as weapons of iniquity"; he is constantly surrounded by "the wisdom of the flesh that is hostile to God." Hence, though he has truly "put on Christ" through Baptism, a weakness is always present to solicit a return to the earthly ways of his old self.

Paul was vitally aware that in the present life the Christian shares only imperfectly in his redemption. The Apostle, therefore, recognizes a constant tension between the two orders, eschatological and temporal. This awareness is reflected in his epistles; his language ceaselessly varies in them from the indicative mood of simple declaration, when he enunciates the truth that the Christian lives Christ's own life, to the imperative mood of command, when he urges his converts to fulfill the exigencies of the heavenly life. On the one hand, for example, he states the fact, "Our old self has been crucified with him"; yet immediately he goes on to command: "Therefore, do not let sin reign in your mortal body" (Rm 6:6, 12).

The actual process of dying is always a painful experience, for it involves separation from what nature clings to. The death of Christ himself was painful beyond measure; he had come "in the likeness of sinful flesh" and underwent real suffering when he had to part with it, in passing through the door of death to heavenly life. Once his passion was over and he had risen from the tomb, this "death was swallowed up in victory" (1 Cor 15:54); for the love and obedience that filled his soul in the moment of death gained power to effect every good. In the application of this efficacy to his members upon earth, however, Christ must often renew the painful experience of mortal suffering. It is characteristic of his Spirit to separate his members from whatever does not accord with God's will—even though it be something as intimate as one's own "flesh" and as homelike as the "world." The daily "dying" of the Christian, therefore, is a prolongation of Christ's own death, just as the abnegation characteristic of Christian service is truly a sacrifice. Such experiences renew in the member that state of death which love and obedience produced in Christ. It is his Spirit, received in Baptism, who inspires and rules all.

In Romans and Galatians Paul affirms an intimate bond between the death of Christ and the inevitable conflict and suffering in each Christian's life. This bond rests on the truth, often repeated in these epistles, that the principle of death in both cases is one and the same. Because they are intimately united by Baptism as body and member, both Christ and the Christian share the same Holy Spirit whose activity inspires the death which loving obedience to God enjoins.

A study of the doctrine on suffering in Romans and Galatians must take into account Paul's statement in chapter eight of Romans. In these verses he brings together the theme of Romans on union with Christ in suffering and an earlier theme of Thessalonians, union with Him in the eschatological tribulation.

This text concludes Paul's analysis of the death principle which the baptized receives from Christ. Paul has identified it as the activity of the Holy Spirit, who infuses the life and love of the glorious Son of God, putting to death all that is inimical to God's will and insuring by his very presence the certainty of glorious resurrection. Paul then describes this *terminus* of Christian experience: "If we are sons, we are heirs also; heirs indeed of God and joint heirs with Christ, since we suffer with him that we may also be glorified with him. For I reckon that the sufferings of the present time are not worthy to be compared with the glory to come to be revealed in us" (Rm 8:17f.).

The thought here is clear enough. Christian sonship, Paul asserts, leads inevitably to full reward through the sufferings which are intimately connected with life in Christ. He has already introduced in chapter five the theme of tribulation, as it develops virtue and leads to glory through the activity of the Holy Spirit. Now in chapter eight he analyzes the contents of this earlier statement and shows that Christian suffering, which has its source in the Spirit's constant war on the flesh, is the necessary consequence of all union with Christ. Furthermore, Paul carefully identifies the "sufferings of the present time" with the tribulations which precede the final, eschatological coming of the Lord. This quasi-technical expression in the Pauline vocabulary—sufferings *of the present time*—refers to the period of tension and trial between the two appearances of Christ. As the Apostle has shown before and as he repeats here, the share which the Christian has in the messianic trials insures an even greater share in the messianic reward.

Because Paul describes the "sufferings of the present time" as a "suffering with Christ," the question arises, what is the nature and measure of the Christian's union with Christ while he passes through the tribulations which Christ's death inaugurated?

As it stands, the term "suffering with" could be interpreted as focusing attention on a bond between the sufferings of Christians and the *historical* passion of the Savior. Though the Apostle has spoken of such a bond in First Thessalonians, he has left this theme underdeveloped in his following epistles. Indeed, the only feature of Christ's earthly life on which he centers attention is his death—and this because it constituted with the Resurrection the unique cause of salvation. Hence, in treating of this death he does not ordinarily delay over external aspects but views it constantly in its redemptive role. He sees it, on the one hand, as the necessary counterpart of the Resurrection. Christ's passage from this world made possible his full messianic activity of Savior. On the other, he traces the involvements of Christ's death in the lives of his members; they share its efficacy through the activity of the Holy Spirit. As J. Moffatt observes, "For the Apostle, what was vital was not the Lord as a heroic individual; it was Christ dying and rising as one who bore in his own person the destiny of God's chosen people, Christ living as the Lord and Spirit in whom they actually shared and reproduced his death and resurrection within their own experience" (*The First Epistle of St. Paul to the Corinthians*, p. 188).

This estimate of Paul's doctrine is particularly relevant in interpreting the phrase "suffering with," or, as the Greek expresses it, *sym-paschomen*, "co-suffering." All similar compounds, in fact, referring directly to union between the Christian and Christ, must be similarly interpreted: co-dying; co-buried; co-rejoicing. It is noteworthy that the Apostle limits these expressions to union with Christ in the salvific mysteries of his death and risen life; he never extends this phraseology to the incidents of the Savior's earthly life, so as to speak of co-praying with Christ, co-fasting, or co-conquering temptation. This significant restriction is consonant with the whole burden of Paul's doctrine in Romans and Galatians. In these epistles he teaches that Baptism, by uniting the Christian to the Savior, confers a share in his death-resurrection. This union constitutes the essential redemptive experience

of Christ the "corporate personality." Life begins with Baptism,
what happened before that moment matters little.

Thus the Christian is not only *in* Christ but also dies and lives
with Him. It is this latter aspect which finds rich expression in
Paul's writing. We have already seen that it is the Spirit, received
in Baptism, who makes the Christian die to all that is apart from
God; like Christ and in Christ, he lives unto God. Hence, because
both body and member share the same principle of life and death,
Paul not only claims for Christ all that his member is and has, but
he also attributes to the member a true share in the salvific death-
resurrection of the Savior.

This must be kept in mind in analyzing the phrase "we co-
suffer *with* him." To interpret the term, as some have done, as
affirming primarily an identity or bond of *resemblance* between
Christian suffering and the suffering of the Passion does not accord with Paul's many uses of this compound: *co*-dying; *co*-
buried. Paul consistently applies these expressions to inner union
with Christ's death-resurrection in their salvific efficacy. Moreover, references to the historical sufferings of Christ are so incidental and so apart from the consistent Pauline motif of death-
resurrection that their presence does not suffice to alter the
obvious Paulinism of Romans 8:17: "If we co-suffer, we will also
be co-glorified."

The denial that the historical sufferings of Christ are the primary term of reference does not exclude this reference altogether.
The fact is that Paul's thought includes by implication a bond of
resemblance between Christian suffering and the Savior's passion.
For Christian suffering flows from the presence in man of the
Holy Spirit and so is always characterized by the fruits of his
activity: charity, joy, peace, patience (Gal 5:22). Paul, accordingly, has explicitly pointed out that Christians must manifest the
dispositions of Christ in meeting the trials of life. He has also
expressed the desire that "the patience of Christ" may characterize
the sufferings of his converts (2 Th 3:5). He was certainly aware,
therefore, of the bond of resemblance between Christians and the
suffering Christ; and he has spoken of this in his letter to the
Thessalonians: "You became imitators. . . of the Lord, receiving

the word in great tribulation, with joy of the Holy Spirit" (1 Th 1:6).

This theme, however, does not come to the fore in the death-resurrection couplet of Romans 8:17-18. Here he merely repeats what he has developed earlier: Christians, because they are incorporated into the body of Christ, share not only his life but also his death (Rm 6). It must be noted, nonetheless, that the juxtaposition of verses 17 and 18 adds a real contribution. Each verse sheds light upon the other. "If we are sons, we are heirs also; heirs indeed of God and joint heirs with Christ, since we suffer with him that we might also be glorified with him. For I reckon that the sufferings of the present time are not worthy to be compared with the glory to come to be revealed in us." The second verse, with its rich background in First and Second Thessalonians, shows how real are the trials involved in suffering with Christ; the other verse stresses the intimate bond which unites the Christian to Christ. The Christian today undergoes the tribulations of the final messianic age, an age which opened the Savior's death. Through this juxtaposition of themes the divine plan of messianic reward through messianic suffering finds its due place in the Christology which dominates all of Paul's thought.

In the highly personal Second Epistle to the Corinthians Paul does not enunciate new themes; but, as a master in complete possession of the doctrine affirmed in the other great epistles, he shows the vital influence of these principles, especially in the apostolate. The attack of critics upon his apostolic authority and his mode of procedure as a minister of the Gospel forced him to reflect on the antimony of his public life. In every respect it manifested both divine force and human weakness. He treats this theme from every angle in the two apologetic sections: 1:12–7:17 and chapters 10–13. Apostolic labor, like Christian life itself, must follow the rule of thumb for all divine activity: power through weakness so that all glory may belong to God alone.

Throughout this epistle he constantly emphasized that, though the apostle is the bearer of God's power, he carries this treasure in a vessel of clay. Apostolic life involves struggle and suffering; it leads to inward tension and outward persecution. Paul's own

endeavor to bring the light of God to man involved a corresponding experience of human weakness. This aspect of his apostolate
had been foretold of him from the beginning; the Lord said to
Ananias: "I will show him how much he must suffer for my
name" (Ac 9:16). And suffer he did. "Whoever would write the
story of Paul the apostle," as J. Schneider observes, "must write
the story of his sufferings." His intimate self-revelation in Second
Corinthians is a tale of suffering from within and from without.
Yet so certain was Paul that this weakness was the human con-
comitant of divine power acting in him and through him, that
the experience of human limitations was for him a cause of joy:
"Of myself I will glory in nothing save in my infirmities" (2
Cor 12:5).

He recounts a personal experience in which God himself
confirmed the conviction that divine power works through human
frailty. Paul was suffering from a "thorn in the flesh" and prayed
for deliverance. God answered: "My grace is sufficient for thee,
for strength is made perfect in weakness." Paul draws the obvious
conclusion in words which echo chapter one of First Corinthians:
"Gladly, therefore, I will glory in my infirmities that the strength
of Christ may dwell in me. Wherefore I am satisfied, for Christ's
sake, with infirmities, with insults, with hardships, with persecutions, with distresses. For when I am weak, then I am strong" (2
Cor 12:9f.). In this epistle he also sums up in a brief statement the
teaching that Christ himself had to follow the pattern which
marks all divine activity—power through weakness: "For though
he was crucified through weakness, yet he lives through the power
of God" (2 Cor 13:4).

But in Second Corinthians he does more than merely reiterate
and apply the "power-weakness" theme of the first epistle. He
here unites to it the vivid coloring of the principles enunciated in
Romans and Galatians on the union of the Christian with Christ.
Several passages are noteworthy.

The first of these passages is 2 Corinthians 1:3-7. "Blessed
be the God and Father of Our Lord Jesus Christ, the Father of
mercies and the God of all comfort, who comforts us in all our
afflictions, that we also may be able to comfort those who are in

any distress by the comfort wherewith we ourselves are comforted by God. For as the sufferings of Christ abound in us, so
also through Christ does our comfort abound. For whether we
are afflicted, it is for your instruction and salvation; or whether
we are comforted, it is for your comfort, which shows its efficacy
in the endurance of the selfsame sufferings that we also suffer.
And our hope for you is steadfast, knowing that as you are par-
takers of the sufferings, so will you also be of the comfort."

Paul here repeats the familiar theme that afflictions abound
in Christian life, and especially in the apostolic ministry. In accord, however, with the fundamental antithesis of death-resurrection, he affirms that such suffering brings its corresponding measure of comfort: "As the sufferings of Christ abound in us, so also
through Christ does our comfort abound." Such comfort, it must
be noted, is not merely personal; whatever the apostle experiences
is of benefit to his converts. "Whether we are afflicted . . . or
whether we are comforted," all serves to strengthen the Corinthians for the endurance of the same sufferings which the apostles
sustain. Paul, therefore, is confident that because the Corinthians
share his sufferings, they will share also the comfort which he has
received.

The trials and sufferings of which he speaks are those that
afflict both the apostle and his converts in the first days of a
Christian community, for the Corinthians are true sharers in the
tribulations which the founder of their Church endures. He
describes his apostolic sufferings, in which the Corinthians
share, as the "sufferings of Christ." It seems unlikely that the
phrase identifies the sufferings of the Corinthians with the historical sufferings of the Passion. It is also unlikely that the phrase refers only to an *extrinsic* bond, based on Christ's command or the
exigencies of His service. Rather, the dominance in Paul's doctrine
of the *intrinsic* bond between the Christian and Christ strongly
suggests that this expression contains richer meaning.

The Corinthians truly belong to Christ who, through his
Spirit, is the efficient principle of all Christian experience in the
lives of his members. This aspect, which is the immediate consequence of baptismal union with Christ, is the quality which gives

richest value to the sufferings of both apostle and converts. Indeed, it is because the *fellowship of their sufferings is really a fellowship of the sufferings of Jesus* and that Paul applies the death-resurrection theme of all his thoughts to establish the certainty that consolation will follow upon trials.

It is legitimate to conclude, therefore, that Second Corinthians 1:3-7 belongs to the thought-pattern already enunciated in Romans: "If we are sons, we are heirs also: heirs indeed of God and joint heirs with Christ, provided, however, we suffer with him that we may also be glorified with him." Both passages affirm an objective and necessary bond between suffering-consolation and suffering-glory. At the same time, these passages refer the trials of Christians directly to Christ, calling them "the sufferings of Christ" and "suffering with Christ." The parallelism of these texts emphasizes that Paul sees verified through the whole course of Christian life the union with Christ in his death-resurrection which was first realized through Baptism. Baptismal union between the body and its members necessarily involves a life process. The Holy Spirit leads the Christian to renew constantly the death of Christ in order to continue living with his life. It is with this context in mind, therefore, that Paul speaks of Christian trial as "the suffering of Christ."

Another striking example of the death-life theme is in chapter four of Second Corinthians. Paul has just spoken of the light which he received as an apostle to communicate to others. He goes on to affirm that the power of his ministry is wholly God's, for the elements of his own temporal life contributed little to its efficacy. "We carry this treasure in vessels of clay, to show that the abundance of the power is God's and not ours." His own experience made him very aware of this duality: "In all things we suffer tribulation, but we are not distressed; we are sore pressed, but we are not destitute; we endure persecution, but we are not forsaken; we are cast down, but we do not perish." His interpretation of the profound meaning of these vicissitudes is significant. He traces these antitheses to his union with Christ, whose death is the source of apostolic suffering and whose life is the source of apostolic strength. For he sums up all by portraying apostles as "always bearing about in our body the dying of Jesus, so that the life also of Jesus may be made manifest in our bodily frame. For we the living are constantly being handed over to death for Jesus' sake, that the life also of Jesus may be made manifest in our mortal flesh."

These words indicate that more than an external bond links the human weakness and suffering of the apostles to Christ. The daily trials of apostolic life borne for Christ are identified as a bearing about of "the dying of Jesus." This latter expression refers to the state of death which is the enduring effect of baptismal death with Christ. This Paul has already indicated in chapter six of Romans where he stated that those who have sacramentally died with Christ must ever after consider themselves dead. Because this state of death involves a constant dying to the deeds of the flesh, it issues necessarily in the activity of self-denial and mortification. But, whether considered in its primary meaning as a passive state of death or in its derived sense of active mortification, this "dying" of the Christian is truly that of Christ, because his Spirit is the effective principle who constantly renews the Savior's death in all the members of his body.

In these verses Paul also states in parallel clauses that the suffering of the apostolic life is inseparably connected with the apostle's manifestation of the life of Christ: "in order that the life also of Jesus may be manifest." Paul speaks here of the actual effects of the labor and suffering of his apostolate. For the manifestation of life takes place in an early state and benefits the Corinthians in the present life. The force of the verb "to be made manifest" cannot be overlooked. Though scarcely appearing outside the New Testament, it shows there an almost technical meaning, referring to the first or second coming of Christ, with the just sharing his glory. Its use in the present case expresses the truth that the life which the apostle diffuses is the life of the risen Christ, "the power of his resurrection." At the same time it suggests that apostolic activity is an anticipated share in the Resurrection.

In Paul's eyes the apostolate is but an extension to others of the life of Christ who already lives in his apostle. Its purpose is to form Christ in men, that he may live in them just as he lives in Paul. Apostolic labor, therefore, follows the same law that governs the personal development of every Christian: life accompanied by death. Paul expressed the pattern of apostolic life this way: "Death is at work in us, but life in you."

In the apostolate the "zone of fulfillment" for Christ's power is enlarged. This means an equally extensive zone of opposition. The apostle has to enter into conflict with a wider "world"; he must "crucify" sin and the hostile flesh in the life of every convert. All this involves struggle and suffering, which Paul can truly call the "dying of Jesus" since he who dwells in the apostle and acts upon him through his Holy Spirit provides the effective principle for such struggle. To make Christ live in his converts, therefore, the apostle himself has to endure the death that Christ underwent to share his life with the world. The principle of death is always one and the same; only the time and manner of its application differs.

A few verses later in chapter four of Second Corinthians, Paul presents another aspect—the psychological—of the union between Christ and his members. Though it is true that Paul does not here speak explicitly of suffering, he brings into sharp focus, nonetheless, the active, psychological influence of the principle which accounts for all Christian suffering.

In the other great epistles he has already shown why all Christians must endure trial and struggle; through the indwelling of Christ's Spirit they share ontologically in the dynamic love-principle of Christ's activity. He now affirms that the very love which the Savior manifested in his life and ministry and which he now continues in his glorious life provides, also, the dynamic psychological impulse of the Christian apostolate: "The love of Christ impels us, because we have come to the conclusion. . . that Christ died for all, in order that they who are alive may live no longer for themselves, but for him who died for them and rose again" (2 Cor 5:14f).

Such fullness of ontological and psychological sharing in the inward spirit of the Savior is required by the very nature of the apostolate, for both Christ and his apostle are engaged in the same work of reconciliation under the guiding inspiration of God's love: "All things are from God, who has reconciled us to himself through Christ and has given to us the ministry of reconciliation. For God was truly in Christ, reconciling the world to himself. . . . On behalf of Christ, therefore, we are acting as ambassadors, God, as it were, appealing through us." This charge and its motivation in love flow from the inward bond between Christ and his members, the bond to which Paul has attributed the whole of Christian suffering.

The same thought of union with Christ in his death-resurrection underlies one of the concluding passages of Second Corinthians. "Do you seek a proof," Paul asks, "of the Christ who speaks in me, who is not weak in your regard, nay, is powerful in you? For he was crucified through weakness, yet he lives through the power of God. Yes, we also are weak in him, yet we shall live with him through the power of God in your regard" (13:3f.).

Paul here stabilizes the "power-weakness" theme of First Corinthians as the law of Christian life; he also identifies it with the intrinsic bond which unites Christians to Christ and gives them a share in his death-life.

Paul deals with the antinomy of his ministry: though personally weak, he is conscious of bearing the power of Christ. Such an experience is inevitable. For the Savior himself had to follow the law that governs all divine activity in this world: "He was crucified through weakness, yet he lives through the power of God." Therefore Paul, too, must follow this rule, not merely because it is a law of God's salvific activity, but especially because he lives by the very principle that produces death-life in both body and its members. Whatever weakness or power the apostle experiences in doing God's work, all is both "in Christ" and "with Christ": "We also are weak *in him*, yet we shall live *with him* through the power of God in your regard."

This passage is a particularly felicitous conclusion to Second Corinthians, since it blends so well the themes of the two preceding epistles. It offers a consummate apologia for the "weakness" of the apostolic ministry. It shows that the "power-weakness" theme of all God's activity applies with special force to the

Christian, who, through his intimate union with Christ, shares the death-life principle which leads both the body and the member through suffering to glory.

A long search through the writings of St. Paul brings us now to the heart of his doctrine on Christian suffering. We read in his letter to the Philippians: "... that I may know him and the power of his resurrection and the fellowship of his sufferings" (3:10).

The very word order of this verse parallels the events of his conversion, as set down in Acts. Its first element was his meeting with the risen Christ on the road to Damascus. This contact illumined his mind and aroused the first stirrings of new life; in very truth, Paul came "to know Christ in the power of his resurrection." But immediately after this experience he learned that suffering was to fill his life: "I will show him how much he must suffer for my name." His surrender to the risen Christ, although lifegiving, involved also a share of suffering. In the story of his conversion, therefore, two elements are essential: vivifying contact with the Lord of glory and a declaration of the necessity of suffering. In the order of actual occurrence, the first preceded the second.

Paul's aim in Philippians, however, is not merely to summarize the incidents of his conversion. He is here writing an apologia for Christianity itself so that, although he speaks of his own conversion, he brings to light the excelling "gains" of which every Christian can boast. Paul understood well that his "I" is the "I" of every Christian and that the new life which he received through conversion is the same reality which every Christian possesses through Baptism. He speaks, moreover, of the benefits of life in Christ from the vantage point of rich experience and mature understanding.

It is clear from the climactic rise in the verses that Paul singles out the parousia-resurrection as the ultimate "gain" dominating all motives. "... that I may know him and the power of his resurrection and the fellowship of his sufferings: become like him in death, in the hope that somehow I may attain to the resurrection from the dead."

Hope for final union with Christ has been a theme throughout the whole epistle. To reach this union necessitates previous labor and suffering. Even the Jews, with their doctrines of the messianic tribulations, recognized that one attained to glory through suffering. But how vastly different was the doctrine of Paul. For him, to attain the ultimate Christian reward, so eminently superior to Jewish resurrection, one had to live and to suffer in the Christian way, so eminently superior to Jewish righteousness. The "gain" of Christianity consisted not only in the excelling *end* at which it aimed—resurrection in and with Christ—but also in the excelling *way* whereby it reached that goal—life in and with Christ. In Judaism men suffered in order to be glorified; in Christianity men suffered *with Christ* in order to be glorified *with Christ*.

Man enters on this way through conversion-baptism. At that moment, the new member is united to the body of Christ and receives the gift of the Spirit. The Spirit vivifies what was dead by infusing the very life of the risen Christ which will one day manifest its full vitality in the parousia-resurrection. As with Paul on the way to Damascus, so too with the Christian in Baptism, the first "gain" of conversion is "to know Christ in the power of his resurrection."

But there is another essential "gain" which Paul describes as "the fellowship of his sufferings." To urge his converts to firmness in the faith, Paul reminds them that their suffering is a sign of salvation, for it is a gift of God like faith itself. There is no question that he sees a strongly active element in the suffering of which he speaks. For he has previously described the activity of the Philippians as a manly strife and immediately afterwards explains their suffering with the parallel phrase, "engaged in the same struggle."

"Fellowship of his sufferings," therefore, could be interpreted as referring to the Christian's share in the passion of Christ. As we have already seen, however, Paul has spoken so rarely of a parallelism between Christian suffering and the historical sufferings of Christ that it does not seem likely he would highlight such a feature in this condensed statement of the essential elements of

Christian life. The reproduction in the Christian of the historical sufferings of Christ, whether by mystical identity or by physical similarity, can hardly be called an essential or even primary element in Pauline doctrine.

On the other hand, the phrase, "fellowship of his sufferings," could refer to sufferings that are borne for Christ, in his cause. Undoubtedly, this element plays a role in Paul's thought. But to limit the content of the phrase to this meaning alone—that is, to a merely external bond between Christian suffering and Christ—does not accord with the demands of Pauline thought. Paul is here speaking of life in Christ and of the fullness of its "gains." He has just referred to the activity of the Holy Spirit which constitutes the "power of Christ's resurrection"; immediately afterwards he speaks of the conformity to Christ's death which leads to resurrection from the dead, a conformity which is effected by the Spirit of Christ working within the baptized. Both of these themes are related essentially to Paul's rich concept of life in Christ. It seems likely, therefore, that the intermediary phrase is also of the same nature.

This inference is wholly consonant with a truth that has emerged clearly from our review of Paul's doctrine: the truth, namely, that Christian suffering has deep theological roots in his teaching on union with Christ. This doctrine, as we have seen, supposes that every Christian receives at Baptism the efficacy of the salvific death and resurrection once accomplished in the body of Christ to which he is now united: "Do you not know that we who have been baptized into Christ have been baptized into His death?" (Rm 6:3). This "gain" of Christian life may be viewed both as it exists in the first moment of conversion when it is simply life-with-Christ and death-with-Christ, and also as it exists in the lifelong process of preparation for the ultimate goal of parousia-resurrection. When Paul speaks of this second aspect, he always sees it as a process involving trial and suffering. For after Baptism the Christian must continue to live in the "flesh" and to deal with the "world," both of which form an ambient, hostile to the love of God and the life of the Spirit. If, therefore, the member of Christ is to live the risen life of the

Savior, he must be crucified to the "world"; he must put to death the "deeds of the flesh." In a word, baptismal death with Christ must be renewed constantly throughout earthly life if one is finally to attain the ultimate goal of parousia-resurrection with Christ.

The "gain" of Paul's conversion, therefore, and of every Christian in Baptism, consisted not merely in momentary death with Christ, but in the fact that it inaugurated a lifelong *state of death*, through the power of the Spirit, to the world, to the flesh, and to sin, both in his own life and in the lives of all whom he must gain for Christ. This Christian experience constitutes the *fellowship of his sufferings*.

This phrase means, undoubtedly, that such suffering is borne for Christ and is incurred in laboring for His cause. It means, too, that such suffering is supported in the spirit of His virtues. But, according to the rich Pauline concept, all this is true because the bond between Christian suffering and Christ himself is rooted in the bond that unites body and member. Such suffering is truly "Christ's," because the love which impelled him to die is the very same love which the Spirit infuses into his members so that they die daily to all that is opposed to God.

It is significant that Paul speaks here of "knowing the fellowship of his sufferings" rather than simply "knowing his sufferings." The word "fellowship" introduces into this phrase the spirit of the whole epistle. Throughout, he has shown himself vitally conscious of the part which all his fellow Christians play in working and suffering for the Gospel; several times, in fact, he has used the word "fellowship" to express the close bond that unites them and to describe the share which the Philippians have contributed. Now, in 3:10, with graceful allusion to the part which his converts play, Paul speaks of his sufferings as a fellowship of his immense suffering. For truly his own daily experiences of "dying" formed but a share of the vast *sufferings of Christ* which all Christians, and especially apostolic laborers, must bear in order to bring the body of Christ to full measure.

"Fellowship in Christ's sufferings" is, therefore, a reality in all Christian living. If Paul here refers the phrase to himself, it is because every Christian can make the same boast and must follow the same example. For all life in Christ is vital with the activity of the Holy Spirit who daily renews in the members of Christ's body the love and obedience which inspired the Savior to undergo the passage of death. This experience involves every Christian in a crisscross of two levels—life in Christ and life in the flesh. Tension and struggle are inevitable. But always the resultant suffering is truly a share in the *sufferings of Christ*, for the glorious Savior claims as his own the sufferings which the dynamic presence of his Spirit occasions in his members.

FAITH: FIRST STEP IN THE ASSIMILATION OF THE EASTER MYSTERY

F.X. Durrwell, C.Ss.R.

The Easter mystery opens out upon men by way of the apostolate and the sacraments; through them it becomes communicable and is communicated. But it remains for men to come to it and take it to themselves. This in the first instance they do by means of faith, and St. Paul has a doctrinal synthesis on this subject.

The Object of Faith

The object of Christian faith is not simply God, but God who raises up Christ. The Jews accepted the Mosaic faith (Dt 6:4), yet they are numbered among the infidels (2 Cor 4:4), for they do not believe in God who raised up Christ.

To St. Paul, the faith of Abraham was a kind of prophetic outline of our faith. The object of Paul's faith, as of Abraham's, was the power of God who gave life to the dead: "Abraham is the father of us all.... He believed in God who quickens the dead, and calls those things that are not into being." He believed the promise made to his seed, "nor did he consider his own body now dead ... nor the dead womb of Sara ... and therefore it was reputed to him unto justice" (Rm 4:16-22).

Our faith is similar: "It is written not only for him [Abraham] that it was reputed to him unto justice, but also for us, to whom it shall be reputed, if we believe in him, that raised up Jesus Christ our Lord from the dead, who was delivered up for our sins, and rose again for our justification" (Rm 4:23-5).

Despite the resemblance, our faith is enormously superior to that of Abraham. Whereas our ancestor believed in a human life being raised from a dead womb, our "faith in the operation of God who raises up" is concerned with a gift of heavenly life: God raised up a man, Christ Jesus, for our salvation, lifting him to his true divine life, in the total gift of the Holy Spirit.

The believer's entire faith centers upon this divine fact. It is briefly defined as "faith in the operation of God who has raised him up from the dead" (Col 2:12; cf. Rm 10:9; 1 Cor 15:2ff., 2 Cor 4:13-14; Ep 1:19; 1 Th 4:14). It believes in God whose will to save us is affirmed in the resurrection of Christ and who judges the world in Christ. So essential is Christ's resurrection to our faith, that if he had not risen, that faith would be simply a dream, void of meaning (1 Cor 15:14-15).

Thus the object of our faith is not God in his serene essence, a God standing in motionless perfection, but the person of God who breaks into our history through the justifying and judgement-giving act of the Resurrection, who obliges us to make a decision, and radically changes the course of our destiny.

The revelation of God's salvation is effected in the person of Christ. The Christian faith is wholly centered upon Christ the Lord, Christ risen from the dead. "Christ is the Lord" (1 Cor 12:3; Ph 2:11; Rm 10:9) formulates the earliest professions of faith. This contains the whole Christian faith, and the whole Creed grows out of it.

Thus the object of faith is essentially soteriological: Christ, Lord of the world to be saved and judged. In the risen Christ faith finds the Father who engenders Christ for us, and gives us the Holy Spirit for our own.

Hope comes so close to faith that the two are hardly distinguishable—hope is faith as a driving force. Abraham believed against all appearances and hoped against hope (Rm 4:18-19), Christians are those who believe, and also those who "hope in Christ" (1 Cor 15:19).

For the power of God effecting the salvation of the world in Christ, which constitutes the object of faith, is also the motive of hope; one cannot be committed to that faith without also having hope (cf. Tt 1:1-2).[1]

Other writers give us outlines and sometimes even exact formulations of this doctrine of faith. For the Synoptics, faith bears upon God in his power to establish the kingdom, and it is inseparable from hope. In the Acts, faith is the response to the announcement of Christ's messianic exaltation, and those who believe call upon the name of the Lord (2:21; 9:14). To St. John the object of faith is "that Jesus is the Christ, the Son of God" (20:31); the idea of Christ as Messiah and Redeemer is essential to it: "I am the Resurrection and the Life....Do you believe this? ... Yes, Lord I have believed that you are Christ the Son of God who have come into this world" (11:25-7). The act of faith consists in believing that Christ has been sent by the Father (17:8, 21), "that I am he" (8:24, 28; 13:19), in other words that he is Jesus who is to come (cf. Mk 8:6), he who, clearly from the context of 8:24, is come to save from death; that he is the bread come down from heaven to feed the world. Above all is that faith demanded and imposed by the exaltation (3:14-15; 8:28); the beloved disciple "believed" when he saw the empty tomb (20: 8); it is to the glorified Christ that the believer must adhere if he is to draw the Spirit from him (7:37-9).

If we leave out the shades of meaning each author supplies, we may conclude that the Christian faith bears upon the redeeming action of God in Christ, an action which culminates in the Resurrection.

Faith as Contact with the Mystery

The believer cannot fail to come in contact with this salvation of God towards which faith moves by its own inner necessity.

The saving mystery of Easter is opened wide and offered to man in the Apostles and in the sacraments; by faith, man is

---

1 Faith is a dynamic virtue, attempting everything, never hesitating. To believe in the resurrection of Christ is to believe that henceforward nothing is impossible. Man enters upon the divine process of justification with complete assurance; the Apostle is never daunted, for the Gospel is the power of God (Rom 1:16), and he works with unshakable certainty for the complete conquest of the world.

borne towards that mystery, lays himself open to it and welcomes it.

In this the virtue of faith consists: it lays man open to the Easter mystery and enables him to take it to himself. "The exceeding greatness of his power [working in the resurrection of Christ is exercised] toward us, who believe" (Ep 1:19). "We have been buried with him in baptism, and we are risen again with him and in him by the faith in the operation of God, who has raised him up from the dead" (Col 2:12).[2]

Where he is not explicitly saying this, St. Paul implies it by what he does say. Our risen life is defined as life "in the faith of the Son of God ... who delivered himself up" (Gal 2:20). The promise of the Spirit, fulfilled in the resurrection of Christ, is made effective for us by means of faith: "that we might receive the promise of the Spirit by faith" (Gal 3:14; cf. 5:5). The presence of Christ in us, that permanent communion in the Resurrection, is the effect of faith: "Christ dwells by faith in your hearts" (Ep 3:17). And similarly our presence in Christ: "That I may be found in him, not having my own justice ... but that which is of the faith" which brings experience of his death and resurrection (Ph 3:9-10). Christ's divine sonship, made manifest in his resurrection, and the privileges flowing from it—such as the freedom of the sons—are all communicated by faith: "After the faith is come, we are no longer under a pedagogue. For you are all the children of God by faith, which is in Christ Jesus" (Gal 3:25-6).

According to the fourth gospel, faith is man's movement towards Christ, the possessor of life. To believe is to come (5:40; 6:35; and *passim*). In his glorified body Christ bears the wellspring of life (7:39; 6:62-3), and man comes to him by faith to drink of the Spirit flowing from his pierced side.

Faith has this power of opening man to the mystery of the paschal Christ because it is not merely an intellectual assent but

---

2 There are two means working together to link the believer to the fact of the Redemption. From the believer's point of view, one is, as it were, the surroundings (ἐν) in which the contact is established, baptism; the other, faith, is an active instrument for taking possession of the Resurrection(διά).

a handing-over of man to God in his total adherence to the risen Christ; it is man's assent, in his inmost being, to another principle of life.

Faith as a Death and a Resurrection

All knowledge presupposes a certain likeness in nature to the thing known, and all adherence to another demands a harmony. The risen Christ, the object of faith, is dead to the flesh and lives in the Spirit. In order to establish contact with him, faith makes man undergo a certain death, and it is in that death that it makes him adhere to the living Christ. It is thus a re-birth.

By faith, man gives up making himself the center of his own life, the basis of his own salvation, and places that center and basis outside himself, in God who gives life to Christ. Whereas the Jew relies upon the privileges of his race and upon his works and remains bounded by the sufficiency of his own justice (Ph 3:9; Rm 9:32; 10:3), the believer considers everything that seemed gain according to the flesh as valueless and even harmful (Ph 3:8); he comes out of himself to seek a justice he has not merited by any works (Rm 3:28; 4:5; Gal 2:16; Ep 2:8-9; Ph 3:9). He believes in the justice of God which is communicated in Christ, and he is in turn glorified, but not for his works, for his glory is in God alone (2 Cor 10:17; Ph 3:9). He has crazily cast his anchor of certainty beyond all the assurances of the flesh to fix it in the death and resurrection of Jesus Christ (Ph 3:3-11).

Intellectual adherence to the teaching of the Apostles is an immediate renunciation of one's own autonomy of thought, and of the security one finds in one's own understanding, by which one lays oneself open to invasion by another's thought. And at a deeper level, it is a complete renunciation of man's right to command himself: faith is obedience (Rm 1:5), it makes man truly captive to God (2 Cor 10:5; Rm 6:17-18). The believer opens himself to God, becomes linked to God, which means the death of the flesh. There is an anguish for man in making this complete reversal, in recognizing his fundamental powerlessness, in handing himself over to another, in delivering himself totally over to the salvific will of God. He lets go the certitudes within his grasp (Ph 3:3-7), abandoning the ground he feels beneath his feet, in order to believe in a world he cannot see; he trusts his weight to something whose very existence (naturally speaking, impossible) he knows only by God's word. He risks all upon the word of God in Christ.

St. Paul speaks of the "sacrificial oblation of faith" (Ph 2:17; Rm 15:16). We say this sacrifice is metaphorical, but we must not therefore miss seeing its real analogy with the sacrifice of Christ.[3]

Faith an Effect of the Resurrection

This faith which subjects man to the raising action of God is itself an effect of that action.

The apostolic preaching which produces it is laden with the raising force of God. Once man has received it, it acts from God and opens him to faith: "It has been given you as a gift . . . to believe in Christ" (Ph 1:29). The confession of faith in the Lord Jesus which assures man the salvation of the Messiah (Rm 10:9-11), is itself a result of the Spirit of the glorified Christ, who is the gift we receive from the Messiah: "No man can say Jesus is the Lord, but the Holy Ghost" (1 Cor 12:3). Faith which involves a death must presuppose a gift of the Spirit; for if it is a death to the flesh it can only be a death with Christ, and one can only die in this way in union with the life of our Savior.

Faith, therefore, not only opens man to the paschal mystery, but itself belongs to that mystery; it is an effect of the Father's action in glorifying Christ. It is at once cause and effect, creating the contact with the Resurrection that it demands. It is numbered both among the means whereby the risen Christ expands, and among the means whereby man assimilates the Resurrection.

Because God's raising force is at work, it exercises a real causality in our justification. It is more than simply "an indispen-

---

3 The martyr is the perfect type of the believer. He lets go the life he has for life in Christ, in which he believes though he cannot see it.

sable prerequisite" for sacramental justification; its action complements the work of baptism: "... buried with him in baptism, in which [or "in him"] also you are risen again by faith in the operation of God" (Col 2:12). Justification results from the combined action of the sacrament and faith.

Though he affirms quite definitely the efficacy inherent in the very administration of baptism, St. Paul attributes to man himself a part of his sacramental sanctification: "You are washed" by baptism (1 Cor 6:11). "They that are Christ's have crucified their flesh with its vices and concupiscences" (Gal 5:24). This crucifixion dates from baptism; but unlike the parallel text, Rm 6:3-4, this one does not attribute the death to the sacramental rite, but stresses the act of the will whereby the believer effects, at the conscious level, the death of his flesh at the moment of baptism.

The efficaciousness of this human activity could hardly be in the order of merit—such an idea would go counter to all Paul's teaching. Yet man does bring his co-operation to God's action in the sacrament. His activity is not alongside God's: the two activities interpenetrate, for man's faith is itself due to the Spirit, and the Spirit is given in the sacrament. Yet man does play an important part. By a positive will, expressed through faith, he puts himself at the disposal of God who justifies the world in the dead and risen Christ. He lets life be implanted in him, consciously submitting to the death of Christ which the sacrament mysteriously achieves.

PAUL AND THE LAW

Joseph A. Fitzmyer, S.J.

Paul's treatment of law is found for the most part in two letters: in Gal 2:16-6:13 and in Rm 2:12-8:7. Though there are scattered remarks about it elsewhere (e.g., in 1 Cor 9:20; 15:56; 2 Cor 3:17-18; Rm 9:31; 10:4-5; 13:8-10; Ep 2:15 [cf. 1 Tm 1:8-9], it is well to recall at the outset that his main discussion is found in polemical contexts. The Judaizing problem in the early Church called forth his remarks on the subject; this was a threat to his fundamental understanding of the Christ-event and he reacted vigorously against it. But it would be a mistake to think that Paul's teaching about the Law occupies the center of his theology. To regard it in this way would be to commit the same error which has plagued much of Christian thinking since the Reformation which identified the essence of Pauline theology with justification. We have finally come to recognize that the essence of the Pauline view of Christ lies in the "new creation" brought about in Christ and through the Spirit, as God initiated a new phase of Salvation History. Similarly we have learned that Paul viewed this Christian condition in terms of justification because of the polemical context of the Judaizing problem. But even though his teaching about the Law is time-conditioned and polemical, nevertheless it has in all parts of it aspects which are relevant and pertinent to our situation today.

Likewise at the outset it is necessary to mention one further minor problem. It concerns the literal and figurative sense of *nomos* used by Paul as well as his use of the noun with and without the article. In a number of instances Paul will make statements such as these: the Gentiles "are a law to themselves" (Rm 2:14);

or "another law in my members at war with the law of my mind" (Rm 7:21-25); or, as he makes use of oxymoron, "the law of the Spirit of life" (Rm 8:2), or "the law of Christ" (Gal 6:2). In all such instances the use of *nomos* is figurative, and its prime analo-gate is the Mosaic Law. These figurative expressions attempt to describe pagan or Christian counterparts of the Mosaic Law in a term that is frankly borrowed from it. But aside from such clearly figurative expressions Paul otherwise speaks only of the Mosaic Law, "the religious system under which the Jews had lived since the time of Moses." He speaks only of it, and makes no distinction between its cultic, ritual, or ethical demands. It may be that he sometimes extends it, designating by *nomos* the whole of the Old Testament and not just the Torah or Pentateuch (cf. Rm 3:19). But it is useless to try to distinguish his statements according to the use of the article or the lack of it. If we empha-size this at the outset, it is only to avoid a misunderstanding; for Paul does not really talk about "law as such." It is true, however, that some statements are couched in terms which are generic and lend themselves to other legal systems than that of Moses; for this reason it is not difficult to apply them to other types of law, Christian or otherwise, and find that they are still relevant.

With such preliminary remarks we may turn to the discussion itself which has three parts: first, Paul's view of the Law and the anomaly which it presents in man's life; secondly, his explanation of the anomaly; and thirdly, his solution of the anomaly.

Paul's View of the Law and its Anomaly

We can best describe Paul's view of the Law by making five brief observations about it.

1. Paul personifies *Nomos*, just as he does *Hamartia* ("Sin") and *Thanatos* ("Death"). This is especially true in the letter to the Romans. Like *Thanatos* and *Hamartia*, *Nomos* is depicted as an actor playing a role on the stage of man's history (see Rm 5:20).

To understand its role, we must recall Paul's view of Salvation History. His conception of it is based on the unilinear view of world history which he inherited from the rabbis of the Pharisaic tradition. Early rabbis maintained that the duration of the world would be 6000 years, divided into three phases: (a) the period of *Tōhû-wā-bōhû* ("Chaos," see Gn 1:2), lasting from Adam to Moses when there was no law; (b) the period of *Tôrah* ("Law"), lasting from Moses to the Messiah when the Law ruled man's existence; (c) the period of the Messiah, when either the Law would cease (according to some rabbis), or the Messiah would perfect it by giving it a new interpretation (according to others). Paul employs a similar threefold division of history: (a) From Adam to Moses the period was law-less; men sinned but there was no imputation of transgressions (Rm 5:13). "For the Law brings wrath; but where there is no Law there is no transgression" (Rm 4:15). (b) From Moses to Christ the Law reigned and men's sins were imputed as transgressions of it; "the Law brings wrath" (Rm 4:15). (c) The Messianic Age began with Christ Jesus, who is "the end of the Law" (Rm 10:4).

Paul apparently followed that rabbinical view which regarded the Law as coming to its end in the period of the Messiah. For him Jesus himself is "the end of the Law" (*telos nomou*), not only in the sense that it was aimed at him as its consummation, its goal, or its *finis* (Gal 3:24), but also in the sense that, as the *Christos* (or "Messiah"), he put an end to it. For he "abolished in his flesh the Law with its commandments and ordinances"(Ep 2:15).Through him "we are discharged from the Law" (Rm 7:6). Upon us "have met the ends of the ages" (1 Cor 10:11), i.e., the last end of the age of the Torah and the first end of the age of the Messiah. In the latter there reigns instead *ho nomos tou Christou*, "the law of the Messiah" (Gal 6:2).

Thus all of man's history has become a stage; and the actors who come upon it to influence his condition are Death, Sin, and the Law.

2. When Paul describes the actor *Nomos* for us, we learn that he is good: "The Law is holy, and the commandment is holy, righteous, and good" (Rm 7:12; see also 7:16). Indeed, it is even said to be "spiritual" (*pneumatikos*, Rm 7:14), i.e., belonging to

the sphere of God and not of earthbound man. For it is "the Law of God" (Rm 7:22, 25; 8:7; cf. 1 Cor 7:19), since it ultimately came from God and was destined to lead men to "life," i.e., to communion with God. It was "the very commandment whose purpose was life" (*hê entolê hê eis zôên*, Rm 7:10). In a broad sense it could even be said to be "the oracles of God" (Rm 3:2), for it manifested to men God's word and his will. In Gal 3:12 Paul quotes Lv 18:5 and is constrained to admit that "he who does them [i.e., the prescriptions of the Law] shall live by them." Even though the Law was secondary and inferior when compared to the promise made to Abraham by God (Gal 3:21), it was certainly not a contradiction of them. It enjoyed, therefore, a fundamental goodness by which the saints of the Old Dispensation were to achieve their destiny, a life of uprightness in the sight of God.

3. This character *Nomos* constituted one of the privileges of Israel. Paul frankly lists it among the prerogatives enjoyed by his kinsmen by race: "They are Israelites and to them belong the sonship, the glory, the covenants, the giving of the Law..." (Rm 9:4). They were privileged in that they possessed a God-given means of seeking their justification. And everything that the Law says is addressed to those who are under its authority and who acknowledge it (Rm 3:19).

But Paul turns the coin, precisely in this regard. For it does little good for a Jew to boast of his possession of the Law and of hearing it read every Sabbath in the synagogue, if he does not obey it (Rm 2:17-24). As a prerogative of Israel, the Law set Paul's kinsmen by race apart from those who were *a-nomoi* and *hamartôloi*, "law-less" and "sinners" (seeing that they were without the Law). But Paul emphasizes the obligation which lay on Israel to observe that Law, and to observe it in its entirety (Gal 5:3), if it is recognized as a norm for life.

4. But in spite of all this *Nomos* is depicted as incapable of producing the uprightness which it was destined to achieve. Though it was "holy, righteous, and good," came from God, and was Israel's prerogative, yet it did not bring "life" to men. Paul is severe in his judgment, as he makes a daring addition to Ps

143:2, "No human being can be made upright in the sight of God —*by observing the Law*" (literally, "from the deeds of the Law"). The last phrase, boldly added by Paul to the Psalm in Rm 3:20, amounts to a devastating accusation which formulates the anomaly which the character *Nomos* brings into the life of man. *Nomos* was supposed to bring life, as Lv 18:5 had promised; but in reality it brought just the opposite. Thus Paul describes the *negative role* of the Law: its inability to give life, because it is nothing more than an external norm. It tells man what he must do without giving him the *dynamis* ("the force") to do it. And so, the Law was not a dynamic force for life.

To prove his point, Paul appeals to the *de facto* situation of the Jews who are just as much subject to God's wrath, even though they possess the Law, as the heathen who do not obey it because they do not know it. Indeed, his accusation implies that the Jews *cannot* really obey it. As proof he cites the Old Testament itself in the words of Hab 2:4, "the upright man shall live by faith" (see Rm 1:17; Gal 3:12); but faith has nothing to do with the Law. This, then, is the negative role of *Nomos*: he fails to give man the ability to fulfill the obligations which he imposes on him.

5. But *Nomos* also plays a positive role by multiplying or enhancing sin and by levelling a curse on man. And herein we find the real anomaly which Paul sees in the Law. Good though it was, the Law really multiplied sin. Paul teaches this explicitly, "It was added [to the promises made to Abraham] for the sake of transgressions" (Gal 3:19); "the Law came in to increase the transgression" (Rm 5:20).

These Pauline statements must be understood in terms of the periods of Salvation History mentioned above. Arriving on the stage of man's history in the second period, *Nomos* became the tool and the instrument of *Hamartia*. In fact, it became the very "*dynamis* of Sin" itself (1 Cor 15:56). While supplying to man no *dynamis* of its own whereby he might find "life," it ironically enough became the henchman of *Hamartia;* and thus it unleashed on man God's wrath: "for the Law brings wrath" (Rm 4:15). Though it was not sin itself, it contributed to sin: "What then shall we say? That the Law is Sin? By no means! Yet, if it had not been for the Law, I would not have known Sin" (Rm 7:7). And the reason is that "in the absence of Law Sin was dead" (Rm 7:8).

This role of *Nomos* is played in three ways: (a) The Law acts as an occasion (*aphormê*) for Sin. It instructs man in the material possibility of sinning, either by forbidding what is indifferent (e.g., the eating of unclean animals, Lv 11:2ff.; Dt 14. 4ff.), or by exciting man's desires in annoying his conscience by the imposition of an external, positive regulation against "forbidden fruit." This aspect of Law, however, as an occasion of Sin, is for Paul only secondary; he alludes to it briefly in Rm 7:5, 8, 11, but otherwise makes very little of it.

(b) Much more important is the role which *Nomos* plays as a moral informer. For *Nomos* gives man "a real and profound knowledge of sin" (*epignôsis hamartias*, Rm 3:20). This deep awareness of the true character of moral disorder shows sin up to be a rebellion, a transgression, an act against a personal God, and an infidelity to the covenant relation and stipulations formulated in the Decalogue. This is why Paul could say, "Sin indeed was in the world before the Law was given; but sin is not imputed where there is no Law" (Rm 5:13). Paul would not deny that men were evil during the period from Adam to Moses (during the "law-less" period of Chaos). But he insists that their sinfulness did not have the character of open rebellion and transgression because the Mosaic Law had not yet been given. Men sinned, but it was not "like the transgression of Adam" (Rm 5:14). Again, "where there is no Law there is no transgression" (Rm 4:15), or "apart from the Law Sin lies dead; I was once alive apart from the Law, but when the commandment came, Sin revived and I died" (Rm 7:8b-9a).

(c) In addition to being an occasion for Sin and a moral informer about the real nature of Sin, *Nomos* also played its positive role by laying a curse on man. This stern view of the Law, which modern Christians may be inclined to tone down, is derived by Paul from Dt 27:26, which he quotes in Gal 3:10, "Cursed be anyone who does not stand by everything which is written in the book of the Law and obey it." This shows, as Paul argues, that the Law itself cursed the very man on whom it imposed its obligations. It brought him under "condemnation" (Rm 8:1), and thus became a "ministry of condemnation" (2 Cor 3:9) and a "dispensation of death" (2 Cor 3:7). And this is the height of the anomaly of man's existence in the period of Torah. Understanding it all in this way, Paul can only exclaim, "Did what was good then prove the death of me?" (Rm 7:13). Did the God-given *Nomos* in the service of *Hamartia* bring man into the clutches of *Thanatos?* His answer is "yes," and it happened that the true colors of *Hamartia* might be shown up: "that Sin might appear as sin" (Rm 7:13). But could this be? How could such a thing happen? To answer this brings us to our second point, Paul's explanation of the anomaly.

Paul's Explanation of the Anomaly

Paul not only recognized and described the anomaly that *Nomos* brought into the life of man, but he also tried to explain how it could have come about. His explanation is twofold, differing according to his letters. In his earlier letter to the Galatians Paul gives an extrinsic explanation, setting forth the temporary role of the Law: "Now before faith came, we were locked up under the Law, kept in constraint until faith should be revealed, so that the Law was our attendant (*paidagôgos*) unto Christ that we might be justified by faith" (Gal 3:23-24). Here in Gal. *Nomos* is depicted as a slave who in the Hellenistic world accompanied the school-age boy to and from classes and supervised his studies. Thus the Law schooled man in preparation for Christ, "the end of the Law." But this was only a temporary disposition of God, permitted until mankind reached the maturity in which it could do without the *paidagôgos* and respond to Christ, who came in the fulness of time, with an adult and personal commitment which is faith. Thus the Law played a role in Salvation History, educating God's people that it might come of age to learn of Christ.

Paul stresses its temporary character by pointing out that it

was added to Israel's promised heritage four hundred and thirty
years after the original promises made to Abraham. Paul's chrono-
logy may be off by several centuries, but in any case the Law came
in later. And this shows that it was in reality inferior to the
promises and could in no way annul them. Its inferiority was
also manifest in that it was promulgated by angels and through
the mediation of Moses (see Gal 3:19-20). Whatever Paul may
have thought about the angels, he certainly relegated them to the
same category as the Mosaic Law as far as Christians were concerned. He chides the fickle Galatians, warning them that to
adopt *any* of the Judaizers' practices would be a return to the
worship of "the elements of the world" (Gal 4:3, 9). As heathens,
they were once enslaved to them; but to adopt any of the
material observances of the Judaizers would be tantamount to a
return to such slavery. Such is the pejorative view of the Law and
its worth that Paul finally developed. Now that Christ's rule has
replaced that of the angels, their role in man's history is over; and
thus their identification with the Law reveals its inferior and
temporary status as well.

But this explanation of the anomaly of the Law was apparently not very satisfactory for Paul, being in effect quite extrinsic. For it did not really come to grips with the problem of man's
incapacity to obey the God-given Law. So when Paul composed
Rm 7:13-24, he abandoned that explanation and sought a more
intrinsic, philosophical explanation. Paul finally realized that the
difficulty was not with the Law as such, but rather with man in
his earthbound condition as *sarx*, "flesh," alienated from God and
dominated by *Hamartia*. In Rm 7 Paul explains the anomaly of
the Law from the fact that man is *sarkinos*, "made of flesh," i.e.,
composed of a principle which ties his whole personal existence,
outlook, and mentality to earth and to a material mode of
existence which distracts him from any consideration of God.
Here we must let Paul speak for himself:

> Did that which was good bring death to me? Not at all!
> It was Sin, producing death in me through what was
> good, in order that Sin might appear as sin, and through
> the commandment might become sinful beyond measure.
> We know that the Law is spiritual; but I am carnal

(*sarkinos*) and sold under Sin. I do not understand my actions; for I do not do what I want, but I do the very thing that I hate. If I do what I do not want, then I agree that the Law is good. But as it is no longer I that do it, but Sin which dwells in me. For I know that nothing good dwells in me, that is, in my flesh; I can will what is right, but I cannot do it. And I do not do the good I want, but the evil I do not want is what I do. If then I do what I do not want, it is no longer I that do it, but Sin which dwells in me.

So I find it to be a law that when I want to do right, evil lies close at hand. I delight in the Law of God, in my inmost self, but I see in my members another law, at war with the law of my mind and making me captive to the law of Sin which dwells in my members. Wretched man that I am Who will deliver me from this body of death? (Rm 7:13-24).

It is the evil force introduced into the world by Adam's transgression, Sin (with a capital S), which keeps man in bondage and slavery. Even if he wants to obey God's Law, he cannot do so because his earthbound self (*sarx*) is dominated by *Hamartia*. Paul even goes so far as to call, figuratively indeed, this indwelling Sin a "law"; it is "the law of Sin" (Rm 7:25).

At the end of chapter 7 in Romans Paul can only exclaim, "Wretched man that I am Who will deliver me from this body of death?" And his answer to his own question yields the solution to the anomaly of the Law. It also provides us with our third point.

Paul's Solution of the Anomaly

Paul's solution is "Thank God! It is done through Jesus Christ our Lord" (Rm 7:25), an answer that is as remarkable as it is simple. He continues, "There is no longer any condemnation for those who are in union with Christ Jesus, for the law of the Spirit of life in Christ Jesus has freed you from the law of Sin and Death" (Rm 8:1-2). It has often been pointed out how in that short answer Paul introduces his great insight into the meaning of the Christ-event for man (viz., freedom from the Law, from Sin, and from Death) and succinctly summarizes the entire second part of the doctrinal section of Romans. For Rm 8:2 is a brief résumé of chapters 5, 6, and 7: "The law of the Spirit of life in Christ Jesus has freed you from the law of sin and death." The three key-words, Law, Sin, and Death, are significantly juxtaposed.

With a slightly different nuance the same message is the burden of the letter to the Galatians, which is Paul's "Charter of Christian Liberty." In it he almost had to thrust his ideas of liberty on reluctant Christian neophytes, who seemed to prefer bondage and restraint in judaizing practices. To those who did not want to be free of the Law he could only exclaim: "For freedom Christ has set us free" (Gal 5:1). And these words sum up his whole message of Christian liberty. In the same context he brands the Law of Moses as a "yoke of slavery." "I testify again to every man who receives circumcision that he is bound to keep the whole Law" (5:3).

But we must specify further the sense in which Paul can say that Christ has freed men from the Law. For it is also obvious that the freedom he preached did not mean a throwing off of all restraint, an invitation to license. Even Paul insisted, "Brothers, you were called to freedom; but do not use your freedom as an opportunity for the flesh" (Gal 5:13). Even in the letter, which is his "Charter of Christian Liberty," Paul inserts the catalogues of vices and virtues which he inherited from the catechesis of the primitive Church. Here as in other letters they serve as norms of Christian conduct. For instance, in Gal 5:21 he lists "the works of the flesh" as "immorality, impurity, licentiousness, idolatry, sorcery, enmity, strife, jealousy, anger, etc." and ends with the warning, "those who do such things shall not inherit the kingdom of God." To put it more bluntly, Paul for all his talk about Christ's abolition of the Law still seems to have in the hortatory sections of his letters elaborate lists of *do's* and *don'ts*. Moreover, he seems to regard them as fundamental to Christian community life. It might seem, then, that Paul has simply done away with the Mosaic Law with its Pharisaic interpretation and casuistry only to set up his own code.

To understand his attitude, we must try to see what he meant by saying that Christ "abolished in his flesh the law of commandments and ordinances" (Ep 2:15), or that Christians "have died to the Law through the body of Christ" (Rm 7:4). For it is noteworthy that Paul in his letters ascribes this freedom from the Law or death to the Law precisely to the crucifixion and death of Christ himself. The explanation of this facet of Pauline theology is found in one of the most difficult verses of the Pauline corpus: "Through the Law I died to the Law that I might live for God; I have been crucified with Christ" (Gal 2:19-20). In these words Paul means that the Christian identified with Christ through Baptism shares in his death by crucifixion. As Christ by his death put an end to the Law, so the Christian has died to the Law; it no longer has any claim on him. But how did this death (of Christ and the Christian) take place "through the Law?" Paul almost certainly means "through the pernicious effects of the law," or, as we might say today, "through legalism." For Paul implies that it is the attitude of mind fostered by the Mosaic Law itself in those who crucified Jesus. He was undoubtedly thinking of the extreme formalism and legalism of the traditions that he knew as a Pharisee which made it impossible for his "kinsmen by race" (Rm 9:3) to accept Jesus of Nazareth as Messiah. So it was "through the Law" that the Christian has died to the Law (by his con-crucifixion with Christ, *synestaurômai*) that he might live for God.

This liberty from the Law brought about by the death of Christ is still further explained in Gal 3. In that and the following chapter Paul develops an elaborate midrash on the Abraham story of Genesis; he shows how God, foreseeing the justification of the Gentiles by faith, announced in effect the Gospel aforetime to Abraham in blessing all nations in him. But by contrast, Paul argues, the Law, which came in after these promises made to Abraham, levels a curse on all who would live by it. "Cursed be every one who does not abide by all the things written in the book of the Law and does not do them" (Dt 27:26). But Christ *by his death* has removed this curse from man.

To show how this was done Paul indulges in a little rabbinical logic. His argument is not marked by Aristotelian logic and any attempt to reduce it to a syllogism fails, for there are actually four terms in the argument. Christ has removed the curse of Dt 27:26 from man because he became the "curse of the Law" in the sense of Dt 21:23, and by dying he blotted it out. When he died as "the curse of the Law," in one sense, the curse of the Law in another sense died with him. "Christ redeemed us from the curse of the Law, having become a curse for us—for it is written, 'Cursed be everyone who hangs upon a tree'" (Gal 3:13). Here Paul cites the curse of Dt 21:23, levelled against the exposed dead body of an executed criminal. It was customary to hang it up as a deterrent to crime, but it was not allowed to remain beyond sundown, for it would defile the Land; in this sense it was accursed. In Roman times, when punishment by crucifixion became frequent in Palestine, the verse was applied to this form of capital punishment. Paul, knowing that Jesus died by this manner of death, realizes that the curse of the Law materially applied to him. So by a free association he maintains that Jesus, the "curse of the Law" (in the sense of Dt 21:23) blotted out by his death the curse levelled against man (by Dt. 27:26). Thus Christ "abolished the Law" (Ep 2:15). Thus he "cancelled the bond that stood against us with its legal demands; this he set aside, nailing it to the cross" (Col 2:14). Thus he became "the end of the Law" (Rm 10:4).

Instead there reigns the "Law of the Spirit of life" (Rm 8:2), which is in reality no "law" at all. The Christian who has been baptized into Christ lives a new life, a symbiosis of himself with Christ. Having grown together with Christ, he can now only think as Christ thinks and conducts his life only for God. "I live, now not I, but Christ lives in me" (Gal 2:20). For he is motivated, energized, and vitalized by the Spirit of the Risen Jesus; it frees him from his condition as *sarx*; it is what later theology calls "grace." The principle of Christian activity is no longer merely an external list of *do's* and *don't's*, but rather the internal whispering of the dynamic Spirit which enables the Christian to cry, "Abba, Father," and which testifies to him that he is a child of God (Gal 4:6; Rm 8:15). For the Christian is "led by the Spirit" (Rm 8:14); it has become for him a *nomos*, a principle, a figurative "law." He is no longer earthbound *sarx* when so activated, but is now *pneumatikos*, "spiritual." Living thus for God, and being so captivated with Christ that he is even his "slave" (*doulos*, 1 Cor 7:22), the Christian has nothing to do with sin, evil, disorder, or transgression. For Paul it is inconceivable that a man identified with the death, burial, and resurrection of Christ in Baptism could ever again think of sin and evil. "How can we who died to sin still live in it?" (Rm 6:2); just "as Christ was raised from the dead by the glory of the Father, so we too must walk in the newness of life" (Rm 6:4). In other words, for the Christian there is no need of a legal system such as was the Mosaic Law, especially as understood in the Pharisaic tradition with its 613 commands and prohibitions.

But how explain, then, Paul's insistence on the catalogues of vices and virtues mentioned earlier? True, Paul does not hesitate to exhort his Christian communities to the practice of virtue. But his norms for individual conduct are now subsumed all under one notion: under love, under concern for others, under the dynamic demand of Christian communal living. In Rm 13:8-10 he makes it explicit:

> Owe no one anything, except to love one another; for he who loves his neighbor has fulfilled the Law. The commandments, 'You shall not commit adultery, You shall not kill, You shall not steal, You shall not covet,' and any other commandment, are summed up in the sentence, 'You shall love your neighbor as yourself.' Love does no wrong to a neighbor; therefore love is the fulfilling of the Law.

Love is the fulfillment of the Law, not because it replaces the Mosaic Law with another external norm of conduct, but because it is itself a dynamic force impelling man to seek the good of others, energizing his faith in Christ Jesus (Gal 5:6: *pistis di' agapês energoumenê*, "faith working through love"). For Paul what does not express love does not lead to life.

It is in this sense that Paul speaks of "the law of Christ." For this Pauline expression is obviously a "take-off" on the expression, the law of Moses. When, however, we look at the context in which the expression is used in Gal 6:2, it is obviously that of brotherly love, and specifically of fraternal correction. "Brethren, if a man is overtaken in any violation, you who are spiritual should restore him in a spirit of gentleness; but look to yourself, lest you too be tempted. Bear one another's burdens, and so fulfill the law of Christ." The example which Paul uses here should obviously be understood as precisely that, an example; for if the "law of Christ" is to be understood in terms of love, as the passage suggests, it is not to be restricted to that form of love which would be manifest only in fraternal correction.

When one sees how Paul does away with the Mosaic Law and its legalism and substitutes for it the "Law of the Spirit of life" and the principle of love, one cannot help but ask how Paul, the former Pharisee, could ever have come to such a view of the Old Testament. But, to my way of thinking, it is precisely his background which has brought him to this reaction. We must remember that Paul's attitude toward the Old Testament is at least double. For if he is very severe in speaking of the Old *Law*, nevertheless he frequently quotes the Old Testament, appeals to it as the source of the promises made to Abraham (Rm 4:13), as "the oracles of God" (Rm 3:2), and sees in it "the book written for our instruction" (1 Cor 10:11; cf. Rm 4:23-24). But his negative attitude toward the Old Testament is undoubtedly due to the "traditions of the Fathers" (Gal 1:14) which surrounded and encrusted it and in which he had been schooled. How often he looked on it as "law," and how infrequently he thinks of it as "covenant." This notion, which looms so large in modern inter- pretation of the Old Testament and in a sense sums it up, is somewhat slighted in Paul's letters. This may well be due to his dependence on the Old Testament in the Greek translation of the Septuagint, where the Hebrew word *berît*, "covenant," was rendered by *diathêkê*, a word which in Hellenistic Greek usually bore the connotation of "last will, testament" (see Gal 3:15). This Greek translation colored the Old Testament covenant with the connotation that it was an expression of God's will; and this aided the tendency to exploit it legalistically and casuistically. It obscured the covenant as "pact," which might have been more appropriately translated as *synthêkê*. The result was a preoccupation with the Old Testament as an expression of God's will that had to be carried out by Israel and as a legal system which had to be interpreted to the extreme of casuistry.

Finally, we conclude our remarks on the subject by referring to one verse which we have not considered so far. It is found in the Pastoral Epistles, but since in modern times it is widely questioned whether Paul wrote these letters himself we have been reluctant to introduce it into our main discussion. Whether it is authentically Pauline or not, it forms a fitting conclusion to our discussion. For it sums up succinctly what has been said above: "Now we know that the Law is good, if one uses it as law should be used, understanding this, that the Law is not laid down for the just but for the lawless and disobedient, for the ungodly and sinners. . ." (1 Tm 1:8-9). This statement fits in perfectly with what Paul wrote about the Law, about its fulfilment in love, about the Spirit as the principle of the "new creation" (Gal 6:15), and about the complete incompatibility of the Christian with what is evil and sinful.

In summary, then, Paul's teaching is a reaction to the Mosaic Law, on the one hand abolished by Christ Jesus who has now enabled man through his own Spirit to transcend the earthbound condition of *sarx,* and on the other summed up and fulfilled in the dynamic principle of love. The grace and favor of Christ enables man to be truly Christian. The norm, however, for the Christian's conduct is no longer an external list of *do's* and *don't's;* such a thing exists for "the lawless and the disobedient." Instead, Paul's specific exhortations and recommendations express not so much a code or a norm to be exploited and interpreted casuistically as examples of the Christian principle of love reacting to communal situations. If my presentation of Paul's reaction to law has stressed the Mosaic over against any generic consideration, it is because this is in fact the perspective from which he viewed and treated it. But it is well to repeat here one phrase that he did write, "The commandments, 'You shall not commit adultery, You shall not kill, You shall not steal, You shall not covet', *and any other commandment,* are summed up in this sentence, 'You shall love your neighbor as yourself' " (Rm 13:9).

PAUL'S GOSPEL OF FREEDOM

Stanislas Lyonnet, S.J.

St. Paul's assertion admits no compromise: The Christian vocation is a vocation to liberty. The Christian is a son, not a hireling, not a slave. "You have been called to liberty, brethren," he writes to the Galatians. And again, "If you are led by the Spirit, you are not under the Law" (5:13, 18). These proclamations, and others like them, were a source of scandal not only to the Jews but even to some of the first Christians. That St. Paul found himself the object of latent hostility, or at least of a painful lack of understanding, from the very beginning of his missionary activity to his last days, was mainly due to his attitude toward the Law and to his preaching of Christian liberty. St. Paul was unyielding whenever the principle of Christian liberty was at stake. For him it was no secondary doctrine, no side issue; the whole religion of Christ was in the balance.

Although the doctrine of Christian liberty which he preached was worked out in his controversies with the Judaizers, and hence in very particular circumstances, still a doctrine can be found in St. Paul's arguments that has undeniable validity and importance for our own day. His doctrine can be summed up as follows: The Christian who is led by the Spirit finds himself freed, in Christ, from the Law of Moses; he is freed from it not only as the Law of Moses, but as law. He is delivered from any law that constrains or coerces (I do not say *binds*) him from without; yet, this in no way makes him an amoral being, outside the realm of good and evil.

When he speaks of law, St. Paul obviously has in mind especially that Law which for him and for his Jewish contemporaries was uniquely worthy of the title, the legislation given on Mount Sinai. To measure the offense his statements must have given to his fellow Jews, we only have to recall how they venerated and honored the Torah. The Law was the word of God, the water that slakes all thirst, the lifegiving bread, the vine laden with fruit; in it were hidden the treasures of wisdom and knowledge. In short, the Law held the place St. John and St. Paul were rightly to announce as that of the Christ.

But from this Law the Christian has been delivered. St. Paul declares: "You are not under the Law but under grace" (Rm 6:14). A wife is bound to her husband as long as he is alive but, when he dies, is completely free from the law that bound her to him, so that she is not an adulteress if she marries another. In like manner the Christian, united to Christ dead and risen, is dead to the Law, delivered from it, no longer its subject (Rm 7:1-6). But had not Law played a role in the history of the chosen people? Indeed, but it was the thankless one of a jailer, or of a pedagogue, the slave whose task it was, not to teach the children, but to lead them to their teacher (Gal 3:23-24). Beyond this, St. Paul paradoxically asserts that the Law, which the Jews revere as the source of life, has been imposed by God on man to bring him death. The economy of the Law was not that of a blessing but of a curse (Gal 3:10).

"What then was the Law?" he asks in the Epistle to the Galatians (3:10), and his answer is that it was given to provoke transgression. This was a shocking statement, even for Christian readers; and well-meaning copyists very soon tried to soften its harshness. But there is no way out—the text is concerned with provoking transgressions, not with repressing them.

Is this witticism? Is it a paradox? Not at all! In fact, the Epistle to the Romans brings out St. Paul's idea with even greater precision. Emancipation from the Law is one of the key links, indeed, the final one, of his argument. Freed from sin, from death, and from the flesh, the Christian cannot be saved unless he is also freed from the Law; only this final liberation will strip sin of its power, its dominion over man: "Sin shall not have dominion over you, since you are not under the Law, but under grace" (Rm 6:14). To be under the Law, then, is the same as to be under the rule of sin. Never before had St. Paul been so incisive.

A source of scandal for the Jews, such assertions run the opposite risk of leaving the modern Christian reader quite indifferent. He has never felt any strong attachment to the Law of Moses. He finds it quite normal not to be obliged to observe its complicated ritual or its many observances—as circumcision, the minute prescriptions for keeping the Sabbath, for preparing food, or for contacts with the pagan world. These, as far as he can see, have no real religious value. As a matter of fact, had St. Paul intended no more than the Christian's deliverance from these obligations, his statements would hardly raise problems. Nor would they offer any great interest for the man of today. But so understood, they would be a caricature of his true teaching.

Under the term "law," St. Paul certainly includes that part of the Mosaic legislation which concerns the moral life in the strict sense; in fact, the Epistle to the Romans speaks of no other aspect of the Law but the moral one. As for the seventh chapter, where the question is expressly treated, one can see if St. Paul has the Law of Moses in mind; it is not in its ritual and ceremonial positions that he considers it, but in its permanent moral content. In other words, he is concerned with the Law of Moses as a positive expression of the natural law. Besides, St. Paul is explicit: The "law of sin and of death"—that is, the Law that provokes sin and leads to death—from which he proclaims we are free, is clearly designated by means of one precept of the Decalogue: "I did not know sin save through the Law. For I had not known lust unless the Law had said: 'Thou shalt not lust'" (Rm 7:37).

Let us press this passage further. The English translation "Thou shalt not lust," may suggest that the Apostle had a particular commandment in mind, the one that prohibits carnal desires. This would be a serious mistake. Not only is the context of Exodus 20:17 or Deuteronomy 5:21, from which this prohibition is taken, utterly opposed to such an interpretation, but in the

Septuagint, the Greek word *epithumein*, whether in its verbal or substantive form, hardly ever evokes the idea of carnal desire. What the commandment forbids, in the most general sense, is the craving for what belongs to another, whether it be his house, his wife, his slave, his ox or ass, or anything else that he owns. In much the same way, Ecclesiasticus sums up the whole Jewish Law in the one precept: "Avoid all evil" (17:22). For Ben Sirach, this precept seems to epitomize not only the legislation of Sinai but all the expressions of God's will that have ever been given to man, expressions that have their synthesis in a unique law and covenant.

It is not surprising, then, that St. Paul in turn should choose an all-embracing formula, one that could be applied to every divine command, even the prohibition imposed upon our first parents, the prototype of all others. In his desire to describe how man becomes conscious of sin, to describe, too, the essential role played by law in this process, Paul thinks of the biblical description of sin that became the pattern of all our sins; all succeeding generations of men unfailingly share in it and reproduce it again and again in their own lives. Many have noticed that more than one detail in chapter seven of Romans is in some way reminiscent of the third chapter of Genesis. In any case, keeping in mind the narrative of Genesis may help throw light on and clarify a passage that is at first sight enigmatic.

Adam and Eve are living in a state of familiarity with God when the serpent comes and persuades them that they will be like gods if they taste of the tree of knowledge of good and evil. Immediately, the fruit, which has become the means of securing this divine privilege, seems to Eve an unknown delight. The Bible brings this out emphatically: "The woman saw that the tree was good for food, pleasing to the eyes, and desirable for the knowledge it would give" (Gn 3:6). But as soon as Adam and Eve break God's command, they find themselves reduced to nakedness, stripped of everything that previously constituted their happiness. Cast out of the garden, they are deprived forever of God's friendship. Unless God himself mercifully intervenes, the gate that leads to the tree of life—of that life which belongs to God alone, and to those who are united to him—is forever shut. Now God's command was unquestionably good, spiritual, divine. It is not the command but the serpent who is responsible for all the world's ills. And yet, according to the biblical account, the command did play a role; the serpent used it to induce our first parents to disobey. Though it was supposed to preserve life in them, in reality it became a cause, or at least an occasion, of death.

This is the point St. Paul is trying to make in the much discussed passage of his Epistle to the Romans. There is only one change in the cast of characters: Sin, personified, plays the part of the serpent. "What shall we say then? Is the Law sin? By no means! Yet I did not know sin save through the Law. For I had not known lust unless the Law had said: 'Thou shalt not lust.' But sin, having thus found an occasion, worked in me by means of the commandment all manner of lust, for without the Law, sin was dead" (Rm 7:7-8). Sin was a powerless corpse.

"But," St. Paul continues, "when the commandment came, sin revived (*anezēsen*)"; heretofore a lifeless body (*nekros*), it rose up (*ana*) a living thing (*ezēsen*), "and I died," that is, I lost that eminently divine privilege of life. "And the commandment that was unto life was discovered in my case to be unto death. For sin having taken occasion from the commandment deceived me" (as the serpent deceived Eve) "and through it killed me" (7:8-11). Hence, for St. Paul, just as for the authors of Gn 3 and Ws 2:24, the one responsible for death is neither the Law nor its author, but the serpent or the devil or sin.

But if "the Law is holy and the commandment holy and just and good," (7:12), how then are we to explain God's strange conduct? If he desires nothing but life, why give man a law that, in fact, will lead him to death? St. Paul provides the answer: "Did then that which is good become death to me? By no means! But sin, that it might be manifested as sin, worked death for me through that which is good, in order that sin by reason of the commandment might become immeasurably sinful" (7:13), in other words, that sin might exercise its full power as sin by means of the commandment.

According to the Jews, the Law gave life. However, a law as such, even if it proposed the highest ideal, could not change a creature of flesh into a spiritual being, alive with the very life of God. If this were possible, it would mean that man has no need of being saved, that he can actually save himself! Far from giving life, far from destroying or even curbing the death-bearing power of sin in man, the purpose of the Law is, as it were, to permit sin to exercise all its virulence, but in so doing, to bring sin itself out into the open and unmask it. The Law does not take sin away, rather it reveals to man his sinful state.

Let us note that, properly speaking, law does not provoke sin, but transgression. St. Paul looks upon transgression as the outward expression of a far more deeply rooted evil, *hamartia*: not merely carnal concupiscence, but an evil power personified, corresponding to that deeply rooted egoism by which man, since original sin, orientates everything to himself instead of opening himself to God and to others. It is this "sin" that must be destroyed in us; and, left to itself, law is incapable of the task. But by permitting "transgression," law makes sin unfold itself and helps man, through his painful experience, to seek his Savior. This is the way St. Paul understands the role of law, a role that is indispensable, ultimately beneficent and salutary. But this role is associated with any law that is truly law, to any rule that is imposed on man's conscience from without. It is from the "rule of law" as such that St. Paul declares the Christian freed.

Is the Christian, then, a man without law, a creature beyond the realm of good and evil? St. Paul issues a flat *no* to this objection. "What then? Are we to sin because we are not under the Law but under grace? By no means!" (Rm 6:15). The eighth chapter of the Epistle to the Romans contains his solution. Chapters five, six, and seven of the Epistle set forth the conditions necessary for the Christian to be saved: deliverance from sin, from death, from the flesh, and the final deliverance, that from the Law. They show that each successive deliverance is secured for the Christian in Christ, and in Him alone. Then, chapter eight begins with a cry of triumph: "There is therefore now no condemnation for those who are in Christ Jesus." St.

Paul states the reason precisely: "For the law of the Spirit, (giving) life in Christ Jesus, has delivered me from the law of sin and death" (8:1-2). So man is delivered from that Law which, according to the incontestable testimony of the Bible, had been the instrument of sin and death, by something that St. Paul also calls a law: the law of the life-giving Spirit.

What does this mean? Can Christ have been satisfied with substituting for the Law of Moses another code, more perfect or less complicated perhaps, but of the same nature, which would thereby keep the Christian under legal rule? This would contradict all that has gone before. St. Paul had just opposed to the Law of Moses, not another law, but grace: If sin no longer exercises its dominion over you, he explains, it is because "you are not under the Law but under grace" (Rm 6:14). Has he changed his mind? Not at all! His choice of expression has changed, but not his thinking.

The "Law of the Spirit," then, does not differ from the Law of Moses—and a fortiori from all non-revealed law—merely because it sets up a loftier ideal and makes greater demands. Nor does it differ because it offers salvation at a bargain, as if Christ had replaced the unbearable yoke of the Law of Sinai with an "easy morality." No, the law of the Spirit is radically different. It is not just a code, not even one "given by the Holy Spirit," but a law "produced in us by the Holy Spirit"; not a simple rule of action outside us, but something that no legal code as such can possibly be—a new, inner source of spiritual energy.

If St. Paul applies the term "law" to this spiritual energy, rather than the term "grace" that he uses elsewhere (Rm 6:14), he probably does so because of Jeremiah's prophecy announcing a new covenant, the "New Testament." For the prophet, too, speaks of law: "This is the covenant which I will make with the house of Israel . . . . I will place my law within them, and write it upon their hearts" (31:33). The Christian who receives the Holy Spirit as an active force within him, becomes capable of "walking according to the spirit," that is, walking in conformity with what the Old Law, "spiritual" though it was, demanded of him in vain. This is why St. Paul, after setting forth man's deliverance by the law of the Spirit, thanks to the redemptive work of Christ, can attribute to that work the following aim: "that the justification of the Law"—that justification which the Law wished but could not obtain from us creatures of flesh—"might be fulfilled in us" (Rm 8:4).

From this basic teaching flows notably the fact that Christian morality is of necessity founded on love, as St. Paul teaches: "The whole Law is fulfilled in one word: Thou shalt love thy neighbor as thyself" (Gal 5:14, Rm 13:8-10). The reason is that love is not first of all a standard of conduct, but a dynamic force—it is precisely because the Law, as a law, was not love that it could not justify man.

Under these conditions, it is easy to see that a Christian, a man led by the Holy Spirit, can at the same time be freed from every external law—"not be under the Law"—and yet lead a perfect moral and virtuous life. Having reduced the whole Law to love, St. Paul adds: "Walk in the Spirit, and you will not fulfill the lusts of the flesh" (Gal 5:16). Nothing could be more obvious, he explains, since these are two antagonistic principles: If you follow one, you must oppose the other.

"If you are led by the Spirit, you are not under the Law." In fact, what need would you have of law? A spiritual man knows perfectly well what is carnal and, because he is spiritual, he will fly from it as by instinct. Since he has no need, then, for a law to constrain him from without, the Christian, led by the Spirit, fulfills every law in the full liberty of the sons of God.

Why, then, does the religion of Christ still require a code of laws? Why should there be kept alongside the chief unwritten element that justifies, an other written element that does not justify? If this state of affairs was strange in the old economy, does it not become unintelligible in the economy of grace? Not at all!

The Pauline principle remains: "The Law is not made for the just, but for the unjust" (1 Tm 1:9). If all Christians were just, there would be no need to restrain them by laws. Law, as a rule, does not enter upon the scene except to arrest disorder. For example, as long as Christians received Communion frequently the Church never thought of obligating them under pain of sin to do so at least once a year. But when fervor declined, she promulgated the precept of Easter Communion to remind her faithful that divine life is nourished by the flesh of Christ. Even though all are subject to this law, it is really not directed to the fervent Christian who continues to receive Communion during the paschal season not because of the Lord's command, but because of that inner need which prompts him to communicate every Sunday or even every day of the year. This does not imply that he is no longer bound by the precept, that as long as he experiences this inner need—which is a fruit of the Holy Spirit leading him—he will in fact fulfill the precept, without even adverting to the fact. On the other hand, as soon as that inner need no longer makes itself felt, the law is there to constrain him and to warn him that he is no longer led by the Spirit.

In the latter case this law will play the same role for the Christian that the Law of Moses did for the Jew. As a pedagogue to lead him to the Christ, it will not only act as a sort of substitute for the light no longer supplied by the Holy Spirit, but will, above all, help him to recognize his condition as a sinner—one who is no longer led by the Holy Spirit. And since such a recognition is for St. Paul the first requirement for man's cure, it becomes evident that the law was made for sinners.

But the law is set down even for the just. Although he is in the state of grace, that is, led by the Holy Spirit, the Christian, as long as he remains on earth, possesses the Spirit only imperfectly, as a sort of pledge (Rm 8:23; 2 Cor 1:22). As long as he lives in a mortal body, he is never so completely freed from sin and from the flesh that he cannot at any moment fall back under their sway. Now in this unstable position, the law—the external, written, objective norm of man's conduct—will guide him in distinguishing the works of the flesh from the fruit of the Spirit and keep him from confusing the inclinations of his sin-wounded nature with the inner promptings of the Spirit. Until the Christian acquires full spiritualization in heaven, there will remain alongside grace (the chief element of spiritualization, alone able to justify) a secondary element, no more able to justify than was the Old Law, but still indispensable for sinners, and by no means superfluous for the just who are still imperfect.

Still it is necessary that this secondary element remain secondary, and that it not tend imperceptibly to assume the role of the principal element, as happened to the Jewish Law in St. Paul's time. To ward off this ever-threatening danger, it is well to recall a basic principle, a corollary of the foregoing doctrine: The external law can be only the expression of the interior law. Works can be commanded only because they bear a necessary relation to the inner grace of the Holy Spirit.

Either they will be works that put us in contact with the humanity of Christ from whom all grace flows, and are therefore necessary to produce in us the inner dynamism that is faith working through charity. Or they will be works that translate and give concrete expression to this inner law of love.

As a consequence, any purely external violation of law, an "involuntary sin," a violation which by definition is unrelated to the interior law, cannot be a genuine violation. On the other hand, an observance devoid of love is also devoid of meaning. Anyone who attaches an independent value to mere observance will try to keep it up at any cost; he may even imagine that he is still obeying the law when in fact he is dodging or "outwitting" it (cf. Mk 7:9-13). But for the man who sees in the outward observance nothing but an expression of the inner law, such an attitude is unthinkable. Since the sole aim of the external law is to safeguard the Christian's inner dynamism, it derives all its value from the latter, not the other way around.

Another consequence of the relationship between love and law is that ordinarily the outward law will not provide the Christian with an ideal, the attainment of which could possibly satisfy him, but simply with a minimum below which the dynamism that constitutes him as a Christian will inevitably fail him. For this reason the code of the New Law, while including a series of positive commands and prohibitions, before all else offers the Christian a complete different norm: The imitation of the person of Christ, particularly of his love, which in turn is a reflection of the love of the Father.

St. Paul hardly knows another norm. Following the example of Christ, who commanded his disciples to be perfect as their heavenly Father is perfect, St. Paul can only repeat to his faithful that they should contemplate Christ and imitate him. "Be you, therefore, imitators of God, as very dear children, and walk in love as Christ also loved us and delivered himself up for us" (Ep 4:32-5:2, 24-26).

The pious Jew, so zealous in his devotion to the Law, strove to know it better and better, so that he might observe its most minute details. For a Christian, the Person of Christ is the whole law, not only with regard to its principal element, the Spirit of Christ imparted to him, but even with regard to its secondary element, which is reducible to the imitation of Christ.

A final consequence of the relationship between love and law is that when a Christian acts in this way, he is free; for "where the Spirit of the Lord is, there is freedom" (2 Cor 3:17). This is a theme dear to St. Augustine as well as to St. Thomas, who comments: "A man who acts of his own accord, acts freely, but one who is impelled by another is not free. He who avoids evil, not because it is evil, but because a precept of the Lord forbids it, is not free. On the other hand, he who avoids evil because it is evil, is free. Now it is precisely this the Holy Spirit accomplishes, by inwardly equipping the soul with an inner dynamism. The result is that a man refrains from evil out of love, as though the divine law were commanding him; and thus he is free, not because he is not subject to the divine law, but because his inner dynamism enables him to do what the divine law requires" (In 2 Cor, cap. 3, 1. 3; cf. S. T. I-II, q. 108, a. 1 ad 2).

PAUL'S ESCHATOLOGICAL MESSAGE
TO THE NATIONS

Lucien Cerfaux

Paul's first great evangelization (commonly referred to as the second missionary journey) took him as far as Corinth. On the way he stopped in Galatia, then for a longer time in Macedonia, at Philippi and at Thessalonica. The letters to the Thessalonians, which were written at this time, and the fifteenth chapter of the first letter to the Corinthians, together with the Acts, provide us with excellent information about the beginnings of his activity in the cities of the Greek world. His message, apart from the themes of propaganda against idolatry, is primarily eschatological. He proclaims the resurrection of Christ and his glorious return; he propounds the doctrines that are naturally linked to eschatology—the resurrection of Christians, the general resurrection, and the last judgment.

The hellenistic world was to a certain extent prepared for this message: this is the first point to be elucidated. We shall then glance at the successive stages of the evangelization and, finally, at the essential eschatological proclamations. The world in which Christianity was implanted had a certain propensity for eschatological ideas. Moreover, in Greek civilization the gospel encountered a tendency toward monotheism.

Eschatological expectations

The time at which Christ appeared was therefore partially responsible for the expression of his message and for the "end of the world" atmosphere which was very soon to envelop the whole of Christianity.

The Hebrew prophets had ceaselessly addressed messages to Israel which directly or indirectly anticipated the end of the age. Many of them announced the "day of Yahweh" with its terrors, like Joel:

> Blow the trumpet in Zion;
>   sound the alarm on my holy mountain!
> Let all the inhabitants of the land tremble,
>   for the day of the LORD is coming, it is near,
> a day of darkness and gloom,
>   a day of clouds and thick darkness! (Jl 2:1-2).

Following this passage there is a moving appeal to penitence (Jl 2:12-18).

Other prophets, however, presented the inauguration of the kingdom of God as "good news." The two forms of expectation are found together in the Gospels. The Baptist announced judgment by fire:

> You brood of vipers! Who warned you to flee from the wrath to come? Bear fruit that befits repentance, and do not presume to say to yourselves, "We have Abraham as our father"; for I tell you, God is able from these stones to raise up children to Abraham. Even now the axe is laid to the root of the trees...he who is coming after me is mightier than I.... His winnowing fork is in his hand, and he will clear his threshing floor and gather his wheat into the granary, but the chaff he will burn with unquenchable fire (Mt 3:7-12).

Jesus was above all the messenger of the good news. It will easily be realized that the expectation of a Messiah is not necessarily linked to eschatological fears or hopes. We could imagine a kingdom of God and an end of the world without a Messiah. Or a purely national Messiah might be hoped for, one who would restore the throne of David.

At the moment when Paul undertook his great evangelization, the Jewish world was in a ferment. The revolution and its terrible repression by the Romans were close at hand. The people were restive under a military occupation that had not fulfilled the hopes at first aroused by the Roman intervention. The Hasmonean dynasty, hardly legitimized by the piety and heroism of Judas

Maccabeus and his immediate successors, had degenerated and then been replaced by the Idumaean dynasty of the Herods. Oppression was stirring up revolt. Political motives were now strengthened by religious reasons, particularly the enduring idea that God alone was the legitimate possessor of that semiroyal semidivine title of "Lord" which the Emperor claimed in order to impose on his subjects worship of himself. Jerusalem and Alexandria barely escaped the mad enterprises of Caligula (another Antiochus Epiphanes) who was fully determined to place a divine statue—his own—in the Jewish Temple and the synagogues.

Wrongly interpreted, the promises of the prophets sustained chimerical hopes. "Apocalypses" in secret circulation prophesied the end of temporal kingdoms and the imminent establishment of the kingdom of God. Sects were founded to keep alive the ancestral faith threatened by the hellenizing authorities. The best known among these are the Pharisees and, recently, the monastic sect of the Essenes. John the Baptist also had disciples organized into a religious community which persisted during the whole of the second century of our era. In Galilee, bands of revolutionaries were getting ready to help.

Everybody was waiting for something or someone: a king sent from heaven to reestablish the throne of David in justice, freedom, and glory; or a divine intervention signaling the end of the existing order after the resurrection of the dead. It was in any case to be the beginning of the final era of the world.

The doctrines of the Pharisees are of especial interest to us. Paul was one of the disciples, almost a "master" of the sect. Their hope for a royal Messiah, a son of David, who would establish justice on earth, was passionately expressed in the "Psalms of Solomon," written in the first century B.C. Later on, their political prudence toned down the messianic expectations; in any case, they left the detailed dreaming to the apocalypses. It seems that before his conversion, Paul was hoping, rather vaguely, for a Messiah-King descended from David (Rm 1:3; 9:5).

The Pharisees gave prominence to the doctrine of the resurrection. A general resurrection was to precede the judgment, with privileges for all those who had lived in observance of the law.

Paul shared these beliefs (Rm 2:5-16). In his appearance before the Sanhedrin convened by the tribune Lysias, he tried to get the Pharisees in the council onto his side by appealing to them in Aramaic: "I am a Pharisee, a son of Pharisees; with respect to the hope and the resurrection of the dead I am on trial" (Ac 23: 6). The resurrection was to become the chief plank in his theology.

The expectations of Judaism existed within the more general anticipations of the Greco-Roman world. The times were as productive of despair as of faith in world renewal, but influences from the ancient Babylonian and Persian religions and from the contemporary mysteries and religions of the East—Judaism among them—were active in the latter direction. Virgil in his fourth Eclogue sang of the wonderful child who would bring back the age of gold.

Greek Monotheism

The early philosophers nursed the dream of unifying the world, which was of one matter according to the Ionians and was numbers for Pythagoras; above this cosmic unity was the idea of a supreme god, the ruler of the universe. "There is one God, sovereign over gods and men; he is not like mortals in bodily appearance, nor in thoughts" (Xenophanes of Elea).

The Pythagoreans, the Orphics, Socrates, and Plato spoke in the same terms. At the syncretist period the multiplicity of secondary gods was reabsorbed fairly easily into a principal divinity—sometimes Zeus, sometimes one or another of the Eastern gods like Isis or Serapis (who became Zeus-Serapis, and later the "Sun").

To this monotheism with its profoundly religious character was naturally attached a belief in immortality and in further rewards and punishments. The old mythology, symbolically interpreted, filled the neo-Pythagoreans of Rome with these aspirations when they descended into the mysterious shadows of their basilica by the main gate.

The message of hellenistic Judaism

Hellenistic Judaism, entrusted with a mission to the Gentiles, had elaborated its line of propaganda. It was based on numerous religious discourses gathered from the ancient Greek "theologians," from philosophers, Orphics, and oracles; it was an impressive collection, enriched by an apologetic literature with faked items, a sacred discourse of Orpheus among others. Here is a confession attributed to Sophocles:

> One, truly, God is one,
>   who created the heavens and the vast earth.
> We mortals, with our wandering hearts,
>   have set up, to soothe our sufferings,
> statues of gods of stone....

It led up to a proclamation of monotheism and judgment. The one God, known through the ancient revelations, manifested by his works and his Providence, had become the unknown God by the fact of idolatry, and he, the only true God, threatened with imminent judgment the disorders of paganism. An urgent exhortation to penitence concluded the Jewish message.

From the gospel of Jesus to the message of Paul

The Christian evangel was preceded by the eschatological message of John the Baptist. John's announcement became, on the lips of Jesus, the "good news." The terrors of the apocalypses were overcome by the optimism of a presence of salvation in the word of the messenger of God, the founder of the kingdom. The good news must be received with "faith," which gives unstintingly to the work of God.

The salvation that Jesus proclaimed was sealed by his death and resurrection, the definitive divine intervention. Then the apostles took the gospel message to the nations: "Having received fullness of strength by the resurrection of our Lord Jesus Christ, and following his orders, with complete trust drawn from the Holy Spirit, the apostles went forth to proclaim the good news of the coming of the kingdom of God" (I Clem. 42).

Henceforth, salvation was present in the Christian community by virtue of Christ's death and resurrection. This was the apostolic message, a message of the remission of sins and the inauguration of the kingdom of God in the exaltation to heaven of Jesus Christ and Lord, and the presence on earth of the Holy Spirit (Ac 2:32-36). From the beginning, the Christian message was undoubtedly eschatological, conditioned by the belief in an overthrow of the old order, but it made men perceive amid the ruins the birth, and even the growth, of celestial realities. Future time is an abstraction; what comes to pass is not time but the realities that are inscribed in it. Christian eschatology, which was already beginning to be realized, was qualitative.

Paul received from Jerusalem, as a tradition, the apostolic message which was later to become the creed of catechesis: "that Christ died for our sins in accordance with the scriptures, that he was buried, that he was raised on the third day in accordance with the scriptures" (1 Cor 15:3-4). He was, among the apostles, the great bearer of the message to the Gentiles. He was an eschatological worker.

The massive evangelization of the pagan world was in fact an event that was itself reserved for the end of the age. So it was understood by the prophets who foresaw the restoration of Israel in the last days, and invited the kings of the nations to come at that time to Jerusalem to worship, bringing their richest presents. So it was still understood by the prophet of the Apocalypse, in his grandiose vision:

> Then I saw another angel flying in midheaven, with an eternal gospel to proclaim to those who dwell on earth, to every nation and tribe and tongue and people; and he said with a loud voice, "Fear God and give him glory, for the hour of his judgment has come; and worship him who made heaven and earth, the sea and the fountain of water" (Rv 14:6-7).

Thus, through the apostles' message, the dream that Judaism saw as happening at the last days was fulfilled—the Gentiles joining in the worship of the one God. It was given to Paul to find the actual adaptation of the message to the Greco-Roman world, to take up the divine task and make it historical.

During the first missionary journey

The story of the missionary journey of Paul and Barnabas reveals an archaic state of the message. Before Jewish audiences, the Apostle develops at length the theme of Christ's resurrection, with the secondary themes of the death and the fulfillment of the promises; in speaking to pagans, he announces the living God whom paganism ignores in the worship of idols, the God who has made heaven and earth, and continues to manifest himself through his Providence (Ac 14:15-17).

At Thessalonica

The Christian message to the Gentiles took definitive form at Thessalonica. Paul reminded his Christians, whom he had hardly left, of the way in which he came among them. He turned them from idols, no doubt using the arguments of Jewish apologetics such as we find in the Book of Wisdom. In this way he led them to worship the true and living God, and then taught them "to wait for his Son from heaven, whom he raised from the dead, Jesus who delivers us from the wrath to come" (1 Th 1:9-10). All these words were rich with meaning which persuaded the Gentiles of humble condition as well as others more cultivated, along with the women of good society (Ac 17:4).

From the themes of monotheistic discourse, with its criticism of idolatry, we pass by the intermediary of the judgment (the wrath to come) to the essential Christian message of the Resurrection. The main lines of the discourse to the Gentiles are thus laid down. Christianity addresses itself directly to the pagans, speaking their language, entering into their minds, giving form to their highest aspirations, bringing them finally to the God whom many of them were seeking without knowing it, and above all revealing to them the supreme act of the power of God in Christ's resurrection.

The oration before the Areopagus

The unaffected discourse which had conquered the Macedonians became a formal oration at the Areopagus in Athens. As Professor Ramsay sees it, it was not to an uncultural Jew but to a former student of Tarsus, a distinguished guest, that the University of Athens, the mother and model of them all, opened its doors. Modern criticism cools enthusiasm, asking whether it is really the Paul of the letters whom we hear at the Areopagus.

Certainly, Luke is the "editor" of the propaganda speech before the Areopagus. He did not hear Paul speak, and if anyone in the audience took notes, they were not communicated to him. But Luke and Paul were united by a profound human and intellectual sympathy. Both of them, the hellenized Jew and the Greek doctor, moved with the same ease in the various societies they met on their travels. Both knew that no one would teach in the "school of Tyrannos" at Ephesus as he would lecture on morals at the Agora or the Areopagus of Athens. If Luke paints the portrait of his hero, he does it with such an understanding love that the personal portrait of the artist and that of the model coincide.

Luke has just been telling us of Paul's indignation at the spectacle of the "city full of idols" (Ac 17:16), and of the superficial curiosity of the Greeks (Ac 17:21), but no hint of contempt and no adverse judgment transpire in the oration which he delivered before the council of the Areopagus. Here it is, transcribed in full:

> [The unknown God] Men of Athens, I perceive that in every way you are very religious. For as I passed along, and observed the objects of your worship, I found also an altar with this inscription, "To an unknown God."

> [The announcement of the true God] What therefore you worship as unknown, this I proclaim to you. The God who made the world and everything in it, being Lord of heaven and earth; does not live in shrines made by man, nor is he served by human hands, as though he needed anything, since he himself gives to all men life and breath and everything. And he made from one every nation of men to live on all the face of the earth, having determined allotted periods and the boundaries of their habitation, that they should seek God, in the hope that they might feel after him and find him. Yet he is not far

from each one of us, for "In him we live and move and
have our being"; as even some of your poets have said,
"For we are indeed his offspring." Being then God's
offspring, we ought not to think that the Deity is like
gold, or silver, or stone, a representation by the art and
imagination of man.

[The message] The times of ignorance God overlooked,
but now he commands all men everywhere to repent,
because he has fixed a day on which he will judge the
world in righteousness by a man whom he has appointed,
and of this he has given assurance to all men by raising
him from the dead (Ac 17:22-31).

Socrates had been condemned to drink hemlock for the crime
of introducing strange gods into the city. In the age of hellenistic
syncretism, there was no one to take up the defense of the
ancient gods. But a few of the Athenians were prepared to be
interested in the serious questions raised by St. Paul.

The resurrection of Christ

This was the central theme of the Christian message. Christ's
resurrection was the beginning of the action in this world of the
promised and long-awaited eschatological events. There was no
question of a prodigy such as might be expected from magicians.
God raised his Son as the "first of the resurrection from the
dead." A movement had started: all the dead were to be raised,
the judgment was near; there would be an end of the present age
and the inauguration of a new world. Already the upsurge of this
new world could be felt. The feeling was penetrating the Christians and all the universe with them.

It must be understood that Paul would never allow anyone to
cast doubt on the fact of the Resurrection, that is, the return to
life of Christ after he had gone down into the tomb. The affirmation rested on the experience of those who *had seen* the risen
Christ, interpreted according to the common and elementary
notions of men's life and death. On philosophical principles the
Corinthians rejected the hope of the resurrection of their dead.
Paul observes that such a negation in principle would involve the

negation of Christ's resurrection also, and the very foundations of Christianity would be undermined. "If there is no resurrection of the dead, then Christ has not been raised; if Christ has not been raised, then our preaching is in vain and your faith is in vain. We are even found to be misrepresenting God, because we testified of God that he raised Christ, whom he did not raise" (1 Cor 15: 13-15).

A faith without foundation, a meaningless faith: if this present life is closed in on itself, if it is not open to the hope of a beyond, what does it mean to have hope in Christ in this world? For this life brings to us Christians, by way of privilege, nothing but permanent dangers, threats of death, promises of suffering. We are the most unhappy of men. It would be better to follow the moral of the Epicureans, "Let us eat and drink, for tomorrow we die" (1 Cor 15:19, 30-33). The Corinthians had not in fact explicitly attacked the message of Christ's resurrection; at least, we have no proof of it. But if they wanted to be self-consistent, that was what it would lead up to. Paul fires off a well-directed barrage.

The witness of the Resurrection is so closely linked to the twelve, then to St. Paul, and therefore to all the apostles, that they take the title of "witnesses." It could be said that their witness preceded their message. By their witness, they were faithful to Christ, were taking his side by affirming that he was alive, and were doing it with the strength given by the Spirit. "With great power the apostles gave their testimony to the resurrection of the Lord Jesus" (Ac 4:33). The denial of the Jewish people and the role of witnesses assumed by the apostles are placed in absolute antithesis (Ac 3:14ff.). We are present at a sort of re-enactment of Christ's trial in public, before the people and the authorities. The apostles testify for him. They do it with the help of the Spirit, which has been promised for the time of persecutions.

The witness is therefore legal, religiously legal, in a trial for or against Jesus. It is nonetheless a human witness, and it has a double value: that of ordinary human witness and that of witness by the Holy Spirit, giving power to the truth that the witnesses express in a religious cause.

The joyous entry of the Lord

Christ's resurrection anticipated his final reign, and was the first of the eschatological resurrections. But Christ had not as yet publicly manifested his glory, which he was to do at the time of his "coming." This coming was to be the signal for the end of time. It was to be preceded by the eschatological battle, the resurrection of the dead, and the judgment. Afterward would remain eternity.

St. Paul, at Thessalonica, painted this glorious coming in colors inspired by the joyous entries of hellenistic sovereigns—kings, emperors, generals, or the higher magistrates.

The joyous entry was an eminently popular festival. Taxes were raised to cover the expenses, and commemorative coins were struck. The ceremonial was carefully regulated. A decree of a city of the kingdom of Pergama, bestowing on King Attales III (138-133 B.C.) the honors of a joyous entry, describes its immediate preparations for us. A procession was to advance from the town to meet the sovereign.

> On his approaching the town, all the crown bearers of the twelve gods and of the god-king Eumenes are to take their crowns, the priests and the priestesses shall open the temples of the gods, scattering incense and offering ritual prayers, in order that now and ever be given to King Attales, Philometor and Evergetes, whether he is making war or defending himself, health, salvation, victory and power over earth and sea, and that his kingdom may endure for ever and in all security. The priests and priestesses above mentioned shall advance to meet him, with the generals, the magistrates, and the winners of the games with the crowns they have won, the ruler of the gymnasium followed by the ephebes and the cadets, the schoolmaster at the head of the children, then the citizens, their wives and all the maidens and inhabitants in white robes with crowns. It is to be a feast day. . . .

Sometimes they improvised, as happened when Titus made his entry into Antioch. The account is from Josephus' *The Jewish War.*

> When the people of Antioch learned that Titus was approaching the city, they could not remain within their walls for joy, but rushed out to meet him, advancing more than thirty stadia, not only the men but a multitude of women and children coming out of the town; and when they saw him approach, they drew up on either side along the road. They saluted him with raised hands as they accompanied him, acclaiming him in every way; in the midst of their acclamations they did not cease from demanding that the Jews be expelled from the town.

St. John Chrysostom, who is so close to the Pauline environment, does not hesitate to copy this profane scenario in describing the coming of the Lord.

> And even as when a city receives the emperor, those persons invested with honors and dignities, or enjoying the favor of the monarch, go out from the city to meet him, while the guilty and the criminals remain under strong guard, awaiting the emperor's sentence; so when the Lord shall come, the men who are in good grace with him shall go up to meet him in the air, but the guilty and those whose consciences are sullied with many crimes shall await their judge on the earth.

The Thessalonians took St. Paul at his word. Swept away by their enthusiasm, they imagined that the coming of the Lord was very near. They even gave up their work. When a few members of their community died, they were filled with grief, believing that the dead would miss the festivities. St. Paul put things straight:

> But we would not have you ignorant, brethren, concerning those who are asleep, that you may not grieve as others do who have no hope. For since we believe that Jesus died and rose again, even so, through Jesus, God will bring with him those who have fallen asleep. For this we declare to you by the word of the Lord, that we who are alive, who are left until the coming of the Lord, shall not precede those who have fallen asleep. For the Lord himself will descend from heaven with a cry of

command, with the archangel's call, and with the sound of the trumpet of God. And the dead in Christ will rise first; then we who are alive, who are left, shall be caught up together with them in the clouds to meet the Lord in the air; and so we shall always be with the Lord. Therefore comfort one another with these words (I Th 4:13-18).

Many commentators have been tempted to short-circuit the unfolding of the scene: "Having met the Lord in the air," they believe, "they will follow him up to heaven in glory: *and thus we shall ever be with the Lord*, in a society and an intimate union which will be one of the essential elements of eternal beatitude." But the Lord, before eternity, puts trust in his elect and associates them with the work of his parousia, combat, and judgment, the crowning of their earthly life.

The eschatological combat

At the beginning of his second message to Macedonia, Paul also uses images gathered from the apocalypses. Particularly since the persecutions of Antiochus Epiphanes, the Jews had placed great hopes in a miraculous intervention by God, and many had dreamed of the time and circumstances of this event.

A collection of visions, in which imagination was mixed with prophetic inspiration, was gradually formed, with a highly original and easily recognizable style. This literature is represented in the bible by the Book of Daniel, the ancestor of all the apocalypses, which was, in fact, written under the influence of the Seleucid persecution, and by Revelation, the masterpiece that so admirably ends our canon.

Paul was familiar with the commonplaces of this literature. In order to explain to the Thessalonians (2 Th 2:3-12) that the coming of Christ was not so very imminent, he reminded them of his teachings: the premonitory signs, the great apostasy, and the revelation of the man of lawlessness, "the son of perdition, who opposes and exalts himself against every so-called god or object of worship, so that he takes his seat in the temple of God, proclaiming himself to be God." Moreover, there was the "obstacle"—"he

who now restrains"—seemingly a man who was blocking the
ultimate development of iniquity. The adversary who was to
take the lead in the struggle was an incarnation of Satan in a
persecuting sovereign imposing his own worship on the Jews, an
Antiochus Epiphanes or, later, a Caligula coming back into the
world. The "restrainer" might perhaps on the other hand be an
emperor who maintained human order in spite of satanic efforts.

According to the first letter to the Corinthians the struggle
has moved into the region of spiritual powers. At this ultimate
moment of time, Christ has overcome all his enemies (the Rebel
Powers), including the last enemy, death, which was the first to
come into the world and was the symbol of the revolt against
God (1 Cor 15:24-26).

The general resurrection and the judgment

Paul's fundamental ideas gradually freed themselves from
sediments; the imagery diminished and disappeared. Here he is
describing the stages of the end of time in First Corinthians (15:
22-28): "In Christ shall all be made alive. But each in his own
order: Christ the first fruits, then at his coming those who belong
to Christ. Then comes the end."

The three stages are announced, because of the context, as
three moments of vivification, that is, the transformation into
glory in the life of the risen Christ. The end is the general resurrection, coming after the resurrection of Christ and the glorification of those who are united to him in faith, Christians who have
died (these are the first to be raised), or are still living. Christ's
resurrection is thus transmitted in concentric circles outward to
the general resurrection. What could the annihilation of death in
fact be, unless it were a general resurrection? And this is what
has been announced in the introductory verse of our description:
"For as in Adam all die, so also in Christ shall all be made alive."

The idea of a general judgment implanted itself in Paul. It
came to him, through his training as a Pharisee, from the depths
of the Old Testament, especially from the prophetic teachings.
All men, the Gentiles and Jews as well, would appear before the

judgment seat of God.The judgment would include the resurrection of the dead because the body had been the instrument of sin or of good works. His horizon reaches beyond the apocalypses, and it is the deepest human conscience, enlightened by divine revelation, which here finds words: "For he will render to every man according to his works: to those who by patience in well-doing seek for glory and honor and immortality, he will give eternal life; but for those who are factious and do not obey the truth, but obey wickedness there shall be wrath and fury" (Rm 2:6-8).

The comparison of the joyous entry and the apocalyptic imagery did not survive the letters to the Thessalonians and the Corinthians. Afterward, Paul continued to use the traditional vocabulary, but it was almost totally denuded. At the end he said, "I have fought the good fight, I have finished the race, I have kept the faith. Henceforth there is laid up for me a crown of righteousness, which the Lord, the righteous judge, will award to me on that Day, and not only to me but also to all who have loved his appearing" (2 Tm 4:7-8).

The elements of the end of time are there, concentrated and unified in the Apostle's hope, in his humility before the Lord Jesus, his master and judge, in his trust in the justice of God, and in his belief that all who have lived in the expectation of Christ's coming will share his reward. This is our hope still, and it banishes both exaggerated fears and despair; we accept for ourselves and our fellowmen the mystery of the conciliation of justice with mercy.

Henceforth, the realities of eternity alone subsist. The Son will have subjected all the cosmos, and he, to whom the Father has put all things in subjection, will himself be subjected to the Father, "that God may be everything to every one" (1 Cor 15:28).

Eternal life

The end of our journey is, in reality, eternal life. Paul tells us of it in two sentences.

We have just met the first of them: "God will be everything

to every one." It resembles some of the old Stoic formulas, with a musty smell of pantheism, identifying the one and the all. But for Paul it is clear that the Son remains the Son, precisely in that he subjects himself to the Father. In the same way Christians, in him, remain the sons of God in eternity. Their personalities persist in eternity, and with them, Christian relationships. We shall find, in God and in Christ, all other men who are our brothers and, like us, are sons of God. "And so we shall always be with the Lord." In that glorification of created humanity, God will exalt his own glory.

The second formula is derived from the Old Testament. We shall see God "face to face" (1 Cor 13:12). The privilege of Moses will be extended to us, but incommensurably enlarged. The face-to-face vision of Moses was ocular and only a symbol of intellectual knowledge; the face-to-face vision of eternity is *knowledge.* No doubt, man is before God in his glorified body, but his *intelligence* lives in the enthusiasm of the knowledge of God. His spiritual existence is born from the act by which God first knew him; his eternal existence is the act that God creates in his intelligence so that it may know him face to face.

The meaning of Christian eschatology

Christian eschatology is fundamentally different from that of the Jewish or pagan apocalyptic writings. For Paul and the Christians, the resurrection of Christ, being already a reality of the end of time present in time now, the things of the eternal beyond have been begun in the existence of Christians and of the Church.

Even while it was centered on the hoped-for future, Paul's message embraced, along with the expected future events, the reality of the resurrection already present in the glorified Christ, and in those who by faith have followed in the path of the risen Lord. Baptism truly unites us to the death of Christ in granting us remission of sins, and it transforms here and now our relations with God and our situation on earth. By this very fact, eschatology is both an expected and hoped-for future and a heavenly future that is already realized; and in the same way, the Christian religion is, for those who accept it, life and experience actualizing our union with God through Christ and the Holy Spirit.

St. Paul had only to develop the virtualities contained in the faith and the efficacy of the sacraments to be able to offer to the Greek world what it was confusedly seeking in the revelation of the unknown God.

THE IDEA OF IMMORTALITY IN PAUL

Frederick F. Bruce

Paul's view of the life to come before his conversion cannot be reconstructed in every detail with complete certainty. That he inherited the common Pharisaic belief in resurrection we know, but we should not assume too readily that the Pharisaic doctrine of resurrection at the beginning of the 1st century A.D. was uniform, or that it can be determined without more ado from later rabbinical teaching. The belief in resurrection seems to have been the principal, though by no means the only, point of theological difference between the Pharisees and the Sadducees: the narrative of Acts records how Paul, appearing before the Sanhedrin after his arrest in Jerusalem, threw the apple of discord among its members by declaring that as a Pharisee born and bred he stood on trial for the hope of the resurrection of the dead (Ac 23:6). Still more explicitly, he is said to have declared before Felix that he held the hope, shared by his accusers—by his *Pharisaic* accusers, of course—'that there is to be a resurrection of good and wicked alike' (Ac 24:15). It is curious—though it may be accidental—that in Paul's letters there is no clear reference to the resurrection of the wicked.

The twofold resurrection is commonly believed to be first attested in Daniel 12:2—"many of those who sleep in the dust of the earth will wake, some to everlasting life, and some to the reproach of eternal abhorrence". But it is possible to render these words otherwise: "many who sleep in the dust of the earth will wake, and these are (destined) to everlasting life; but those (the others, who do not wake) are (destined) to the reproach of eternal abhorrence" (cf. Pr 10:7, "the memory of the righteous is for a blessing, but the name of the wicked will rot").

Josephus' account of the Pharisees' teaching is based on inside information, but it suffers from his eagerness to assimilate it to the Greek outlook, especially in *Antiquities* xviii. 14: "They believe that souls have power to survive death and that there are rewards and punishments under the earth for those who have led lives of virtue or vice: eternal imprisonment is the lot of evil souls, while the good souls receive an easy passage to a new life." Nothing here would cause much offence to a Platonist. In his earlier work, his *Jewish War*, Josephus had spoken more explicitly of the Pharisees' belief in resurrection: "They hold that every soul is incorruptible, but that the soul of the good alone passes *into another body* while the souls of the wicked suffer eternal punishment" (ii.163). Here it appears that the bodily resurrection of the righteous only is contemplated—although an uninitiated Greek or Roman reader might well have taken Josephus' words to imply a belief in metempsychosis. Later in the *Jewish War* the Pharisaic belief finds fresh expression, where Josephus represents himself as trying to dissuade his comrades at Jotapata from committing suicide to avoid falling into the hands of the Romans: "those who depart this life in accordance with the law of nature [which would be violated by suicide] . . . win eternal renown; . . . their souls, remaining spotless and obedient, are allotted the most holy place in heaven whence, in the revolution of the ages, they return to find a new habitation in pure bodies" (iii. 347).

The varieties of expectation among religious Jews in the last two centuries B.C. are well illustrated by the intertestamental literature. Ben Sira thinks that posterity's remembrance of a good man's virtues is the most desirable immortality[1]: the author of Wisdom, influenced by Greek thought, thinks in terms of the survival of souls—especially of "the souls of the righteous" which "are in the hand of God", so that no evil can befall them.[2]

---

1 Si 4:1ff.
2 Ws 3:1ff.

From the second century B.C., however, the idea of the Garden of Eden (Paradise) as a place of bliss for the righteous and of Gehinnom as a place of fiery punishment for the wicked after death took hold of popular imagination among the Jews— partly, no doubt, under the influence of Iranian belief, in which fire is a means of testing at the last judgment (*Yasna* 47:6, 51:9). In Pharisaism the fire of Gehinnom for the ungodly is not always purely penal; according to the school of Shammai those whose merits and demerits were evenly balanced had first to purge their sins in its flame and only so enter into Paradise (TB *Rosh ha-Shanh* 16b, *Baraitha*). This implies the idea of some sort of personal survival between death and resurrection.

In the first century A.D. the souls of the dead, or at least of the righteous dead, are kept in store-chambers or treasuries between death and resurrection—of all the dead, apparently, in 4 Ezra 7:32, 75-101, and 2 Baruch 21:23; of the righteous dead in 2 Baruch 30:2.

The Qumran texts speak plainly enough of eternal life for the righteous and annihilation for the wicked, but throw no clear light on the question of resurrection. Those who hold fast to God's house (cf. Heb 3:6) "are destined for eternal life and all the glory of man is theirs" (CD iii.20); the disobedient "have no remnant or survival" (CD ii. 6f) but suffer the doom of the antediluvian sinners who "perished and became as though they had never been" (CD ii. 20).

The men of Qumran looked forward to the day of requital when God would "render to man his reward" (1 QS x. 18). His elect would inherit the lot of the holy ones—indeed, in their community life they anticipated this inheritance, for God had "joined their assembly to the sons of heaven, to be a council of the community, a foundation of the building of holiness, an eternal plantation for all time to come" (1 QS xi.7-9). They are "adorned with God's splendour and will enjoy many delights with everlasting peace and length of days" (1 QH xiii. 17-18). When the last battle between good and evil is fought, "there shall be eternal deliverance for those belonging to the lot of God and destruction for all the nations of wickedness" (1 QM xv.1-2). But just how the godly pass from mortal life, or from a martyr-death, to their state of endless bliss is not so clear.

If we could be sure that the men of Qumran were Essenes, then we might associate the former's expectation of eternal bliss with Josephus' statement (*Jewish War* ii. 154ff) that the latter look for the soul, consisting of the finest ether, to be released from the bonds of the flesh and enjoy an elysian retreat. His description of this retreat is not unlike the oasis in which, according to 1 QH viii.4ff, the godly man finds his abode—"beside a fountain of streams in an arid land, . . . beside a watered garden [in a wilderness]".

> No [man shall approach] the well-spring of life
> or drink the waters of holiness
> with the everlasting trees
> or bear fruit with [the planting] of heaven
> who seeing has not discerned
> and considering has not believed
> in the fountain of life.

But Josephus' tendency to conform Jewish beliefs and practices to those rendered respectable by Greek philosophy counsels caution once more in taking his information *au pied de la lettre*. Hippolytus, whose account of the Essenes in the ninth book of his *Philosophoumena* largely follows Josephus but seems to be indebted to a further source, says that in addition to the immortality of the soul they believed in the resurrection of the body: the soul, he says, is regarded by the Essenes as imperishable, resting after death in an airy and well-lighted place, until it is rejoined by the resurrected body on the day of judgment.[3] Our ignorance of Hippolytus' additional source prevents us from adequately evaluating his information where it contradicts that of Josephus, but a certain suspension of judgment is plainly the wise course to adopt.

Whatever Paul's earlier position on immortality may have been, it was decisively modified by his conversion to Christianity.

---

3 Hippolytus, Philosophoumena (=Refutation of All Heresies), ix. 18ff.

This conversion resulted immediately and inevitably from his vision of the risen Lord, who called him to be his apostle. What he had previously refused to admit—that the crucified Jesus had been raised from the dead by the power of God, as the earlier apostles maintained—was now born in upon him by testimony too compelling to be doubted. Jesus was therefore the Messiah, the Son of God, the highly exalted Lord—but, more especially for our present purpose, with Jesus' rising from the dead the expected resurrection had begun to take place. What had been for Paul previously the resurrection *hope* was now, so far as Jesus was concerned, more than a hope; it was a *fait accompli*. Since God had raised Jesus from the dead, he would assuredly raise all his people in due course.[4] At least, he would raise those of them who passed through death before the *parousia* of Jesus—his advent in glory when their resurrection would take place—whether they belonged to the patriarchs and prophets of the old age or to believers of the new age. But many believers of the new age would not require to be raised from the dead, for they would still be alive at the *parousia*. Here and now believers of the new age continued to live in mortal bodies, but inwardly they already enjoyed a foretaste of the coming resurrection life—eternal life—because they were united by faith to the risen Christ, incorporated in him. This incorporation was effected by the Spirit of Christ whom they had received, and by his power the life of the risen Christ was already imparted to all his people. In baptism, indeed, they had died with Christ and been buried and raised with him; at his advent they would share his manifested glory, but by the in-dwelling Spirit they were able to anticipate the hope of glory and live in the good of it.[5] It was no mere intimation of immortality that they thus received; it was an initial experience of immortality, though the full experience must await the *parousia*. Here and now they knew that Christ, once raised from the dead, is never to die again: he is no longer under the dominion of death (Rm 6:9),

---

4 Cf. I Th 4:14; I Cor 6:14; 2 Cor 4:14, etc.
5 Cf. Rm 5:2; Col 1:27.

and what was true of him must be true of his people who through him possessed as the gift of God the life of the age to come. "If the Spirit of him who raised Jesus from the dead dwells within you"—so Paul's argument runs—"then the God who raised Christ Jesus from the dead will also give new life to your mortal bodies through his indwelling Spirit" (Rm 8:11).

These last quotations from Paul's writings express the full maturity of his understanding; but, while we can trace a progression in his thought and language on this subject, his central belief and teaching do not appear to have undergone any essential change throughout his Christian career.

The main body of Paul's correspondence that has been preserved to us comes from a period lasting not more than from ten to twelve years—from his Corinthian ministry in the early 50's of the first century to his Roman imprisonment at the beginning of the 60's. So short a period may see but little development in some men's careers when they have reached this stage of life, but Paul's life during these years was so full of intense activity and, latterly, a spell of enforced inactivity, coupled with an ever deepening awareness of what it meant to be Christ's apostle among the Gentiles, that it would be surprising if his experiences had no influence at all on his outlook on the future.

At the beginning of this period Paul visited the Macedonian city of Thessalonica and founded the church there, but circumstances beyond his control forced him to leave the place before he had given his converts all the teaching he believed they required. It is clear that he taught them not only "to be servants of the living and true God" to whom they had turned from pagan idolatry, but also "to wait expectantly for the appearance from heaven of his Son Jesus, whom he raised from the dead, Jesus our deliverer from the terrors of judgment to come" (1 Th 1:9f). Such expectant waiting implies survival to witness the great event. But in the weeks and months that followed Paul's departure some of his converts died. The death of believers before the *parousia* was something that the Thessalonian church had not been prepared for, and a problem was thereby created in their minds on which they sought enlightenment. Through Timothy, probably, whom Paul had sent back from Athens to visit them, they submitted their problem to Paul; in fact, they seem to have put two questions to him:

1. At Christ's *parousia*, what will be the lot of those believers in him who have died before he comes?

2. When may the *parousia* be expected?

In answering the former question Paul assures them that those of their number who have died before the *parousia* will suffer no disadvantage when it takes place; "we who are left alive until the Lord comes shall not forestall those who have died". On the contrary, when the Lord descends from heaven with the shout of command, the archangel's voice and the trumpet blast, those who respond to his summons first will be the dead in Christ; when they rise at his call, brought to life with him who died and rose again, "then we who are left alive shall join them, caught up in clouds to meet the Lord in the air" (1 Th 4:14-18). This assurance is conveyed to them "by the word of the Lord"—on the authority of an utterance of Jesus himself (whether given before his death or subsequently we need not now inquire). The language and imagery are those associated with Old Testament theophanies of redemption and judgment—we may think of the trumpet blast which calls home the dispersed of Israel in Isaiah 27:13 and the clouds of heaven on which one like a son of man is brought to the Ancient of Days in Daniel 7:13—but what is here communicated in these terms is new and distinctively Christian. Because Jesus died and rose again, those who die believing in him cannot fail to rise with him; and all his people must live forever with him.

As for the latter and more general question, when the *parousia* would take place, Paul does little more than repeat the words of Jesus, that it would come unexpectedly, "like a thief in the night."[6] The call to the people of Christ therefore is to "keep awake and sober"—"for God has not destined us to the terrors of judgment, but to the full attainment of salvation through our Lord Jesus Christ" (1 Th 5:1-9).

---

6 cf. Mt 24:43; Lk 12:39; Rv 16:15.

Paul's best-known contribution to the subject is his reply to those members of the church of Corinth who held, as he put it, that there was "no resurrection of the dead" (1 Cor 15:12). In these people's eyes the doctrine of the reanimation of corpses, as they took it to be, was perhaps an uncongenial Jewish super-stition which was a handicap to the acceptance of the Christian message by thoughtful Gentiles. It was a pity, they thought, that Paul had not been able to disencumber himself of this as he had of so many other Jewish peculiarities. Happily, they themselves were more completely emancipated. It stood to reason that (in words which Aeschylus places in the mouth of the god Apollo) "when the earth has drunk up a man's blood, once he is dead, there is no resurrection"[7]—and Aeschylus used the same Greek word *anastasis* as Paul uses in 1 Cor 15.

What these Corinthians positively believed about the life to come is more difficult to determine. They may simply have believed in the inherent immortality of the soul, or in some kind of assumption into glory at death or at the *parousia;* but there are hints elsewhere in Paul's correspondence with them that they held what has been described as an "over-realised eschatology." Earlier in this letter he tells the Corinthian Christians, ironically, that they have "arrived" ahead of time: "You have come into your fortune already. You have come into your kingdom—and left us out. How I wish you had indeed won your kingdom; then you might share it with us!" (1 Cor 4:8). Presumably they thought that with the gift of the Spirit they had received all that the religious man could desire. One suggestion is that they anticipated the outlook of Prodicus, a second-century Gnostic, whose followers claimed to be 'by nature sons of the first God' and therefore "royal sons far above the rest of mankind" (Clement of Alexandria, *Stromateis* iii. 30).

If a Gnostic link is sought, a more promising one may be provided by the *Epistle to Rheginus,* a short Valentinian treatise on resurrection, included in the 'Jung papyrus' (one of the Nag

---

7 Aeschylus, *Eumenides,* 647f.

Hammadi codices) and published for the first time in 1963.[8] According to this document (p. 45, II. 14ff):

> The Saviour swallowed up death. . . . For he laid aside the world that perishes. He changed himself into an incorruptible *aeon* and raised himself up, after he swallowed up the visible by the invisible, and he gave us the way of our immortality. But at that time, as the apostle said, we suffered with him, and we rose with him, and we went to heaven with him. But if we are made manifest in this world wearing him, we are his beams and we are encompassed by him until our setting, which is our death in this life. We are drawn upward by him like beams by the sun, without being held back by anything. This is the spiritual resurrection which swallows up the psychic together with the fleshly.

The first editors of this document interpreted its contents in terms of an over-realised eschatology such as that for which Hymenaeus and Philetus are reprobated in 2 Tm 1:17f: "they have shot wide of the truth in saying that our resurrection has already taken place, and are upsetting people's faith." More recently Dr. Malcom Lee Peel has pointed out that there is an element of not-yet-realised eschatology in the document: bodily death must be undergone even by the elect, and it is followed by resurrection, albeit a spiritual resurrection.[9] But when the transformation which follows death is described as a spiritual resurrection, the word 'resurrection' is used in an extended sense, one which it does not bear in the New Testament. If the deniers of the resurrection at Corinth held some form of incipient Gnosticism (a possible, though not a necessary, view), they may have anticipated some such view as that expressed in the *Epistle to Rheginus*, for the 'spiritual resurrection' envisaged in the *Epistle* would in Paul's

---

8 *De Resurrectione* (*Epistula ad Rheginum*), ed. M. Malinine, H.-Ch. Puech, G. Quispel, W. Till (Zürich and Stuttgart, 1963).
9 *The Epistle to Rheginus* (London, 1969), pp. 143ff; cf. also M.L. Peel, 'Gnostic Eschatology and the New Testament, *Novum Testamentum*, 12 (1970), pp. 141ff.

eyes have been no resurrection in the true sense of the word. In this "spiritual resurrection" it is the inward and invisible "members' that ascend, clothed in a new and spiritual "flesh", for which the appearance of Moses and Elijah on the mount of transfiguration is cited as a precedent.

Nevertheless, Paul himself taught his converts that believers in Christ had been raised from death with him; why then should they think of any further resurrection? It is evident from Paul's argument that the men to whom it was directed had no thought of denying the resurrection of Christ: if they accepted that, he urges, they must logically accept the resurrection of his people. The resurrection of Christ was the first-fruits of the general resurrection-harvest which the people of Christ would experience at his *parousia*, when death, the last enemy, would be abolished.

For Paul, this further resurrection could only be bodily resurrection. True, the immortal resurrection body would be of a different order from the present mortal body; it would be a "spiritual" body whereas the present body was "natural" or "psychic"—*sōma psychikon*, a body animated by "soul". This language is bound up with his distinction between life "in Adam", who in Gn 2:7 is described as "a living soul"—"an animate being" —and life "in Christ," who in resurrection has become "a life-giving spirit" (1 Cor 15:45). But in this argument Paul goes beyond the assurance he had given to the Thessalonian Christians a few years earlier. Then, he declared that those who survived to the *parousia* would enjoy no advantage over the faithful departed; now he affirms, and that on the strength of a special revelation, a "mystery" newly disclosed (1 Cor. 15:51), that those who survive will then undergo an instantaneous transformation, so that they too will be adapted to the conditions of the resurrection age. We may compare and contrast the expectation found later in the first century in the Apocalypse of Baruch where the bodies of the dead, raised without change of form in order to receive equitable judgment, are thereafter transformed in accordance with the verdict—those of the justified being clothed in angelic glory, while those of the condemned waste away in torment (2 Ba 49: 1ff). According to Paul, the dead—that is to say, the dead in Christ, who alone come into his purview here—will rise in bodies which are not liable to corruption, while the living will exchange mortality for immortality. To much the same effect he tells his converts at Philippi that "from heaven we expect our deliverer to come, the Lord Jesus Christ, who will transform the body belonging to our humble state, and give it a form like that of his own resplendent body" (Ph 3:20f). Basic to his thinking throughout is the conviction that Christ and his people are so vitally and permanently united that his triumph over death must be shared with them, not only in sacramental anticipation but in bodily resurrection.

But in all this nothing has been said about a question which, to our way of thinking, is of the essence of this topic of immortality: what happens at death? Not until 2 Corinthians does Paul approach this question, so far as his extant correspondence is concerned. This may have been due in part to his expectation that he would survive until the *parousia*. In the nature of the case he could not *know* that he would survive until then, but in his earliest references to the subject he associates himself with those who will survive: "we who are left alive until the Lord comes shall not forestall those who have died" (1 Th 4:15)—"those who have died" are mentioned in the third person but the survivors are mentioned in the inclusive first person plural. In 1 Cor 6:14 the first person plural is used of those who will experience resurrection: "God not only raised our Lord from the dead; he will also raise us by his power"—but here no distinction is drawn between those who have died and those who will still be alive, for Paul is emphasizing that the body comes within the scope of God's redemptive purpose and that present bodily actions have therefore a serious relevance for the future state of Christians; by "us" he means "us Christians" in the most general sense. No significant shift of perspective is involved in 1 Corinthians: "we shall not all die, but we shall all be changed", for at the *parousia* 'the dead will rise immortal and we [the living also] shall be changed' (1 Cor 15:51f).

It is when we come to 2 Corinthians that we are conscious of a change of perspective on Paul's part. Probably not more than a year separated the writing of the two letters, but the experiences of that year affected Paul profoundly. This is clear, even if we do not go all the way with C.H. Dodd in locating in this interval a 'spiritual crisis' which was 'a sort of second conversion' (*New Testament Studies*, 1953, p. 81).In addition to the 'fightings without and fears within' to which Paul refers in 2 Cor 7:5, there was one specially serious danger which overtook him in proconsular Asia, one from which he could see no way out but death. Confrontation with death was no new thing for Paul: "I die daily", he could say some months before this trouble befell him (1 Cor 15:31). But on this occasion he felt like a man who had received the death-sentence. On earlier occasions the way of escape had presented itself along with the danger, but no such way could be discerned this time. Commentators are not agreed about the nature of the trouble: it may have been a nearly fatal illness or (as seems rather more probable to me) it may have been a nearly successful judicial attempt on his life. One thing is certain: when at last, beyond all expectation, escape did come, Paul welcomed it as little short of resurrection from death—a miraculous deliverance wrought by "God who raises the dead" (2 Cor 1:9).

Paul had frequently experienced the risk of death before, but never before had he faced for a period what he believed to be certain death. Whatever other changes this experience occasioned in his outlook, it modified his perspective on death and resurrection. For one thing, he henceforth treats the prospect of his dying before the *parousia* as more probable than otherwise. This change would no doubt have come about in any case with the passage of time, but it was precipitated by his affliction in Asia. Be it noted, however, that while it affected his personal perspective, the "deferment of the *parousia*" caused no such fundamental change in his thought as it is sometimes held to have caused in the thought of the church as a whole. Now it is as a personal confession of faith that he says: "we know that he who raised the Lord Jesus to life will with Jesus raise us too, and bring us to his presence, and you with us" (2 Cor 4:14).

But, if death before the *parousia* was now the more probable prospect for Paul, what would be his state of existence (if any) between death and the *parousia?* As we have seen, this question did not exercise him before (so far as can be judged from his extant writings); now in 2 Corinthians he tackles it. But in tackling this question he could appeal to no "word of the Lord" as he had done when clearing up the Thessalonians' difficulty, nor had he any special revelation to guide him as when he unfolded to the Corinthians the "mystery" that the *parousia* would witness the transformation of living believers as well as the resurrection of those who had fallen asleep (1 Cor 15:51). Nonetheless he speaks with confidence: "we know," he says (2 Cor 5:1). But what do "we know"? Not simply that for the believer to depart is to be "with Christ," which is better by far," as he puts it in Phil 1:23, but that, for this to be so, some kind of new embodiment is necessary at death—and his assurance is that such embodiment is available.

Paul evidently could not contemplate immortality apart from resurrection; for him a body of some kind was essential to personality. Our traditional thinking about the "never-dying soul", which owes so much to our Graeco-Roman heritage, makes it difficult for us to appreciate Paul's point of view. It is, no doubt, an over-simplification to say that while for the Greeks man was an embodied soul, for the Hebrews he was an animated body; yet there is sufficient substance in the statement for us to say that in this as in other respects Paul was "a Hebrew born and bred" (Ph 3:5). For others, including several of his Corinthian converts, disengagement from the shackle of the body was a consummation devoutly to be wished; but if Paul longed to be delivered from the mortality of this present earthly "dwelling", it was with a view to exchanging it for one that was immortal; to be without a body of any kind would be a form of spiritual nakedness or isolation from which his mind shrank. But he sees the resurrection principle to be already at work in the people of Christ by the power of the Spirit who indwells them; in some sense the spiritual body of the coming age is already being formed: while the "outward man" wastes away under the attrition of mortal life, the inward man experiences daily renewal, so that physical death will mean no hiatus of disembodiment but the immediate enjoyment of being "at home with the Lord" (2 Cor 5:8).

It is in 2 Cor 5:1-10 that Paul makes his most personal contribution to the subject of immortality. The number of articles and monographs devoted to the interpretation of this passage is beyond counting, and shows no sign of abating. Without waiting for the *parousia*, Paul begins by stating his assurance that "if the earthly frame that houses us today should be demolished, we possess a building which God has provided—a house not made by human hands, eternal, and in heaven" (2 Cor 5:1). What is in these words called a "building" is afterwards described in terms of a garment: "we yearn to have our heavenly habitation put on over this one"—since, of course, "being thus clothed, we shall not find ourselves naked" (5:2f). But whether building or garment is spoken of, it is a body—the new, immortal body—that is meant: "we do not want to have the old body stripped off. Rather our desire is to have the new body put on over it, so that our mortal part may be absorbed into life immortal. God himself has shaped us for this very end; and as a pledge of it he has given us the Spirit" (5:4f).

It is difficult to distinguish the new body to which Paul here looks forward from the spiritual body to be received when the last trumpet sounds, according to the teaching of 1 Cor 15. Attempts have indeed been made to explain the heavenly body as a corporate entity, the body of Christ; but believers have already "put on Christ" (Gal 3:27), and the Pauline concept of the body of Christ and believers' membership in it is related to the present mortal existence rather than to the life to come. If, however, the new body referred to here is the spiritual body of 1 Cor 15, Paul no longer thinks of waiting until the *parousia* before he receives it. Nor is it a merely temporary integument that he hopes to receive at death, pending his investiture with the resurrection body at the *parousia*; it is the eternal "housing" which God has prepared for him and his fellow-believers, and of which the present gift of the Spirit is an anticipatory guarantee. So instantaneous is the change-over from the old body to the new which Paul here envisages that there will be no interval of conscious "nakedness" between the one and the other. The change-over takes place, as he says in 1 Cor 15:52, "in a moment, in the twinkling of an eye"—only there the split-second transformation takes place at the *parousia*, whereas here Paul seems to imply that for those who do not survive until the *parousia* the new body will be immediately available at death. If he does not say so quite explicitly, this may be because he has received no clear revelation to this effect.

Perhaps Paul's pre-Christian conception of the life to come had little to say about the state of affairs between death and resurrection. The dead were dead, and that was that, but they would be brought back to life by the power of God on the resurrection day.

But, for Paul the Christian, the resurrection of Christ made a vital difference to this pattern. For Christ, having died, had already been brought back to new life by the power of God, and by faith-union with him his people were already enabled to share the power of his resurrection and walk in newness of life. Was it conceivable that those who were united, right now in mortal life, with the risen and ever-living Christ, should have this union interrupted, even temporarily, by bodily death? We have it on Dr. Samuel Johnson's authority that a man's expectation of imminent execution "concentrates his mind wonderfully"[10] and it may have been precisely such expectation that concentrated Paul's mind on this question in the months preceding the writing of 2 Corinthians, to the point where he reached the conclusion set forth in this fifth chapter. It was not the nature of the resurrection body that caused him chief concern, although he could not conceive of conscious existence and communication with his environment in a disembodied state. What he craved, and received, was the assurance that absence from this earthly body would mean being "at home" with the Lord, without any waiting interval. The immediate investiture with the new body is valued only as a means of realising and enjoying a closer near-

---

10 'Depend upon it, Sir, when a man knows he is to be hanged in a fortnight, it concentrates his mind wonderfully' (J. Boswell, *Life of Johnson*, ed. G.B. Hill and L.F. Powell, iii [Oxford, 1934], p. 167). And it may well be that Paul had been literally sentenced to death (2 Cor 1:9).

ness and a fuller communion with the Lord than had been possible in mortal life. Therefore, says he, "we never cease to be confident" and meanwhile we "make it our ambition, wherever we are, here or there, to be acceptable to him" (5:6, 9). Appearance before the tribunal of Christ, to give account of deeds done in mortal body, is still a future certainty; so also is the participation of the people of Christ in their Lord's glory when he is manifested—that "revelation of the sons of God" for which, according to Rm 8:19, "the created universe waits with eager expectation." The coming consummation is in no way diminished, but those eschatological features which are realised in life on earth at present do not cease to be realised in the interval between death and the final consummation; they continue indeed to be more intensely realised than is possible during life on earth. Paul's last word on the immortality of men and women of faith is the logical outworking of his teaching on their union with the living Christ.

The tension between our experience of mortality and our hope of immortality is as real to us as it was to Paul. He shows us how in faith we may live with tension. Those who know the fellowship of Christ in this world will know it in the world to come. In the Synoptic record our Lord puts the questions of resurrection and immortality on a firm basis when he subsumes it under man's relation to the living God: "for him all are alive" (Lk 20:38). In the gospel our relation to the living God is realised in Christ, whose assurance to his followers is preserved thus by the Fourth Evangelist: "Because I live, you too will live" (Jn 14:19). With the Paul of the Pastoral Epistles, then, each believer in Christ may say, "I know the one whom I have trusted" (2 Tm 1:12)—and what more need be said?

THE PAULINE MEANING OF MAN'S RISEN "SPIRITUAL BODY" (1 Cor 15:44)

Léonard Audet, C.S.V.

The combination "spiritual body" occurs in the Bible only once as Paul's own invention. It has given rise to a welter of fantasies concerning the nature of bodily being after the resurrection. Even Aquinas debates soberly whether the nails will grow and the intestines function. Such speculations give us no help in penetrating to what Paul really meant by a body that would be "not in the order of the soul (*psychē;* "animated") but in the order of spirit (*pneuma;* "spiritualized")" 1 Cor 15:44.

Sōma in Paul

"Body" itself has in Paul a specialized sense which has been adequately set forth by research. *Sōma* does not mean that part or aspect of bodily being which decomposes after death. That is called *sarx* (1 Cor 15:50): to which, in the Septuagint, corresponds the Hebrew *baśar*, while *sōma* is really without any proper Hebrew equivalent. *Sōma* can absolutely never designate a human corpse. Nor does it even mean the really material element which we would today call "the body composed of molecules." It is far more than that.

It is commonly assumed that the body is an individuating factor, the thing that recognizably sets off one individual from others of the same species. For Paul, on the contrary, *sōma* effects solidarity rather than distinction; "it is what makes all men into a live bundle." It is the necessary vehicle of man's relation to the cosmos, to other men, and even to God; it is the mode of expressing the self and of being present to others.

Insofar as he is *sōma*, man relates to the realities external to him, including even those which transcend him, like God, or like "the Spirit." This is precisely how *sōma* differs from *sarx*, which also expresses solidarity with the created but not with the transcendent. *Sōma* is the most comprehensive concept of Pauline anthropology in that it expresses the human person all the way from his situation as sinner and up to his definite glorification in God.

The dualism which sees two different components in the human being (for example, "body-soul) is incompatible with Paul's notion of *sōma*. Body may be defined "the whole man insofar as he is in relation to other realities." The background of the whole of chapter 15 is Paul's rejection of those at Corinth who consider that a part alone of man will survive, whether this be *psychē* as for the Platonists or *pneuma* as for the Gnostics. What survives is the entire man. Therefore that is what rises again.

Since *sōma* is essentially a relational rather than a static/ontological description of man, *sōma pneumatikon* from the outset specifies that the relation in this case is "to the Spirit," without of course obliterating other more basic relationships.

Pneumatikos in Paul

The adjective *pneumatikos*, itself already meaning "in relation to the Spirit," occurs twenty-four times in Paul, besides the two occurrences in 1 Peter 2:5 (the community is a "spiritual edifice" to offer "spiritual sacrifices"). This adjective never occurs in the Greek Old Testament, because it has no proper Hebrew equivalent despite its basic affinity with *ruach*. From this angle its best rendition with *sōma* would be "the whole relational man as influenced by the Spirit." But *pneumatikos* occurs often in the Gnostic and mystery literature of Paul's background, in a more constitutive/ontological nuance: from which its rendition with *sōma* would be "the whole relational man made up of Spirit." Which of the two alternatives best fits Paul?

In a first series of texts (Gal 6:1; Col 1:9) it is *man* who is spoken of as *pneumatikos*, which in 1 Cor 2:4 as in 15:44 is contrasted with *psychikos*. In these texts the adjective *pneumatikos* expresses not a spiritual substance but an inspiration or dependence in relation to the Spirit.

In a second series, it is the *charisms* which are "spiritual" (1 Cor 12:1; 14:1, 37)—here, too, not ontologically but inspirationally or dependentially. These Corinthians' passages about charisms understand *pneumatikos* in a Jewish and not Hellenistic purview.

Finally there are texts where *any* supernatural gift is spiritual (Ep 1:3; Rm 1:11; 13:27; 1 Cor 9:11; 10:3). Here, too, the nuance is not Hellenistic but rather eschatological.

An Original Intuition

We conclude that just as *sōma psychikon* never implies that the body itself is made up out of soul, so *soma pneumatikon* never implies the Hellenistic/Gnostic "body made up out of spirit." The antithesis between these two "ways of being body" is an original intuition of Paul based upon his notion of *pneuma*, and is without precedent in either Hebrew or Hellenistic literature.

Remarkably, Paul uses the noun *psychē* only thirteen times as against one hundred forty-five occurrences of *pneuma*. And yet *psychē*, plainly corresponding to the Old Testament *nefesh*, is very frequent in the intertestamental literature. *Nefesh* is the core of the Semitic philosophy of man, and may be defined "man himself precisely in his relation to life." Significantly, Paul (or Christianity itself) has abandoned this centrality of *nefesh*, and made rather *pneuma* the key-word. *Psychikos* always has a pejorative sense, almost "fleshly" like *sarx*, in its six New Testament occurrences, four of which are in Paul.

When Paul said the body will rise again spiritual, he was countering objections from his Corinthians. But what precisely were those objections? Three options are left open by the complexity of the data:

(a) Paul addresses himself to Greeks who feel that since the *soul* is immortal, it is profitless that the body should survive. Indeed, for them its survival would destroy all hope of a happy future life, since the body is prison and millstone of the soul. To

.such objectors Paul says in 1 Cor 15:17f: "If Christ is not risen. . .
those who died in Christ are perished."

(b) Paul answers Christians imbued with the Gnostic conviction that at death man is delivered from both body and soul
(whether or not there is thus released a third entity lurking un-
noticed beneath them, the *pneuma*) so that in total nudity he can
recover the quintessence of "being a man."

(c) Paul envisions the same blunderers as those in 2 Tm 2:17f
who claim that all those who have already risen and have conquered death, will never die.

The first option is probably best, but rather in the more
generalized sense that Paul is addressing himself to both Jewish
and Greek superstitions about that ghost-world Sheol or Hades.
The supposedly-surviving *nefesh* or *manes* had such a tenuous
and miserable existence that believers suspected they would be
better off annihilated.

The cause of our resurrection

Throughout chapter 15, Paul considers Christ's resurrection
not the "cause" of ours in any Thomist sense, but rather "a case
in point." Since we are all one, what one can do, all can do. Since
the man Christ "resurrected," we are all "resurrectible." As
Adam died, so all men die; as Christ rose, so all rise. And really
for Paul, not Christ but the Father is the cause of any resurrection.

Person Remains Identical

"Spiritual body" seems a contradiction; the body we are
familiar with is the "fleshly body" or *sarx*. How could there be
happiness in an eternity of flesh? Or even if there is a "spiritual
body," will it be in continuity or discontinuity with that other?

Paul answers in images drawn from agriculture. But to grasp
their force, we must realize that for him and his hearers, the
growth of a seed into a plant was no "natural" process due to
what we call "secondary causality." God has to intervene directly
each time, just as he had to intervene in the first creation. And

neither more nor less than this is what God does in making the body rise again.

The seed is not the plant, and could never become it without that miraculous intervention; and yet, still and all, there is truly some continuity of the seed in the plant. So also between the corruptible body and the surviving glorious one.

Ultimately it is *not* in our old wornout body that we will rise, but in a *new* one; it *must* be "different" if it is "spiritual." Paul rejects the view which had come to prevail in Judaism: Namely that the future life will be like this life only more so. The new body will be even of different constitutives; it will have no blood, no flesh even. It will not be numerically the one left in the grave! *Sōma* in 1 Cor 15 thus means ultimately not "material body" but "personality." The person remains identical in the transit from one kind of body to another. Paul tries to make his point clear by analogy with then-current beliefs that there are also different kinds of bodies (verse 39). Stars are bodies, but they have no flesh at all; they have luminosity instead. In the resurrection we will have a body, but a new one, not made up of those material elements which constitute flesh.

The citation of Gn 2:7 in 1 Cor 15:45 takes on a pejorative nuance: Adam became "(mere) *nefesh hayyâ*, living being," the last Adam will be "*pneuma* which *gives* life." Again, this is not by scholastic causality, but insofar as Christ is the key-example of a dynamic quality which every risen *sōma* will share, just as all make up one body in him.

The risen body will also be "heavenly" (verse 47), not a spatial but an eschatological characterization: it will belong to a different world. It will have no corruption and weakness; it will have a new kind of *time* also to go with it. The new *sōma* will be unimaginably docile to the guidance of the Spirit.

And yet the same old "person," the same Ego will still be there, which Paul tries to convey by the expression "the man inside," *esō anthrōpos*: "not the soul or spirit in contrast to the body, but a sort of seed of the glorious future man." "Soul" (*psychē*) passes away no less than "flesh" (*sarx*); *person* continues, but solely in virtue of the *pneuma*.

Conclusions

We conclude in noting some key contentions: (1) 1 Cor 15 gives not a description of the risen body but a proof of its "resurrectibility." (2) The risen or spiritual body differs from the present one not only in its orientation but also in its constitution. (3) The Jewish notion of the material body continuing numerically one but transformed is rejected. (4) Personal identity survives in the transit from one kind of body to another. (5) There is no definitive salvation without the corporal resurrection; body is the vehicle of all man's relationships to the universe and even to God. (6) The resurrection is a new creation setting the man under the entire guidance of the Spirit; hence it is in no wise implied that the *wicked* also will rise again! (7) The empty tomb is not exactly a stumbling-block to Paul's idea of what resurrection means, but neither is it necessary, except possibly as a symbol. (8) Hence, other parts of the New Testament (Jn 20: 1-10, 24-29) exhibit a view of the risen body more material than Paul's, though others approach his (in Lk 24:13-35 the risen body is hard to recognize). We need not recoil from this pluralism of views on the resurrection, but strive to understand them as factors within the broader spectrum of the Church's authentic teaching.

TO LIVE IN CHRIST:
REFLECTIONS ON "PAULINE MORALITY"

Ceslaus Spicq, O.P.

Gratitude is clearly the dominant inspiration of the moral life. This being true, we must determine how Christians are to express their gratitude to God and to live their lives in charity before Him. The all-inclusive response of St. Paul is: *in Christ Jesus.* It is in terms of His Son that God the Father conceived and accomplished all things:

> God, who is rich in mercy, was moved by the intense love with which he loved us, and when we were dead by reason of our transgressions, he made us live with the life of Christ. By grace you have been saved. Together with Christ Jesus and in him, he raised us up and enthroned us in the heavenly realm that in Christ Jesus he might show throughout the ages to come the overflowing riches of his grace springing from his goodness to us (Ep 2:4-7).

Since it is in Christ that God, out of love for us, conceived and executed His plan of salvation, it is clear that no supernatural reality can exist or can even be thought of apart from Christ. It is in Christ that God chooses and predestines His elect (Ep 1:4, 5, 11), that He manifests His grace (Tt 2:11, 3:4), that He communicates His charity (Rm 8:35-39) and peace (Ph 4:7), liberty (Gal 2:4) and light (Ep 5:8-14), knowledge (Ep 4:21) and strength (Ep 6:10).

> They are sanctified freely by his grace through the redemption which is in Christ Jesus. God has publicly exhibited him as a means of expiation available to all through the shedding of his blood (Rm 3:24-25; cf. Gal 3:13). All this comes from the action of God, who has reconciled us to himself through Christ.... God

reconciled the world to himself in Christ (2 Cor 5:18-19; Ep 2:16). God proves his love for us, because, when we were still sinners, Christ died for us. Much more now that we are sanctified by his blood shall we be saved through him from God's avenging justice. Surely, if when we were enemies we were reconciled to God by the death of his Son, much more, once we are reconciled, shall we be saved by his life (Rm 5:8-10).

Not only does God give everything through Christ; He receives only what is united to Christ, what passes through Christ, and what comes from Christ. There is, then, only one moral problem for the Christian: participation or union with Christ, in whom he possesses all the treasures of salvation and by whom alone he rejoins God. "From him comes your union in Christ Jesus, who has become for us God-given wisdom and holiness and sanctification and redemption" (1 Cor 1:30; cf. 6:11). For the converts of St. Paul's day who, humanly speaking, were without reputation or power, who literally "did not exist," this was a prodigious enrichment (1 Cor 1:28). By means of Christ they passed from nonbeing to being. Supernaturally, they did not exist apart from Him!

St. Paul coined the expression "in Christ," which he uses more than one hundred and sixty times. What precisely does it mean? First of all, it must be emphasized that he is speaking not of the Christ according to the flesh (Rm 1:3-4; 1 Tm 3:16), but of the risen Christ, living now in heaven, of Him whom the primitive Church described as the *Christ Spirit*, the Lord possessing in its fullness the divine mode of being (2 Cor 3:17). The heavenly Christ is "spiritual" (1 Cor 15:45-49). Sharing the same nature and the same attributes of power and glory as the Father, Christ is able to endow His disciples with life and make them divine, "according to his spirit of sanctity." There, from the moment he believes, the Christian is defined as one united to the glorious Christ:

Moses writes that the man who realizes that holy living which is required by the Law shall find life by it. But the sanctification that comes of faith says, "Do not say in your heart: Who shall ascend into heaven?" (that is, to bring Christ down); or "Who shall descend into the

abyss?" (that is, to bring Christ up from the dead). But
what does Scripture say? "The message is near you, on
your lips and in your heart" (that is, the message of faith
which we preach). For if you confess with your lips that
Jesus is the Lord, and believe in your heart that God
raised him from the dead, you shall be saved. Because
with the heart a man believes and attains holiness, and
with the lips profession of faith is made and salvation
secured (Rm 10:5-10). Christ dwells through faith
in your hearts (Ep 3:17).

But how are we to understand this vital relationship? To call
it mystical explains nothing, for mystical means merely secret.
We gain little in precision by, as it were, localizing the Christian
"in Christ," implying that he lives in the atmosphere of Christ
and under His influence, for this is to treat the bond with Christ in
terms of space or place, when in reality it is a question of two
persons who are in each others' presence and who communicate
with each other. It is true that the relationship of love between
two persons makes it possible for lovers to be always united, in
that the one loved lives in the one who loves. But this union remains on the moral and even metaphorical level; whereas the
union of Christ and the Christian takes place on the level of
being. To explain this absolutely unique case, St. Paul had to coin
a new phrase.

In designating the Christian as a "being in Christ," thus
directly excluding the notion of fusion or absorption, St. Paul presents much more than a psychological relationship of knowledge
and love. He describes a union that is personal, a communion that
is reciprocal; or better, an organic and living relationship, a union
of life that is the result of our incorporation into Christ. He
declares explicitly that we have been grafted onto Christ and
implanted in Him (Rm 6:5), so that we constitute but one being
with Him. "All of you who have come to Christ by baptism have
clothed yourself with Christ. No longer is there Jew or Greek;
no longer is there slave or freeman; no longer is there male or female. You are all one in Christ Jesus" (Gal 3:27-28). Even though
the differences of race, sex, and social conditions subsist, each
Christian, in his religious being, is *incorporated* into the Lord,

becoming *one in Him* and *with Him;* just as, in the words of our Lord, the branch is a part of the vine (Jn 15:1).

"To be in Christ Jesus" expresses not so much a bond between the faithful and their Savior, which remains extrinsic to those it unites, as an existential notion, conveying the idea of a "Christian being." Just as every creature is completely dependent upon his Creator and has being only in this "relationship," so the Christian exists supernaturally only in his relationship to Christ. Somewhat like a limb that has life only when it is attached to a body and to the degree in which it receives a vital influx from the head and heart (1 Cor 6:15), a Christian has his being of grace through dependence on Christ. One who receives everything he is from another cannot be conceived of apart from this other. In the same way the Christian can be conceived of only in relation to Christ because without Christ he would not exist, that is, supernaturally: "If any man is in Christ, he is a new creation; the old state of things has gone; wonderful to tell, it has been made over, absolutely new!" (2 Cor 5:17).

And so, to be Christian means to be in Christ, for Christ, and by Christ. Tradition has understood this in the most realistic sense possible. The Syriac version translated Heb 3:4—"participants of Christ"—as "those mixed with Christ," and St. John Chrysostom comments even more frequently: "We form but one with him . . . . We are consubstantial with Christ." At the opposite pole from the pagan, who is a "being in the flesh," the Christian is essentially "a man in Christ" (2 Cor 12:12). Just as he is described as *deified* by the grace of the Father, or *spiritualized* by the action of the Holy Spirit, we ought to speak of him as *Christified*, to explain his being and his existence "in Christ." St. Athanasius spoke of the Christian as "wordified," that is, made the Word.

The pagans who were converted by hearing the message of the apostles believed both in the infinite love of God and in the resurrection and omnipotence of Christ: "He whom God raised to life did not see decay" (Acts 13:37; cf. Rm 10:9; 1 Th 1:9-10). The faith that saves is our belief in Christ (Rm 3:26; 1 Th 4:14), the glorious Savior (2 Th 2:14) and the Son of God (Ac 9:20, 13:33), from whom we receive life (1 Th 5:10; Ep 2:5). The convert's act of faith procured for him the pardon of his sins and the purification of his soul. But it was at his baptism, the regeneration and renewal of his very being (Tt 3:4-7), that he was incorporated into Christ and that he participated fully in His grace. In fact, baptism unites the Christian so completely to his Savior that not only does he live "in Christ" and in union with Him, but his life is henceforth that of Christ Himself living in him. Christ died and rose again, and the baptized person shares in this death and resurrection. He relives them for himself, and renews them so truly that it can be said that he dies and is buried with Christ, and then rises, lives again, and reigns with Christ.

> Do you not know that all of us who have been baptized into union with Christ Jesus have been baptized into union with his death? Yes, we were buried in death with him by means of baptism, in order that, just as Christ was raised from the dead by the glorious power of the Father, so we also may conduct ourselves by a new principle of life (Rm 6:3-4).

The consequence is evident. The Christian life—a symbiosis with the Lord, to borrow a term from biology (Rm 6:8; Col 2:13) —will be nothing other than the living and the putting into effect of this baptismal grace, a continuous, progressive death to sin and a life of renewal and victory:

> We carry about with us in our bodies at all times Jesus' condemnation to death, so that in these same bodies of ours the living power of Jesus may become evident (2 Cor 4:10-11). Buried with him by baptism, you also rose with him by your faith in the power of God who raised him from the dead (Col 2:12).

This double rhythm of the crucifixion and resurrection of the Savior, impressed like stigmata on the very being of the Christian (Gal 6:17), marks his whole existence. What he has acquired once and for all ontologically, he must develop and perfect psychologically and morally:

> Since we have grown to be one with him through a death like his, we shall also be one with him by a resur-

rection like his. We know that our old self had been crucified with him, in order that the body enslaved to sin may be reduced to impotence, and we may no longer be slaves to sin; for he who is dead is once and for all quit of sin. But if we have died with Christ, we believe that we shall also live with him, since we know that Christ, having risen from the dead, will die no more; death shall no longer have dominion over him. The death that he died was a death to sin once for all, but the life that he lives is a life for God. Thus you too must consider yourselves dead to sin, but alive to God in Jesus Christ. Do not then let sin reign in your mortal body so as to obey its lusts. And do not go on offering your members to sin as instruments of iniquity, but once for all dedicate yourselves to God as men that have come to life from the dead, and your members as instruments of holiness for God; for sin shall not have dominion over you, since you are not subjects of the Law but of grace (Rm 6:5-14).

Such is the end to strive for. The baptized Christian is no longer subject to the demands of the flesh, itself a slave of the reign of sin, but rather to Christ: "Those who belong to Christ have crucified their flesh with its passionate cravings" (Gal 5:24). A transfer of property and authority has taken place: "All of you who have come to Christ by baptism have clothed yourself with Christ.... You are Christ's (Gal 3:27, 29; Rm 13:14). So true is this transfer that the converts of St. Paul's day found themselves in a state of irreconcilable opposition toward the world; they were about to live in conditions completely different from those that preceded their conversion. Won by Christ and paid for by Christ—the contract of sale in Greek antiquity was sealed by the payment of the price—they would henceforth live for Christ: *"Our Lord Jesus Christ died for us in order that we might find life in union with him"* (1 Th 5:10).

Love for Christ impels us. We have come to the conclusion that since one died for all, therefore all died, and that Christ died for all, in order that they who are alive may live no longer for themselves, but for him who died for them and rose again (2 Cor 5:14-15). None of us lives for himself, and none dies for himself. If we live, we live for the Lord, and if we die, we die for the Lord.

Whether we live or whether we die, we are the Lord's.
To this end Christ died and lived, that he might be Lord
both of the dead and of the living (Rom 14:7-9).

St. Paul's insistence in reminding Christians that they no longer
belong to themselves but are become the property of Christ, is
based first of all on their profession of faith at baptism, when they
proclaimed: "Jesus is the one Lord" (1 Cor 8:6); secondly, it is
based in this sentence of our Lord: "A man cannot be the slave of
two masters. He will either hate the one and love the other, or, at
least, be attentive to the one and neglectful of the other" (Mt
6:24); and finally, on the contemporary custom of emancipating
slaves under the form of a sale to divinity. Slaves could free themselves by paying their owners a sum of money that they had
laboriously earned. Many masters, however, after having received
the "ransom," kept their slaves in servitude. From this abuse
arose the practice of paying money to the treasury of the god
Apollo, who would then "ransom" the slave from his master and
guarantee him protection against every evil. For example, a
"receipt" is extant that reads: "Cleon, son of Cleoxenos, sold to
Pythian Apollo a male body (the customary designation of a
slave), bearing the name Istiacos, a Syrian, for the price of four
minas, on the condition that Istiacos be free and that no one be
permitted to touch him for the rest of his life." The purpose of
this bill of sale was to transfer the right of ownership. As soon
as the stipulated sum was paid, the slave ceased to belong to his
former owner; redeemed by the god he became free and was
henceforth his own master. It is explicitly stated that at no time
could he be seized by anyone, that he could do what he wished
and live where he wished for the rest of his life.

For St. Paul, Christ had poured forth His blood in ransom to
liberate the slaves of sin. His disciples are 'bought at a price" (1
Cor 6:20), and therefore are free. So true is this that we can substitute for the word "redemption," which is no longer meaningful, the word "liberation," so significant to contemporary ears.
There is this difference, however, between the man ransomed by
Apollo and the man ransomed by Christ. The former could
henceforth "do what he wanted," according to the terms of the

contract; the latter belongs body and soul to his Savior. Freed from sin, he becomes the slave of Christ, whom he recognizes as his new Master. Because of his desire to live in sanctity, he submits voluntarily and joyfully to this yoke which is sweet and light: "He who was called in the Lord, while he was a slave, has become a freedman of the Lord, just as he who was called while he was a freedman has become a slave of Christ. You have been bought with a price! Do not enslave yourselves to men" (1 Cor 7:22-23).

Expressive though they are, juridical metaphors are insufficient when it comes to plumbing the depth of the "mystery of Christ," of explaining how the Christian, who is now the property of his "Redeemer," has no existence and no life apart from Him. Therefore, St. Paul coins neologisms and uses them over and over to convey the truth no matter what his state of life or what his work, the Christian is not only united to Christ, but lives his life in and with Christ, *cum Christo.* Just as he suffers and dies with Christ, he lives with Christ, grows with Christ, is conformed to Christ; a co-heir with Christ, he is glorified and enthroned with Christ and reigns with him. His very being is defined in terms of a Person, and so, too, is his life: "Your life is hidden with Christ in God" (Col 3:3).

What most clearly characterizes this "new man" (Ep 2:15, 4:24) or "new creature" (2 Cor 5:17; Gal 6:15) is the loss of his autonomy. Since he is formed by insertion into Christ and by belonging to the Lord (Gal 3:29), the Christian could not possibly be the source of his own life or the guide of his own actions. Apart from the fact that he is in Christ and lives with Christ, it is Christ who, living in him, makes him live: "With Christ I am nailed to the cross. *It is now no longer I that live but Christ lives in me.* The life that I now live in this body, I live by [the union of] faith in the Son of God who loved me and sacrificed himself for me" (Gal 2:19-20).

Here we reach the heart of Pauline ethics: the moral life is a prolongation, an extension, an unfolding of the life of Christ in His disciples. The "rule of life" of the Christian is to *conform* his thought and his conduct to Christ, who is the perfect model, and thus to become ever more perfectly incorporated into Him. This is the express will of God, the reason for the creation of the world and the predestination of the faithful. Indeed, just as God established His Son as center of the plan of salvation and head of the universe, "gathering all creation both in heaven and on earth under one head, Christ" (Ep 1:10, 20-23, 2:14-22, 4:15), so He sees and loves the elect only in Christ. "Those whom he has foreknown he has also predestined to be conformed to the image of his Son, so that this Son should be the first-born among many brothers."

Every Christian is *called* to be a sharer in the glory of the Son of God, and, in so doing, to contribute to this glory. The risen Lord is to be surrounded in heaven by the multitude of men whom He has saved. More precisely, Christians resemble the glorious Christ as the younger members of a family resemble their elder brother (Heb 2:10-12). Christians are authentic children of God even here on earth, possessing by grace the same divine nature as their Father in heaven (Ep 1:5; Gal 4:5). If Christ is the Son of God by nature, the faithful are sons by adoption and by an adoption as real as any generation (Rm 8:15-17). Now each son resembles his Father. Jesus is the exact reproduction, "the radiant reflection of God's glory and the express image of his nature" (Heb 1:3); and the adopted sons must try to be "imitators of God, as his very dear children" (Ep 5:1). But because God is invisible and because it would be impossible to reproduce a model that one has never contemplated, it is the image of the Father in Christ that Christians must make their own. St. Paul presents himself as an example to his disciples in this way: "Become imitators of me as I am of Christ" (1 Cor 4:16; cf. 11:1, 1 Th 1:6).

The orientation of life of the sons of God is clear beyond all doubt. Since they have become the property of Christ by the baptismal rite, their consecration must be so total that they will live and die only for their Lord. United to Christ as a member is to its body, they must try to assimilate this new life, which is the life of Christ Himself. The moral life is nothing other than the pursuit of an ever more profound assimilation, and ever more total *conformity*. *Mimesis*, the Greek word used in the above text, signifies "reproduction" and "representation." Consequently, as one becomes more fully the possession of the Lord, the transformation into His image becomes a more perfect resemblance to Him, more exact and manifest. The true Christian life, which comes from the glorious, immanent Christ—*Christus in vobis* (2 Cor 13:5; Ep 3:17; Col 1:27)—is a gradual metamorphosis, by means of which the copy becomes each day an ever more exact likeness of the model: "All of us, reflecting as in a mirror the Lord's glory, are being transformed into his very image from one degree of splendor to another, such as comes from the Lord who is the spirit" (2 Cor 3:18).

We are true Christians in the measure that the traits of the Lord can be discerned in us: *Christianus alter Christus!* It goes without saying that the similarity can never be total. But since our predestination, our very reason for being, is to be an "image" of the well-beloved Son, then we must pursue throughout our lives this quest for a more complete resemblance "until we all attain to unity in faith and deep knowledge of the Son of God. Thus we attain to perfect manhood, to the mature proportions that befit Christ's fullness" (Ep 4:13).The glorious resurrection of the body will bring the ultimate completion of this "configuration": "Just as we have borne the likeness of the man of dust [Adam], so shall we bear the likeness of the Heavenly One [Jesus]" (1 Cor 15:49).

This law of the imitation of Christ is so truly the unique moral rule of Christianity that it applies to all ages, all conditions, and all stages of life:

> Strip off the old self with its deeds and put on the new, which is being progressively remodeled after the image of its Creator and brought to deep knowledge. Here there is no Gentile, no Jew, no circumcised, no uncircumcised, no barbarian, no Scythian, no slave, no free man, but Christ is everything in each of us (Col 3:9-11; cf. Gal 3:28).

Men or women, rich or poor, great or small, the faithful are members of the divine family and they conduct themselves according to the principles of their heavenly Father, as they see them realized in Christ.

It is not that Christians must reproduce the deeds and accomplishments of the Savior materially, and thus superficially, but they must adopt His manner of thinking and judging (1 Cor 2:16), be inspired with His sentiments, copy His virtues, imitate His charity, and have the same filial piety toward the Father. The golden rule is: *To have in oneself the same sentiments which were in Christ Jesus* (Rm 15:5; Ph 2:5). It is not a question of practicing some particular virtue, of reforming oneself, of controlling one's acts by reason, or of conducting oneself as a man of principle, but of acting as Christ would act, of forming judgments *analogous* to His, of loving with the same generosity and the same delicacy as He would love, of being patient and humble as He would be, since, once again, it is Christ in person who lives in the Christian and gives him his life. Efficient causality produces in him whom it moves a formal or "conformed" resemblance.

Consequently, whatever the particular act in question may be, it must be adjusted to the thought and the charity of Christ. For example, when St. Paul has to recall the Romans or the Philippians to humility, he reminds them that "Christ did not please himself" (Rm 15:3), that they should

> be of the same mind as Christ Jesus, who, though he is by nature God, did not consider his equality with God a condition to be clung to, but emptied himself by taking the nature of a slave, fashioned as he was to the likeness of men. . . . He humbled himself and became obedient to death; yes, to the death on the cross (Ph 2:5-8).

When he seeks to encourage the Corinthians to give generous help to the poor of Jerusalem, he writes: "You know the graciousness of our Lord Jesus Christ. Although he was rich, he became poor for your sakes that by his poverty you might become rich" (2 Cor 8:9); thus must you act toward one another. When he finds the Ephesians lacking in charity he admonishes them to consider the example of the Lord:

> Let all bitter resentment, and passion, and anger, and

loud abusive speech, in a word, every kind of malice, be banished from your minds. On the contrary, be kind to one another, and merciful, generously forgiving one another, as also God in Christ has generously forgiven you. Therefore, follow God's example, as his very dear children, and let your conduct be guided by love, as Christ also loved us and delivered himself for us (Ep 4:31-5:2).

The same exhortation is given to the Colossians:

Therefore, as God's chosen ones, holy and well beloved, clothe yourselves with the sentiments of compassion, kindness, humility, meekness, long-suffering. Bear with one another and forgive whatever grievances you have against each other. Just as the Lord has forgiven you, so you must forgive (Col 3:12-13).

The delicacy and devotedness of fraternal charity are inspired by the example of Christ: "Welcome one another cordially, even as Christ has welcomed you to himself for the glory of God" (Rm 15:7). Any division among Christians is the same as dismembering Christ, for Christ, living in each one of them, has made of them one body (1 Cor 1:12-13, 12:12). "You are all one in Christ Jesus" (Gal 3:28). Out of foolish vanity the Corinthians have scandalized a brother who is weak and have thus made him subject to destruction; how can they forget that Christ died for this brother (1 Cor 8:11-13; cf. Rm 14:15)? It is inconceivable that a lie should come from the lips of a disciple of Christ who was veracity itself: "The Son of God ... did not prove to be Yes and No .. in him was realized the Yes" (2 Cor 1:17-20).

The reason we must keep ourselves pure is that our bodies are the members of Christ; to sin against one's body is to impair the consecration that unites it to the Lord (1 Cor 6:15-18). Even spouses are united in the Lord (1 Cor 7:39; 11:11); marriage can be lived in a Christian way only if the husband and wife love each other after the manner of Christ who on the cross united Himself to sinful humanity in order to engender it to grace:

Let wives be subject to their husbands who are representatives of the Lord, because the husband is head of the wife just as Christ is the head of the Church and also the savior of that body. Thus, just as the Church is subject to Christ, so also let wives be subject to their husbands in all things.

Husbands, love your wives, just as Christ loved the Church, and delivered himself for her, that he might sanctify her by cleansing her in the bath of water with the accompanying word, in order to present to himself the Church in all her glory, devoid of blemish or wrinkle or anything of the kind, but that she may be holy and flawless. Even so ought husbands to love their wives as their own bodies. He who loves his wife, loves himself. Now no one ever hates his own flesh; on the contrary, he nourishes and cherishes it, as Christ does the Church, because we are members of his Body. "For this cause a man shall leave his father and mother, and cling to his wife; and the two shall become one flesh." This is a great mystery—I mean in regard to Christ and the Church (Ep 5:22-32).

It is precisely in this reproduction of the union of Christ and the Church that marriage has its "significance," its *sacramental* value. Conjugal union symbolizes and "imitates" the Savior's total gift of self to his beloved spouse. The love of marriage is a love of union and fecundity; it is "Christianized" by the *imitation* of the charity by which Christ is united to men and regenerates them.

There is no act, no matter how slight, which the Christian is not able to accomplish in the spirit of Jesus Christ. He will speak and he will say the truth in Christ (Rm 9:1; Ep 4:21), just as St. Paul exhorted and commanded in the Lord (1 Th 4:1; 2 Th 3:6, 12), just as he had confidence or was proud in him (1 Cor 1:31; Gal 5:10). The Christian, rooted and established in the Lord, will conduct himself in conformity with what he has learned from him (Col 2:6). To hold fast and to persevere is possible only in him (1 Th 3:8; Ph 4:1). Therefore, the Christian will receive his brothers (Rm 16:2) and will greet them in the Lord (1 Cor 16:19; Rm 16:22). Children will obey, just as a wife will be subject, in the Lord (Ep 6:1; Col 3:18).

Likewise, if we struggle and toil, our struggle and toil will have value only in the Lord (Rm 16:12) and in the fact that we experience the sufferings of Christ Himself (2 Cor 1:5). Prisoners in the Lord (Ep 4:1; Philem. 23) and weak in Christ (2 Cor 13: 4), we are united to Him in a communion of sacrifice, and thus we participate in his death (Ph 3:10; Col 1:24); we endure all things with his patience (2 Th 3:5). In the same way, we are filled with joy (Ph 3:1, 4:10), with courage (Rm 15:17; 1 Cor 15:31; Ph 3:3), and with strength in Christ (Ep 6:10); we possess and reproduce his kindness and gentleness (2 Cor 10:1), His truth (2 Cor 11:10), His exceedingly tender mercy (Ph 1:8), and His peace: "Let the ruling principle of your hearts be the peace of Christ" (Col 3:15; Ph 4:7). The phrase "in the Lord" or "in Christ" could often be translated "in a Christian manner," which expresses the mode of thinking, of loving, and of acting, proper to "those who are of Christ."

St. Paul calls this imitation of Christ the accomplishment of the Law of Christ (Gal 6:2), or again his "teachings and methods," rules of life which he taught everywhere, to every congregation (1 Cor 4:17), and by means of which they now walk according to the Lord (Rom. 15:5; 2 Cor 11:17; Col 2:8). This ethic is simply the consequence of the union of being and life with Christ. As one is, so he lives, thinks, and loves. Little by little, the life of Christ appears in our bodies (2 Cor 5:10), since Christians in effacing themselves, only manifest more clearly what they are interiorly: other Christs. The resemblance is so exact that in St. Paul's hymn to charity (1 Cor 13:4-8), where he presents his ideal of life for each Christian, we can, by replacing the word *charity* with the word *Christ*, have a portrait of the Savior: "Christ is long-suffering; Christ is kind; he is not self-seeking; he takes no note of injury; always he is ready to make allowances, always to be patient. . . ."

Each baptized person is called to say again, with the assurance of St. Paul: "For me to live means Christ" (Ph 1:21). To make this notion of life precise, one would expect a verb here or some term expressing an action or a state, but St. Paul names a Person, who represents to him his all: the Lord! This mode of expression is truly a creation inspired by love, but also by genius, since St.

Paul transfers to the new religion the great principle of ethics in antiquity: *Become what you are!* St. Thomas Aquinas later expressed this in the words: *Viventibus, vivere est esse.*

The Spirit says:

> Awake, sleeper,
> And arise from the dead,
> And Christ will give you light (Ep 5:14).

"I solemnly assure you, unless the grain of wheat falls to the earth and dies, it remains just a grain of wheat. But if it dies, it bears much fruit. The man who loves his life destroys it; while the man who hates his life in this world, preserves it to live eternally" (Jn 12:24-25).

THE SPIRIT OF *KENOSIS*:
A PRINCIPLE OF PAULINE SPIRITUALITY

Mitchel B. Finley

Thus the Fourth Gospel teaches that through self-forgetfulness and complete concern for the faith-realities of the gospel, through genuine love of God and neighbor, the Christian "hates" his life, thus preserving it "to live eternally."

St. Paul, too, manifests an explicit awareness of the need for death to self as vital for life in Christ. It is this awareness as it manifests itself in Paul's letter to the Philippians that we are concerned with here. Paul expresses the faith-principle which supports the idea of the grain of wheat attaining fulfillment through death in his use of the word *kenōsis*. As we shall presently see, the ideal of this attitude is exemplified in the self-emptying undergone by Jesus out of obedience to the Father. Becoming man, Christ emptied himself of the divine glory he rightfully possessed *en archē*, before anything in creation ever came to be. *Kenōsis*, means "emptying," and for Paul this word describes that sharing in the Cross of Christ, that death or detachment from self which is required for the life of the Kingdom. By emptying oneself of ego-centered concerns, by desiring to serve rather than be served, by accepting the death of the Cross (out of love for God and neighbor), the Christian faithfully gives himself to *kenōsis*, that emptying of self characteristic of the One who came into the world to proclaim the universal reign of his Father.

Overview

Paul's letter to the Christians of Philippi seems to be a brief though concentrated manifestation of the Apostle's understanding of *kenōsis* and of its central place in Christian faith, life, and spirituality (all of which are aspects of the same reality). The letter opens in Paul's characteristic manner: a greeting of "Grace and peace. . . from God our Father and from the Lord Jesus Christ!" Paul's affection for the Philippian Christians is evident from the outset. Immediately, however, we see reflected what will become the central theme of the whole letter, Paul's admiration for Christian unity, service to others, forgetfulness of self—manifestations of *kenōsis*. The high point of this letter is Paul's well-known hymn, wherein the kenotic attitude of Christ is held up for emulation: ". . . he emptied himself (*eauton ekenōsen*) and took the form of a slave, being born in the likeness of men" (2:7).

Paul's enthusiasm for this essential spirit of Christian faith continues to inspire his words; then once again the strength of the Pauline spirit shines forth in the equally well-known lines which begin: "I have come to rate all as loss in the light of the surpassing knowledge of my Lord Jesus Christ" (3:8). Spontaneously expressing his own faith and dedication to Christ, Paul thus buoys up his readers with a genuinely inspiring exhortation to the spirit of *kenōsis*. Then, finally concluding his message, Paul maintains his theme of admiration for Christian *kenōsis* by expressions of gratitude for having been the recipient of precisely this kind of unselfish concern.

It is our intention to search out in more detail the Pauline understanding of *kenōsis* which appears throughout this letter to the church at Philippi.

Examination

Following Paul's initial greeting, expressed for both him and his companion Timothy, he assures the Philippians of his confidence that "he who has begun the good work in you will carry it through to completion, right up to the day of Christ Jesus" (1: 6). Clearly implicit in this statement is Paul's awareness that it is only through abandonment of self to the Father that any "good work" of value to the Kingdom will be accomplished. He then goes on to observe that precisely because of his present imprisonment (Paul was probably writing from Ephesus), the Gospel is being proclaimed more widely. Though being done from both good and less than admirable motives, all that matters to Paul is that the Gospel be proclaimed. Thus we see that he seeks no honor for himself; he is empty of any desire for personal aggrandizement.

Reflecting yet more clearly his own kenotic spirit, Paul proclaims that "Christ will be exalted through me whether I live or die" (1:20). For him, "life means Christ; hence dying is so much gain" (1:21). However, Paul is not saying here that what he would *really* like to do is die, get rid of the bothersome body, escape this vale of tears, and finally gain eternal life. Rather, a deeper underlying attitude is to be observed. To be "freed from this life" (1:23) means final union with Christ (via the emptying and abandonment of self in faith required by natural death); yet to "remain alive for your sakes"(1:24) requires that self-emptying demanded for service to others. In other words, an attitude of *kenōsis* is called for in both cases. Both death and laboring in the service of the gospel are opportunities wherein Paul's more radical desire—to act in union with Christ—may manifest itself to the glory of God the Father.

After a brief exhortation to communal unanimity as the "way worthy of the Gospel" (1:27), Paul states flatly that it is the special privilege of the Philippian Christians to suffer (*paschein*) for Christ. This is a quite concrete description of faith which runs far more deeply than either natural death or this life as an ultimate value. Indeed, it calls for genuinely kenotic self-emptying, for only thus can such deep faith be received as one's own.

Building up to his great hymn on the *kenōsis* of Christ, Paul lauds a unity of many persons in the Lord, a unity which can be attained only as each individual, through his own *kenōsis,* prefers others to himself: "... let all parties think humbly of others as superior to themselves, each of you looking to others' interests rather than his own" (2:3-4).

The Great Hymn

The moving and majestic hymn to the love of God which follows marks what is certainly the apex of St. Paul's reflections on how vitally important the spirit of *kenōsis* is to Christian life. Our subject requires that we quote it in its entirety: "Your attitude," writes Paul, "must be that of Christ."

> Though he was in the form of God he did not deem equality with God something to be grasped at. Rather, he emptied (*ekenōsen*) himself and took the form of a slave, being born in the likeness of men. He was known to be of human estate, and it was thus that he humbled himself, obediently accepting even death, death on a cross! Because of this, God highly exalted him and bestowed on him the name above every other name, so that at Jesus' name every knee must bend in the heavens, and on the earth, and under the earth, and every tongue proclaim to the glory of God the Father: JESUS CHRIST IS LORD (2:5-11)!

Though he possessed equality with God (*morphē theou*), it was precisely through losing himself, as it were, giving up his divine rights and status, that Jesus fulfilled the mission given him by his Father. At this the mindboggling incredibility of the mystery of the Incarnation hits us with full force.

Being "of human estate" (*Jerusalem Bible:* "being as all men are"), he humbled himself; the Infinite entered the realm of the finite. Then, as if to compound the enigmatic nature of the situation yet further, Paul reminds the Philippians that Jesus, infinite Son of the eternal Father, even went so far as to drink the cup of human existence to the last drop: he submitted to human death, the death of an obscure criminal at that! This, for St. Paul, is the ultimate witness of love—a *kenōsis* so complete and so unselfish that it can never be surpassed. And yet, as stated earlier,

Paul teaches that this same attitude is to be that of the Christian: no equivocation, no qualification—the statement stands to challenge and call to account every Christian way of life. The call to conversion, to *metanoia*, by a self-emptying life in Christ, is a call which is never fully responded to this side of natural death.

However, "because of this" emptying of himself and of his taking "the form of a slave," continues Paul, Jesus of Nazareth was raised up by his Father and given "the name above every other name," that is, Jesus is given the divine name, "Lord," and all creation worships this Jesus as Lord of the universe.

Application

What, then, does this mean for the Christ-like *kenōsis* which Paul insists must be that of sincere faith? It means that it is through a *no* to selfishness, through concrete identification of oneself with the Passion of Christ, through a hope which is not for this life only, that union with Christ is to be attained. This is indeed the message of the Cross which is absurdity to any mind except that of Jesus Christ (cf. 1 Cor 1:18-25).

As if to emphasize the vital importance of personal effort, Paul moves on once again by admonishing his readers to "work out your own salvation with fear and trembling" (2:12). Efforts to attain Christian unity, to live at peace, and to grow in faith will require much giving way to others in matters which are merely relative to the penultimate goal of communal and personal peace and concord. And yet, paradoxically, "It is God who, in his good will toward you, begets in you any measure of desire or achievement" (2:13). In other words, regardless of how much good the Philippians may do or how admirable their life in Christ may be, the proper attitude is one of humble gratitude to the Father. True emptying of self requires the renunciation of smug pride or complacent self-satisfaction. As Paul remarks elsewhere: "Name something you have that you have not received" (1 Cor 4:7).

Waxing somewhat poetic, Paul encourages his readers in this kenotic attitude, reminding them that thus they will prove themselves "children of God beyond reproach"; indeed, they will "shine like the stars in the sky (*en kosmō*)" (2:15).

Once again we are able to witness something of Paul's own excellent forgetfulness of self for the sake of Christ as he comments that he rejoices if his life is to be a self-emptying "sacrificial service of your faith" (2:17). Then, becoming somewhat scornful, he says that "Everyone is busy seeking his own interests rather than those of Christ Jesus" (2:21)—manifestations of that attitude directly contradictory to the spirit of *kenōsis*. Paul's Philippian comrade, Epaphroditus, however, because "he came near to death for the sake of Christ's work," well exemplifies Christian unselfishness.

Entering now upon the second high point of his letter, Paul writes that he sincerely desires to share in "the resurrection from the dead"; so important is this that he has "forfeited everything... accounted all else rubbish so that Christ may be my wealth" (3:8f). The interior attitude of *kenōsis*, then, extends to the whole Christian life. Christian freedom is freedom from mere law as a final word in itself, from material wealth, from power and prestige: all is "rubbish" for one who seeks only union with Christ. Paul is quick to remind his readers, however, that he is by no means claiming to have "made it"; he keeps his eye on the goal, keeps on running the race. What is important is that "we continue on our course, no matter what stage we have reached" (3:16).

Regretfully, Paul acknowledges that "many go about in a way which shows them to be enemies of the cross of Christ" (3:18). He is referring to people whose "god is their bodily desires." "I am talking," Paul explains, somewhat dryly no doubt, "about those who are set upon the things of this world" (3:19). We might say therefore, that Paul's complaint is based on his conviction that true Christians must live a faith which attains its freedom and strength from the belief that, on the deepest level of reality, "we have our citizenship in heaven" (3:20) rather than in "this world." (As Karl Rahner states it, "... man's existential center no longer lies in the realm of the tangible and the empirical.")

In other words, Christian life simply transcends what Paul refers to as "the things of this world." It is in fact, he says, "from there (i.e., heaven) that we eagerly await the coming of our Savior, the Lord Jesus Christ" (3:20). The *kenōsis* required for such faith as this is once again clear: only abandonment of self, sharing willingly in the death of Christ (really and spiritually at baptism, in an immediate way in one's own death), and a fundamental hope which rests on the resurrection alone can qualify one's faith as fully Christian.

After further admonitions to live unselfishly and to rejoice always in the Lord, as well as encouragement to abandonment in prayer, Paul tells the Philippians that when they actually live Christian faith, then "the God of peace" will be with them (4:9).

Again referring to his own good example, Paul writes that he does not depend on exterior conditions for his peace in Christ, for "In him who is the source of my strength I have strength for everything" (4:11). He then commends the unselfish kindness of the Philippian church in coming to his aid by sharing his hardships. Such manifestations of the kenotic spirit are "a fragrant offering, a sacrifice acceptable and pleasing to God" (4:18).

Finally, Paul concludes his letter with assurances of God's blessings, greetings from himself and his fellow-workers, and a typical Pauline ending: "May the favor of the Lord Jesus Christ be with your spirit. Amen" (4:23).

Conclusions

What, therefore, may we conclude from our examination of the letter to the Philippians? It would seem that woven throughout this letter there are two specific modes or forms of Christian activity which Paul understands as necessary manifestations of the spirit of *kenōsis*. Although both depend upon and express kenotic faith in Christ as Lord, each has specific characteristics of its own, and each depends upon and supports the other.

The first manifestation of this kind of faith seems to show itself in references which Paul makes to interior attitudes of the heart, e.g., his indifference concerning death (1:20-22), and his sharp awareness of the limitation which characterizes created realities when compared with the life of the Kingdom (3:8-11). This framework of faith is also apparent in Paul's teaching on the primacy of the Cross, particularly when he notes that "enemies of the cross" are precisely those whose "god is their bodily desires" (2:18-19). For such people do not concretize in their own lives the belief that Christians (ultimately) have their "citizenship in heaven" (3:20).

This first expression of kenotic faith, therefore, is one which might manifest itself in Christian spirituality through positive asceticism, i.e., concrete identification of oneself with the Passion of Christ in order to grow in a more Easter-oriented kind of faith, a faith which takes courage from what Paul says in another of his letters: "Food is for the stomach and the stomach for food, and God will do away with them both in the end" (1 Cor 6:13). Such asceticism (which may never despise the goodness of creation) is a positive and personal acceptance of death in Christ in order also to rise with him and to share even now in the power of the resurrection. In Paul's own words, "The message of the cross. . . is the power of God" (1 Cor 1:18).

The second manifestation of the spirit of *kenōsis* is perhaps more readily understandable, for it is much more outwardly oriented than the first and is characterized more obviously as what we today might call "social service." In this letter Paul clearly praises unselfish service to others. His mention of those who "have struggled at my side in promoting the gospel. . . whose names are in the book of life" (4:3) is a good example of this. In addition, Paul's gratitude to those who "sent something for my needs" well expresses his admiration for this more directly observable concern for the welfare of others.

These two expressions of the basic spirit of *kenōsis* appear side by side in the hymn of 2:5-11. First: ". . . he emptied himself" of personal divine glory out of obedience to the Father. Second: ". . . and took the form of a slave" (or "servant" [*doulos*], as it may also be translated).

It seems, therefore, that the proper identification of oneself with the self-emptying of Christ must include these two kenotic movements. Traditionally, this has meant the practice of personal asceticism as well as dedicated service to others.

PAUL ON THE DISCERNMENT OF SPIRITS

Jacques Guillet, S.J.

Although Paul enumerated among his charisms the gift of
"discernment of spirits" (*diakrisis pneumatōn*), he, nonetheless,
never elaborated a systematic doctrine of discernment. Still the
place that the discernment of the Spirit and his action holds in
Pauline thought is worthy of study. To recognize its importance,
a grouping of texts in which the apostle speaks of discernment or
shows the criteria on which it is based is not sufficient. It is necessary to look at the apostle actually practicing this discernment,
and this might be in most diverse circumstances: while justifying
his mission, settling a difficulty, or judging the actions of a community.

All his actions consisted in practicing discernment. Whether
he is making known to the Christians of Thessalonica God's work
in them; or is appraising the merits and weaknesses of the people of
Corinth; or is revealing to the Romans the spiritual power which
animates Judaism, Paganism, and Christianity, and which dominates the religious history of the world; or is teaching the authentic ways of the Spirit to the Christians of Asia, led astray by
Gnosticism—he is always projecting the light of God on the situation of the churches and on hearts. He is practicing the discernment of spirits.

Without claiming anything other than an empirical approach,
it will be helpful to study this very complex subject under three
headings: a) discernment in the Christian life; b) the discernment
of spirits; c) the criteria for a discernment of spirits.

a) *Discernment in the Christian life.* At the base of man's
religious life, Paul sees a discernment that is able, by means of the
visible world, to recognize the true God. The sin of idolaters is

an error in discernment: "Since they did not see fit (*dokimadzein*) to acknowledge God, God gave them up to a base mind (*adokimos*) and to improper conduct" (Rm 1:28). The theoretical advantage of the Jew over the pagan is the possession, thanks to the Law, of a criterion for discernment by which he can know God's will "and approve (*dokimadzein*) what is excellent" (Rm 2:18). This superiority makes his responsibility more weighty, but it is also a sign of divine predilection. In these two texts we find a fundamental constant of discernment according to St. Paul, the discerning of God or his Spirit, which, in turn, will always be the discerning of his will, his ways in relation to man and his Church.

Christian life, too, is a continuing discernment, an attention always on the alert, maintained by the twofold concern of keeping out of sin and continually seeking the better course.

"Do not be conformed to this world but be transformed by the renewal of your mind, that you may be convinced of (*dokimadzein*) what is the will of God, of what is good and acceptable and perfect" (Rm 12:2). This is a frequent theme. "For once you were in darkness, but now you are in light in the Lord; walk as children of light (for the fruit of light is found in all that is good and right and true), and try to be interiorly convinced of (*dokimadzein*) what is pleasing to the Lord. Take no part in the unfruitful works of darkness, but instead expose them (Ep 5:7-11); "therefore do not be foolish, but understand what the will of the Lord is" (Ep 5:17); "that your love may abound more and more, with knowledge and all discernment so that you may be interiorly convinced of (*dokimadzein*) what is excellent" (Ph 1:9-11).

There is here something more than total adherence to a marked general movement toward what is good. There is sensitivity always on the alert and, at the same time, a spiritual maturity that makes the Christian capable of assuming his responsibilities with clearheaded resoluteness:

"So that we may no longer be children tossed to and fro and carried about with every wind of doctrine, by the cunning of men, by their craftiness in deceitful wiles; rather, speaking the truth in love, we are to grow in every way into him who is the head, into Christ" (Ep 4:14-15). The same doctrine is in the Epistle to the Hebrews: "For everyone who lives on milk is un-skilled in the word of righteousness, for he is a child. But solid food is for the mature, for those who have their faculties trained by practice to distinguish (*diakrisis*) good from evil" (Heb 5:13-14).

This perfection of the adult Christian, if it presupposes the persevering use of all personal resources, and if it produces a type of perfect man, is a perfection, not of the world, but of the Spirit, for it has plumbed divine depths: "What person knows a man's thoughts except the spirit of the man which is in him? So also, no one comprehends the thoughts of God except the Spirit of God. Now we have not received the spirit of the world, but the Spirit which is from God, that we might understand the gifts bestowed on us by God. And we impart this in words not taught by human wisdom but by the Spirit, interpreting spiritual truths to those who possess the Spirit" (1 Cor 2:11-13).

b) *The discernment of spirits.* All Christians are not capable of this discernment, only those whom Paul calls "perfect" or "spiritual." As the context indicates, they do not constitute a privileged group that has attained perfection. Quite the contrary; they are those who, having had genuine spiritual experience, are able to discern at every moment of life an invitation to perfection. This sensitivity is not simply an ordinary grace, but rather the result of a charism.

This charism does not, of necessity, imply visible signs. In I Cor 12:10, in a series of phenomena characterized by striking supernatural power, it is spoken of as discernment of spirits. Paul speaks in the same manner of the manifestations of the varied services, emphasizing in this way their spiritual function and their real efficacy. In a list found in Rm 12:5, where he names charisms such as service, teaching, exhortation, the giving of one's goods, almsgiving, mercy-gifts marked by the most simple and efficacious actions, we note that he includes prophecy, a gift closely related to that of discernment. If in charisms there is always the element of a powerful and discernible intervention of God, the importance of the charism is not gauged by its extraordinary aspects, but by its constructive and enriching elements. The gift of discernment, in itself, compels respect because of the insights, certitude and light it gives, without involving any extraordinary states.

Discernment is associated with the charism of prophecy and seems to constitute with it a separate group as is the case with cures and miracles, on the one hand; the gift of tongues and the interpretation of them on the other hand. The objective of prophecy and discernment is to reveal the secrets of the heart; and for Paul, this explains their value. Reacting against the excessive concern of the Corinthians for the gift of tongues, he expresses opposition because the community derives little value from tongues, since this phenomenon cannot be communicated; and he favors the fruitfulness of prophecy: "But if all prophesy, and an unbeliever enters, he is convicted by all, he is called to account by all, the secrets of his heart are disclosed; and so, falling on his face, he will worship God and declare that God is really among you" (1 Cor 14:24-25).

Although in this text the discernment of spirits is not mentioned, it is clear that prophecy ends in discernment; moreover, such a sequence should be in conformity with the whole prophetic tradition of Israel. If a prophet is capable of foretelling the future, it is not in virtue of some sort of second sight. He figures out a divine plan in the world, discerns the secrets of hearts and there discovers the work of sin and the activity of the spirit.

c) *The criteria for a discernment of spirits*. St. Paul never gave a comprehensive statement on the criteria of discernment. To know what he thought, we must examine his own exercise of discernment. Moreover, his experience is always instructive because the apostle joins to unerring intuition a constructive and pedagogical concern that leads him to justify the judgment given by throwing light on the principles involved:

I - Good and evil spirits are recognizable by their fruits. In the measure that they are good or evil, their origin is apparent: "Now the works of the flesh are plain: immorality, impurity, licentiousness, idolatry, sorcery, enmity, strife, jealousy, anger, selfishness, dissension, party spirit, envy, drunkenness, carousing, and the like... but the fruit of the Spirit is love, joy, peace, patience, kindness, goodness, faithfulness, gentleness, self-control" (Gal 5:19-22). More exactly, the Spirit of God alone is fruitful, the spirit of darkness produces perishable results only: "The fruit of light is found in all that is good and right and true; try to learn what is pleasing to the Lord. Take no part in the sterile works of darkness" (Ep 5:8-10).

The contrast is immediately positive and clear—darkness and light, life and death: "I do not do the good I want, but the evil I do not want is what I do... it is no longer I that do it, but sin that dwells within me" (Rm 7:19-20). "You have died to the law through the body of Christ, so that you may belong to another, to him who has been raised from the dead in order that we may bear fruit for God. While we were living in the flesh, our sinful passions aroused by the law were at work in our members to bear fruit for death" (Rm 7:4-5). "I, through the law died to the law, that I might live to God. I have been crucified with Christ; it is no longer I who live, but Christ lives in me" (Gal 2:19-20). Paul realized that his life showed the fruitfulness of the Spirit that guided him: "By the grace of God I am what I am and his grace toward me was not in vain" (1 Cor 15:10).

II - The authentic gifts are those that "edify" the Church (1 Cor 14:4, 12, 26); "bring some improvement" (1 Cor 12:7); and contribute to the growth and unity of the body of Christ. From the instant this body was born of the Spirit and drank of the Spirit (1 Cor 12:12-13), the Spirit cannot act except to make it grow in unity. Paul attached so much value to the gift of prophecy (and therefore to the gift of discernment, closely related to prophecy), precisely because of its positive and constructive effects: "He who prophesies speaks to men for their upbuilding and encouragement and consolation" (1 Cor 14:3).

When Paul wished to prove that his action derived from God, he adduced its wondrous results: "I worked harder than any of them, though it was not I, but the grace of God which is with me" (1 Cor 15:10). "If to others I am not an apostle, at least I am to you, for you are the seal of my apostleship in the Lord" (1 Cor 9:2). "You yourselves are our letter of recommendation, written on your hearts, to be known and read by all men; and you show that you are a letter from Christ delivered by us, written not with ink but with the Spirit of the living God" (2 Cor 3:2-3). "In that which touches the work of God ... by the power of the Spirit of God, from Jerusalem even to Illyria, I have procured the fulfillment of the gospel of Christ" (Rm 15:17f).

III - The Spirit shows itself by powerful signs: miracles, the certitude of expressing God's word, and meeting with persecution: "We know, brethren beloved of God, that he has chosen you, because our gospel came to you not only in word, but also in power and in the Holy Spirit and with full conviction" (1 Th 4: 6). "The signs of a true apostle were performed among you in all patience, with signs and wonders and mighty works" (2 Cor 12: 12).

So striking are these signs that they contrast with the natural weakness of the apostle. "My speech and my message were not in plausible words of wisdom, but in demonstration of the Spirit and power" (1 Cor 2:4). "My grace is sufficient for you, for my power is made perfect in weakness. I will all the more gladly boast of my weaknesses that the power of Christ may rest upon me" (2 Cor 12:9).

IV - Among these signs, God's direct communication by revelation is fundamental for St. Paul. The vision of Damascus is at the heart of his whole apostolate, the certainty of having been "called to be an apostle" (Rm 1:1), "set apart" by God "to reveal his Son... among the Gentiles" (Gal 1:15-16), "because Christ Jesus has made me his own" (Ph 3:12). Not only does this vision motivate his activity, it constitutes in his eyes an authentic manifestation of the Spirit that confers on him his particular mission and authorizes it before the whole Church (Gal 2:9).

In circumstances under which Paul arrived at the faith and under which his apostolate developed, there was all that was necessary to give rise to illuminism, but Paul did not found a new religion on the basis of his revelations. He entered into one already constituted; he was never able to accept the idea of a break from those who represented it prior to him. At the cost of most serious difficulties he insisted on remaining in contact with them.

Authentic revelation harmonizes with or deepens a revelation already confided to the Church.

In this regard Paul's teaching on the resurrection is significant: "I delivered to you as of first importance what I also received from tradition: that Christ died for our sins in accordance with the Scriptures; that he was buried; that he arose on the third day in accordance with the Scriptures; that he appeared to Cephas, then to the twelve... last of all, as to one untimely born, he appeared also to me" (1 Cor 15:3-8).

Such is Paul's spontaneous attitude, and it clarifies what he expects from those who receive spiritual communications from God: "If any one thinks that he is a prophet, or spiritual, he should acknowledge that what I am writing to you is a command of the Lord. If any one does not recognize this, he is not recognized" (1 Cor 14:37-38). God cannot reveal himself to any one who does not recognize the authority of the Apostle.

V - Authentic gifts are marked by light and peace. They are not blind impulses that stir up discord and commotion:"The spirits of prophets are subject to prophets, for God is not a God of confusion but of peace" (1 Cor 14:32-33). This is a valid principle not only for extraordinary phenomena but also for all movements of the heart. "Godly grief produces a repentance that leads to salvation and brings no regret, but worldly grief produces death" (2 Cor 7:10). "To set the mind on the flesh is death, but to set the mind on the Spirit is life and peace" (Rm 8:6).

This peace is not only an interior state, it spreads into the community and he who believes himself strong and scorns the sin of the weak, condemns himself by opposing the action of the Spirit: "For the kingdom of God does not mean food and drink but righteousness and peace and joy in the Holy Spirit; he who thus serves Christ is acceptable to God and approved by men" (Rm 14:17-18).

We are not sure that the warning given in I Cor 12:2 may be added to the texts quoted above, "You know that when you were heathen you were led astray to dumb idols, however you may have been moved." The vocabulary used seems to indicate the blindness of idolatry under the sway of paganism rather than frenzied emotional outbursts.

VI - Fraternal charity holds the most important place among the fruits of the Spirit. Under one form or another and with all its constituent elements, it is mentioned constantly in all the texts that enumerate the manifestations of the Spirit. "The fruit of the Spirit is love, joy, peace, patience, kindness, goodness, faithfulness, gentleness, self-control" (Gal 5:22-23). "While there is jealousy and strife among you, are you not of the flesh, and behaving like ordinary men?" (1 Cor 3:3). "Therefore, if food is a cause of my brother's falling, I will never eat meat" (1 Cor 8:13; cf. Rm 14:15). "As servants of God we commend ourselves in every way: through great endurance, in afflictions, hardships, calamities, beatings, imprisonments, tumults, labors, watching, hunger; by purity, knowledge, forebearance, kindness, the Holy Spirit, genuine love, truthful speech and the power of God" (2 Cor 6: 4-7).

VII - Charity is not only an unchanging sign of the Spirit, it is in the same manner a principle related to discernment. Living in charity, one becomes more and more sensitive to the promptings of the Spirit: "It is my prayer that your love may abound more and more with knowledge and all discernment" (Ph 1:9). "So that we may no longer be children, tossed to and fro and carried about with every wind of doctrine, by the cunning of men, by their craftiness in deceitful wiles. Rather speaking the truth in love, we are to grow up in every way into him who is the head, into Christ" (Ep 4:14-15).

It is noteworthy that charity itself instinctively practices discernment. Paul describes it as assuming spontaneously an authentic outlook: "Love is patient and kind; love is not jealous or boastful; it is not arrogant or rude. Love does not insist on its own way; it is not irritable or resentful" (1 Cor 13:4f).

These are the criteria of love and the criteria of the Spirit; but it is love itself, a direct and privileged gift of the Spirit, that sets the pattern of its ways and proclaims on this earth the love of God.

VIII - The supreme criterion of discernment is for Paul as for the evangelists one's attitude in relation to Jesus Christ:

"No one speaking by the Spirit of God ever says 'Jesus be cursed'!" (1 Cor 12:3). It may be that Paul is recalling here some extreme cases of pneumatism when its adherents were struggling against the spirit of Jesus with which they thought themselves endowed.

Because this principle has a universal value, Paul continues: "No one can say 'Jesus is Lord' except by the Holy Spirit" (1 Cor 12:3b). Any one not discerning the body of the Lord in the bread and wine of the Eucharistic meal "eats and drinks judgment upon himself" (1 Cor 11:29), for he is cutting himself off from the Spirit. On the other hand, to confess the lordship of Jesus, to proclaim his divinity, is to reach the secret of his person; no one can have access to this secret except through the Spirit of the Lord.

This confession of the divinity of Jesus is much more than an empty formula. For a truly "spiritual" Christian who enjoys a mature familiarity with the Spirit it means that he has entered into the mystery of wisdom and divine power revealed by Jesus; it means that he has discovered how Jesus has unveiled himself as Lord only on the Cross; and consequently he will desire "to know nothing except Jesus Christ and him crucified" (1 Cor 2: 22). This discernment of divine ways, missing in "the rulers of this age who crucified the Lord of glory" (1 Cor 2:28) and in Christians who are unable to see the Lord's meal as a gathering of love, is revealed to the "spiritual man" by the Spirit: "for the Spirit searches everything, even the depths of God" (1 Cor 2:10, 15).

Concluding his study on inspiration in St. Paul, J. Mouroux gives this excellent summary: "This dissertation on inspiration gives us a triple list of values: the primacy of theological charisms and above all that of charity; the primacy of charisms of service over extraordinary charisms; the charism of spiritual judgment over that of feeling and suffering. The inspired person is not truly spiritual, and his experience is not authentic, unless he is incorporated into the total life of the Church, committed to works of charity and with that purity of mind that pays homage to God" (*L'expérience chrétienne*, p. 143).

THE CHRISTIAN'S RELATIONSHIP TO THE WORLD

Ignace de la Potterie, S.J.

Can the Christian find and follow God in the world where providence finds him at the moment of his conversion? Comparing the new faith with Judaism Paul shows quite clearly the novelty of Christianity on this important point. The Jew who wanted to be perfect, that is, to observe the law in all its rigor, had to cut himself off from the pagan world, not only by not practicing its vices but by renouncing all dealings with it. The law raised up between the Jew and the non-Jewish world a "hatred" intended to protect the follower of Yahweh, an insuperable barrier which Paul will mention (Ep 2:14) and which is symbolized by the wall in the Temple of Jerusalem which separated the courtyard of the Jews from that of the Gentiles; everyone not circumcized was forbidden to cross it under penalty of death.

The New Testament gives us enough information about the requirements of the Jewish law in this area so that we can appreciate the revolution that Christianity brought. The centurion Cornelius was a "devout man" who gave much alms to the people and prayed to God continually (Ac 10:2), "a just and God-fearing man, to whom the whole nation of the Jews bears witness" (v. 22). And yet, even after Pentecost, St. Peter needed a formal order from God, received in revelation, to respond to that pagan's call and enter his house. And no doubt in order to avoid the scandal of those who accompanied him, Peter explained his conduct: "You know it is not permissible for a Jew to associate with a foreigner or to visit him; but God has shown me that I should not call any man common or unclean; therefore I came without hesitation when I was sent for" (Ac 10:28-29). In the Epistle to the Galatians, Paul tells how later on the same Peter thought he should yield to the pressures of those of Jewish background, who were still attached to a past they had not thought changed, and would cease eating with the converts from paganism, influencing by his example all the Christians of Jewish origin, including Barnabas himself. So serious was the problem that Paul intervened and protested publicly against an inconsequential matter which endangered Christian freedom and the "truth of the Gospel" (Gal 2:11-14).

In light of these facts, which could easily be multiplied, we understand better the importance of the principle stated three times by Paul in 1 Cor 7: "As God has called each, so let him walk" (v. 17). "Let every man remain in the calling in which he was called" (v. 20). "Brethren, in the state in which he was when called, let every man remain with God" (v. 24). Conversion to Judaism included not only a break with the customs of paganism; most often, if the proselyte to Judaism wanted to observe the law and observe it to perfection, it demanded that he change his state in life. The "publican," for example, whose business forced him into those contacts with non-Jews forbidden by the law, was by definition a "sinner," and the two terms are equivalent in the Gospel. The Corinthians who were converted to a religion which in many ways resembled Judaism—whose Scriptures were in large part the same and whose moral requirements often coincided— could, indeed automatically tended to, think that their conversion implied a similar separation from the society in which they had previously lived.

To forestall such an error regarding the nature of the new religion, Paul, who was so concerned about reminding his followers of their obligation to renounce pagan practices (e.g., 1 Cor 5, 1ff; 6:9ff), not only refrained from imposing on them anything that would imply a change in their state of life, but made it a rule that they should remain in the state in which they were when called to the faith, so long as this state did not endanger their faith or morals.

The most typical case was that of the slave, especially since he frequently had to go to the cosmopolitan city of Corinth, where slaves were very numerous and Christianity had recruited largely among the poor and the ordinary people (cf. 1 Cor 1:26). In virtue of his very condition, the slave obviously could not observe Jewish law: how could he observe, for example, the very strict commandment of rest on the Sabbath or the many rules regulating the serving of meals, based on the distinction of pure and impure animals and the consumption of blood. As a result, the first duty of a slave who became a convert to Judaism was naturally to obtain his freedom. But in the case of slavery Paul does not hesitate to apply the general principle which he had just stated regarding those who were circumcised or not before their conversion: "Let every man remain in the calling in which he was called. Were you a slave when called? Let it not trouble you. But if you can become free, make use of it rather" (vv. 20-21).

Paul's advice, as we know, was cause for scandal. More than one modern commentator has concluded that Christianity was uninterested in social progress. In order to preclude such accusations, others, beginning with the sixteenth century, Protestants and Catholics alike, strove to give the words used by the Apostle another interpretation: while, faithful to the principle given, they stated that slavery is not completely incompatible with the profession of Christianity, they maintain that Paul would not go so far as to invite the Christian slave to remain a slave, "even if he had the opportunity to become free." This would be to attribute to Paul feelings that would run counter to the goodness of his soul and the saneness of his judgment. On the contrary, Paul would advise such a slave not to lose the opportunity to emerge from his state, when such an opportunity presented itself. Noble intentions, no doubt, but perhaps they do not take sufficiently into account the problem that arose in the community of Corinth and to which Paul tries to give a solution. If indeed he does foresee this extreme case, it is not because the slave's condition seems to him to be a good thing (still less a condition to be preferred over that of the free man) inasmuch as it would favor the development of certain virtues, such as humility.

The New Testament never identifies the slave's condition

with, for example, that of the poor man—he who does not have an abundance of material possessions—a condition which was deliberately chosen by Christ for himself and his family and which constitutes, in fact, a *conditio optima* for salvation and perfection, in itself better than riches. The Apostle does not intend to forbid the Christian slave from accepting freedom, if this becomes possible; the context clearly shows that a counsel is involved here. The only motive that inspires this counsel is to make clear to those who are automatically convinced of the opposite how much the law of Christ is different from the Jewish law and to what extent the Christian can work for the perfection of Christianity while remaining part of society and retaining the place he occupied before.

The consequences of such a rule are quite clear. The Christian slave, while remaining a slave, became in his own environment a living witness of Christ much more by his life than by his words; and so too in all the milieux, all the concrete situations that make up each and every day. The only exception envisaged is that of the husband or wife who would convert and whose spouse would refuse to live with him. But when the spouses continue to live together, "the unbelieving husband is sanctified by the believing wife, and the unbelieving wife is sanctified by the believing husband" (v. 14).

Thus the Christian will continue to live in the state in which he was when he was a pagan: externally there will be no change, but internally his conduct will be radically transformed and such conduct, completely new, will affect everything, without exception. For in the Apostle's mind a second, but no less important, principle governs the Christian's relationship with the world. It is expressed in this same chapter a little further on. In this world the customary activities of the Christian are identical with those of the pagan; but a new spirit penetrates all his efforts. It does not regulate only his dealings with God, or what could be called his "life of prayer"; it transforms even those of his efforts which others would consider secular. Like the pagan, he "weeps," he "rejoices," he "buys," in short, "uses this world." But he does so differently, which is what Paul means when he says he "weeps, as though not weeping," "rejoices, as though not rejoicing," "buys as though not possessing," "uses this world, as though not using it." All these activities he engages in, not with less seriousness and sincerity than the pagan, but with more, for he is not motivated by self-love but by disinterested love, that very love with which God and Christ love us and which is given to him by his conversion to Christianity.

It is not by chance that the Apostle states this principle in regard to Christian virginity and applies it above all to the conjugal life of married Christians. For there is perhaps no area that shows more clearly how the Christian "led by the Spirit" is both in the world and yet not of the world, and how, while remaining in the world, he can transform the realities of the world. Christ, who wanted to communicate his own life—grace—to us, through the medium of matter—the water of baptism, the oil of the sacrament of the sick, etc.—did not hesitate to consecrate the union of married couples and make of carnal reality a sacrament, a bearer of the Spirit, to such an extent that conjugal love becomes the symbol of the most spiritual love imaginable, that of Christ for his Church (Ep 5:25). But in assimilating the most authentic conjugal love to the strictly supernatural and divine, theological love of *agapē*, celebrated by the Apostle in chapter 13 of the First Epistle to the Corinthians, Paul was not playing on words, no more than is the Church when she commands the spouses on the day of their marriage, in the words of Paul: "Husbands, love your wives, just as Christ also loved the Church" (Ep 5:25). As proof, the lived experience of Christian couples is enough to demonstrate this. To take but two examples, chosen from among many. The first comes from a Protestant, a victim of Hitler's persecution, who was hanged at the age of thirty-eight in his prison at Berlin, "for having dared," he said, "to discuss with some Protestant and Catholic friends certain ethical and practical imperatives of Christianity." The person involved is Count Helmuth von Moltke, grand nephew of Marshal von Moltke. During the days preceding his execution, he was able to write three letters to his wife, in which he reveals the most intimate thoughts of his noble soul, which profoundly trusted in and was nourished on the Bible. He describes in these letters his experience of conjugal love:

> And now I wish to speak of you. I have not yet mentioned you, for you occupy in my life a place far different from the others. You are not an instrument of God to make of me what I am. You are rather myself. For me you are chapter 13 of the First Epistle to the Corinthians, a chapter without which a man is not a man. Without you, I would have received love, as I accepted it from my mother, with joy and gratitude, as one is grateful to the sun for warmth. But without you I would not have known love.... You are that part of me that can only be lacking to myself. Together we form one idea of the Creator. Thus am I also certain that you will not lose me on this earth, not even for a minute. And this reality we may symbolize once more by our common participation in Holy Communion, for me the last communion.... I hope that one day our children will understand this letter.[1]

The second example, that of a "broken home," is perhaps no less significant. We will reproduce it here, despite its length, according to the text published after World War II in a collection containing numerous examples of laymen's witness in the world.[2] It is entitled "Witness of a Broken Home."

> Feeling the ground give way under my feet, rolling at a dizzying pace into an abyss—this was the sudden feeling I had in regard to the catastrophe that was breaking up my home. Then I was seized by an immense sadness, composed of anguish, fear, disillusion, and humiliation, regret, abandonment, and solitude. Thereafter came the determination to fight with my own means, which proved to be ineffective: that is, maintaining a permanent state of legitimate defense, attacks corresponding to those

---

1 "Lettres de la prison de Tagel" by Helmuth von Moltke, in *Esprit et Vie* (ed. Maredsous), August 1949, 358-359. An English translation of the German original appeared under the title *A German of the Resistance*, Oxford.

2 "Parmi les hommes," a special issue of the A.C.I., Easter, 1946, 39.

that came from the intruder, attempts at awkward moral-
izing with respect to the deserter, sadness or simulated
indifference, falling back on myself, finally lassitude
ending in bleak resignation.

At that moment, tired of fighting alone and overwhelmed by this interior drama and the problems of
daily life, the Christian that was within me came alive.
With all my strength I called out to God. Many years
before, when fortune smiled on me, unsatisfied, however,
and looking for something, I had asked God to help me
love him more than anything else, but instead I gave
preference to the many goods that surrounded me.

After months of struggling against the temptation to
rebel, months of prayer and reflection, the Spirit dictated
to me a line of conduct and gave me the strength to hold
fast over the course of long years. Despite his failing,
my husband remained my husband before God. It was
necessary to love him, not with the affection and love
that drew me to him at the start of our marriage, but
with the completely disinterested charity which had to
be the fruit of the sacrament that still united us. It
was necessary to live with my husband; and although his
mistress passed me by every day, it was necessary to live
as if all that did not exist. And again I showed gentleness
and sincere kindness in an attempt to make our household pleasant, even though he spent a very small part of
his time there.

At that moment I really understood what was meant
by "He who loses his life finds it". . .

—Exterior peace, my attitude disarming necessarily
"the enemy";

—Interior peace, above all, consciously obeying the
suggestions of the Spirit.

But what I did not imagine was that in the meantime
there was taking place within me a complete stripping
of self that would draw me to the God whom I had
prayed to in vain when fortune smiled on me. Detached
from my bitterness and egotism, I was then, and only
then, free enough to love God with an immense love
and in it all those whom he had put on the road of my
life. I was overwhelmed with joy. And little by little,
in the opinion of several friends, serenity displaced the
pitiful shrinking up of my features. I felt lighthearted,
borne on wings. I have since found out that my husband,

although he was caught in a web from which he could
not free himself, respected and admired me. But it was
not in God's plans that our household should be restored. But this stripping of self aroused in me an ardent
desire to allow others to profit from the experience of
my life and the graces that had been given me.

Such examples of witness amply show how the Christian
state of perfection, far from separating one from the world,
enables one to become part of it and to transform it.

PRAYER IN PAUL

Pierre-Yves Emery
Frère de Taizé

The Damascus Road

The prayer of St. Paul is that of a Jew accustomed to the
liturgy of the synagogue and the temple, and the intimate and
personal prayer of the pious man in Israel. Yet this is a Jew who
has come through that overwhelming and outstanding experience
that was the Damascus Road for Paul. This is generally called his
conversion, yet it is less a matter of a conversion event than an
event and an account of vocation. Indeed one has here the equivalent and the echo for the New Covenant of the vocation of the
great prophets of Israel. The clearest reference in this respect is to
be found in the Epistle to the Galatians: "When he who had set
me apart before I was born, and had called me through his grace,
was pleased to reveal his Son to me, in order that I might preach
him among the Gentiles, I did not confer with flesh and blood. . . .
I went away into Arabia" (1:15). "Before I was born," "set apart"
are expressions that had been used for the prophets. Like Isaiah
and Ezekiel, Paul has seen the glory of God, but he has seen it in
the face of the Risen Christ and it is this that determines his
apostolate and his prayer. As he says, "Have I not seen Jesus our
Lord?" (1 Cor 9:1), "Last of all, as to one untimely born, he
appeared also to me" (1 Cor 15:8), and he has seen him "who has
shone in our hearts to give the light of the knowledge of the
glory of God in the face of Christ" (2 Cor 4:6).

He has seen the glory of God in the face of the Risen Christ,
and in his existence this determines what can truly be called a

mystical life, a spiritual experience that is extremely profound
and lasting. Little is known of this, other than through a kind of
confidence that is reluctantly drawn from him in his concern
to defend his ministry among the Corinthians, "I will go on to
visions and revelations of the Lord. I know a man in Christ who
fourteen years ago was caught up to the third heaven—whether in
the body or out of the body I do not know, God knows. And
I know that this man was caught up into Paradise—and he heard
things that cannot be told, which man may not utter" (2 Cor 12:
2-4).

From now on, St. Paul's whole ministry is lived before God, in
his presence, as he puts it, face to face in a way that is truly that
of prayer and contemplation. Here we find an indication of the
very close connexion that exists for the Apostle between his
ministry and his prayer. Here are some examples: he feels joy for
the sake of the Thessalonians "before God" (1 Th 3:9), and he
remembers "before God" their faith, their charity and their
hope (1 Th 1:3), he recommends himself to every man's
conscience "before God" (2 Cor 4:2), and if he has been severe
with the Corinthians it is in order that their zeal for him may be
revealed to them "before God" (2 Cor 7:12), etc. In this
expression there can be discerned the mystical experience of the
face to face with God that the Apostle lives even through his
ministry.

The Book of Acts shows us this ministry woven through with
prayer, and in the epistles too, prayer breaks through continually.
The difficulty of our subject is precisely in that in order to do
justice to prayer in St. Paul, one would have to take in nearly
every chapter of every epistle. The Apostle prays without
ceasing, at every moment, at all times, night and day. In the
Epistles to the Thessalonians alone, the insistance on continuous
prayers comes up six times (1 Th 1:2; 1:3; 3:10; 2 Th 1:3; 1:11;
2:13).

The closeness of God, the revelation of the glory of God in
the life of the Apostle, and the closeness of Paul with regard to
God belong too to his consciousness of being the ambassador of
God, of being as it were hoisted up by God to the loftiness of

his charge. To the Corinthians, he throws out, "our sufficiency is from God, who has qualified us to be ministers of a new covenant" (2 Cor 3:5). His vocation, from the Damascus Road on, has introduced the Apostle into the very mystery of God and to the active awaiting on the full realization of that mystery. Finally, the unity of his prayer and his apostolate is sealed in an exemplary way in St. Paul in the reality "your life is hid with Christ in God" (Col 3:3).

Abba, Father

The prayer of St. Paul is addressed to God rather than to Christ, but to the God whom he very often qualifies thus: "the Father of our Lord Jesus Christ" (Rm 15:6, etc.). This is no mere formula, but the way in which the paternity of God expresses itself for him. This means that the prayer of the Apostle bursts forth with the novelty of the Christian economy that was revealed to him on the Damascus Road. That economy consists as follows: Jesus reconciles us with his Father. Through the bond of faith in Christ we become sons of the Father of Jesus Christ in the Spirit that the Son gives us after his resurrection. This is why, like Jesus, Paul says to God "Abba, Father," with that nuance of intimacy and affectionate closeness that is expressed in the Aramaic "Abba." It is with Jesus, entering into the prayer of Jesus, that the Apostle expresses himself like Jesus: Abba.

The source of the prayer of St. Paul is also to be found in God-Abba, through the Spirit of adoption sent by the Father. The Spirit, interior principle of our spiritual life, infuses his power into the weakness of man who does not know how to pray.

Not only does the Spirit place within us that which is the heart of prayer, the knowledge of the spirit of sonship, but he even expresses that filial spirit within us: he cries within us Abba, Father. This cry of the Spirit within us is to be understood in at least two ways. Firstly, as the expression of a burning desire to be with the Father, but also as a solemn declaration of attestation on the part of the Father of our sonship. Thus in our filial prayer

there is the extraordinary event that, in one and the same movement, the attestation of the Father through the Spirit that we are
sons is also the essential of our prayer addressed to the Father.

"Because you are sons, God has sent the Spirit of his Son into
our hearts, crying, 'Abba, Father'" (Gal 4:6). And the parallel,
"For all who are led by the Spirit of God are sons of God. For
you did not receive the spirit of slavery to fall back into fear, but
you have received the spirit of sonship. When we cry, 'Abba!
Father!' it is the Spirit himself who bears witness with our spirit
that we are children of God" (Rm 8:14ff).

It is not that the Spirit dictates within us or formulates the
words of our prayer. He is there too within the words, inter-
ceding within us in ineffable groanings that in us are the great
desire of our redemption, an expecting that is ardent and infinite,
founded on what we have already received, namely, the Spirit as
the first fruit and the earnest of the Kingdom. It is in this way that
the Spirit comes to the help of the weakness and the hesitation of
our prayer. This prayer, aroused inexpressibly within us by the
Spirit, must not even be said to go up to God; rather, the Spirit
puts in man, in his prayer, the very will of God and God hears
this prayer within us through his Spirit. "He who searches the
hearts of men knows what is the mind of the Spirit, because the
Spirit intercedes for the saints according to the will of God"
(Rm 8:27). Finally the dialogue between the Father and the
believer through the Spirit becomes so close that one can almost
no longer distinguish what is of the Father and what is of man.

Christ the Mediator

We have noticed that generally speaking the prayer of St. Paul
is addressed to the Father. Yet, as in the whole economy of the
New Covenant, Christ is in the center as the mediator of an
initiative which always remains with the Father. If the Father
of our Lord Jesus Christ is for us source and ultimate goal of
our prayer, Christ is always united with him as he who reveals
the Father, as he who realizes his initiative, and as gift. This is
expressed by the frequent use of the preposition "dia," meaning
"through" in English. Here is a typical example. "For us there

is one God, the Father, from whom are all things and for whom we exist, and one Lord Jesus Christ, through whom are all things and through whom we exist" (1 Cor 8:6). By the use of prepositions, we are enabled to discern the initiative of the Father and the mediation of the Lord in the common work of Father and Son.

The rapport of the Apostle to God is that of son to Father, the rapport of the Apostle to Christ is as a rule that of servant to his Lord, engaged in the work of the Lord, mediator and saviour.

Thus the prayer of Paul is in general addressed to the Father in order to express the Father's radical initiative. This statement should be slightly qualified however. Referring to the messenger of Satan that harrasses him, Paul writes, "Three times I besought the Lord about this" (2 Cor 12:8). Perhaps it is intentional that he does not speak about "*praying*" here, but of "*parakalein*" meaning to beseech, to send for. Elsewhere, he addresses himself to those who "call on the Name of our Lord Jesus Christ" (1 Cor 1:2), which means to confess his Lordship and call upon his mediation. Paul presents this invocation, which is nevertheless a form of prayer, to the Thessalonians, calling upon the Lord that he may make them increase and abound in love (1 Th 3:12).

If God is the pole of Christian worship, Jesus Christ is the center. This is expressed particularly in certain hymns in the epistles: the hymn in Philippians on the emptying and raising up of Christ, the hymn in Colossians on Christ the image of the Father, mediator of creation and salvation, and in certain hymns in the Pastoral Epistles.

Three passages that are especially typical of the mediation of Christ in the prayer of the Apostle should be noted: "Whatever you do, in word or deed, do everything in the name of the Lord Jesus, giving thanks to God the Father through him" (Col 3:17). We should note once again here the link between prayer and action in the widest sense of the term: that they be always accomplished in the name, that is to say through the mediation, of the Lord, so that they be thanksgiving to God also through him, the mediator.

"For all the promises of God find their Yes in him. That is why we utter the Amen through him, to the glory of God" (2 Cor 1:20). In the first part of the sentence, Christ appears as the mediator of the yes that God pronounces on our life in order to save us. In the second part, he is celebrated as the mediator of the amen that is our reply, prayed and lived, to this yes of God. But Christ is not mediator through placing himself between God and man, after the manner of Moses who at one moment goes up towards God and at another comes down again to the people. Christ is mediator because he is in his person God and man, and in his incarnate life, he is inseparably yes of God and amen of man.

"Through him we both have access in one Spirit to the Father" (Ep 2:18). Our whole life is caught up in the love of the Trinity, and especially so our prayer. We are not merely in face of God, but truly introduced into the exchange of love of the Father, the Son and the Holy Spirit.

The Forms of Prayer of Paul

The indications given here are very summary, being content to pick out a few of these forms that are close to Hebrew prayer, even though their content is Christological.

First of all there are what are called the solemn *doxologies*. "Now to him who by the power at work within us is able to do far more abundantly than all that we ask or think, to him be glory in the church and in Christ Jesus to all generations, for ever and ever" (Ep 3:20). One that is even longer and perhaps even more solemn is to be found in the last verses of the Epistle to the Romans.

Very close to doxology there is the *benediction*, that made by the Apostle as if in passing: "The God and Father of the Lord Jesus, he who is blessed forever, knows that I do not lie" (2 Cor 11:31). Another example, less occasional: "Blessed be the God and Father of our Lord Jesus Christ, the Father of mercies and God of all comfort" (2 Cor 1:3). For the Jews the benediction is the central form of prayer, the prayer of the festivals and the passover. Yet a change in terms that can be remarked in St. Paul is that he speaks less frequently of benediction and eulogy and more often of thanksgiving: *eucharistia*. This change of vocabulary is noteworthy. The Jewish benediction in passing into the New Covenant, especially in Paul, is given a new extension and breadth. This is so because that which was expected in the form of promise is realized in Christ. St. Paul's thanksgiving, in comparison with the Jewish benediction, expresses the attitude before God of the man who has entered into the new existence, that of grace, that of *charis*, to which the *eucharistia* replies. A typical phrase of the Apostle in this regard: "So that as grace extends' to more and more people it may extend thanksgiving" (2 Cor 4: 15). Here seems to be the key in the progression from Jewish benediction to Christian thanksgiving. We now live from the grace that had been previously announced. The benediction, and still more the thanksgiving, consist in giving witness before God to that which has been received from him: benediction and grace.

Perhaps most important of all to underline is the extremely close conjunction in St. Paul between thanksgiving and intercession. Prayer beginning in thanksgiving and continuing in intercession thus expresses the situation of the Christian, on the one hand in what still brings him close to the Jew, for he still expects the fulness of grace, yet on the other, it expresses too what distinguishes him from the Jew, for the Christian has entered the "already" of the Kingdom that has fully come.

After the Jewish manner, St. Paul's prayer is thanksgiving and intercession that extends to include petition. It is in this way that the majority of the epistles begin. Paul inserts the most typical form of Jewish prayer (which is also the schema for Christian thanksgiving) into an epistolary procedure of his day, a formula of politeness towards the gods. Take an example from Colossians: First of all the Apostle expresses thanksgiving, "We always thank God, the Father of our Lord Jesus Christ when we pray for you" (Col 1:3). The motif for this thanksgiving is finally the reception they have given to the Word of God. Then comes the petition: "And so, from the day we heard of it, we have not ceased to pray for you" (v. 9), and the motif of this prayer is the same as that of the thanksgiving, namely, their receiving the

Word. The request is rooted in the thanksgiving. One prays for that for which one awaits because one has already received the earnest and the first fruit. The same can be said for Romans, Philippians and Thessalonians.

On the question of forms of prayer, one could go on to consider what the apostle has to say about certain aspects of the liturgy. Let us consider in particular a passage from the Epistle to the Ephesians (there is a parallel in Colossians). The passage begins in an astounding way, namely, in an exhortation that appears fairly ordinary, on the plane of ethics or practical morality, "Do not get drunk with wine, for that is debauchery," but then comes the surprising justification, "But be filled with the Spirit." The most surprising thing is the "but"! One could say: Do not get drunk, for you must expect of the Spirit that which you are seeking in wine. It is a matter here of that sober ecstasy of which the spirituals speak later on, and in St. Paul, there is question of this in the liturgy. It is therefore legitimate that the latter comprise a certain exaltation of an interior kind. The fulness of the Spirit must be found in the common recitation of the psalms (perhaps it means here the O.T. psalms or else Christian compositions corresponding to them), of canticles (liturgical pieces which would have Christ for the center), and inspired hymns (perhaps songs that were improvised suddenly), "singing and making melody to the Lord with all your heart, always and for everything giving thanks in the Name of our Lord Jesus Christ to God the Father" (Ep 5:18).

Elsewhere, the Apostle shows how the liturgy is the occasion for building up the community (Col 3:16ff; 1 Cor 14). Here it is presented rather from the angle of a personal fulness, and a certain spiritual exaltation to which it gives rise.

The Object of Intercession

It has been possible to say that the characteristic of Christian prayer is the certainty of its being heard, a certainty entirely founded on the love of the Father shown in Jesus Christ. From now on there is no more need to wonder what one can or ought to ask: every desire that lives in the heart of a man whose light and trust are in God is an object of prayer.

For St. Paul, what lives in his heart, what makes up more than his desire, his care, even his constant obsession (2 Cor 11:28) is his apostolic ministry, the fruit of his word in the churches he has founded or to whom he writes, and the fruit of his word in his correspondents. Here is the essential of the prayer of the Apostle. In a single stroke, it is boldness and freedom that he asks for his apostolate, and in the case of the Romans it is his desire to go to them, if God wills, to see them and to communicate a spiritual gift to them, but also to receive with them the consolation of a common faith (Rm 1:9ff).

Rather than go through all the epistles to discover the object of prayer in them, we shall pause only at two passages which are particularly important; two passages where we shall see the close link between prayer and love.

"It is my prayer that your love may abound more and more, with knowledge and all discernment, so that you may approve what is excellent, and may be pure and blameless for the day of Christ, filled with the fruits of righteousness which come through Jesus Christ, to the glory and praise of God" (Ph 1:9-11).

The themes of this passage form a close succession of ideas. Paul prays that charity whose source is God may grow in us without ceasing, and that in this particular case it may produce two things. Firstly, a contemplative type of knowledge, i.e. the knowledge of the mystery of God which is no mere exterior information but a knowing that is lived in charity. Secondly, a refinement of the moral sense with a view to (literally) testing things that differ, i.e. having a spiritual discernment concerning attitudes that have to be adopted in practice. The prayer starts out by asking for love of one's neighbour, so that therefore the knowledge of the mystery (in which we live the meeting with our neighbour, all the while trying to discern what is to be done and what not to be done) may give us to live a life that is pure and blameless, awaiting and preparing the Kingdom and the coming of Christ: his day, which supposes also his judgment. This is the opportunity to recall that holiness or purity of life does not consist, as is often believed, in withholding from evil in a purely negative way, but rather to live positively more and more in charity. "Filled with the fruits of righteousness." It is in this that consists the famous adult state of which so much is said today. The adulthood of the Christian is the maturity of charity. The movement of this passage, prayer that charity fill our life and that our life, filled with charity, become prayer to the glory and praise of God, is the prayer of St. Paul for the Philippians and for us.

The second passage to be noted is the prayer of St. Paul for the Ephesians (3: 14-19). Once again, and this time even more profoundly, the Apostle's prayer is expressed in a single sentence in which the prepositions succeed one another very closely. May God "grant you to be strengthened with might through his Spirit in the inner man and also that Christ may dwell in your hearts by faith." Here are two requests, parallel and conjoined, but which distinguish between the work of the Spirit in the interior man and that of Christ which is evoked as an indwelling in man. The conjoint effect of the coming within us of the Spirit and Christ is a rooting in charity—charity as a force, for charity means here the charity of God for us, in which we have been rooted and grounded.

Here is the basic movement of this prayer. May the work of the Son and the Spirit make us persons that are founded in the love of the Father, so that you "may have power (the power of charity) to comprehend (here there is the movement from love to knowledge) with all the saints what is the breadth and length and height and depth, and to know the love of Christ. . ." The rooting in the love of the Father is thus the starting point from which we can enter into the knowledge of the love of Christ. The terms used here show that he is speaking of laying hold of an object that is very far off, beyond the reach of man. This object of contemplative knowledge that starts from the love of the Father is no other than the love of Christ whose four dimensions signify that it cannot be measured, that it is immense. What are we really to understand from this? Finally, that we cannot understand: the

love of Christ goes beyond all knowledge. This is the summit
of the Christian's contemplative knowledge. God is infinitely
beyond every movement of our spirit toward him, and the love
of Christ surpasses all representation. But in this knowledge
that discovers that finally it can be but unknowing, there takes
place a movement of the whole being which consists in being
"filled with all the fulness of God." "Pleroma" is a passive
term used to describe that which is filled by God. Is not the
fulness of God Christ himself?

An openness on our part, starting from the love of God
where the Son and the Spirit root us: an openness on the love
of Christ, and an openness that is without measure as his love
is without measure: a movement of knowledge in love that
does not close up on its object but opens itself ever more
towards the person of Christ in whom is the fulness of God.
This endless succession of love and knowledge and the growing
openness to the very life of God evoke a very high Christian
mystic. And all this is what the Apostle asks for his readers,
nothing less.

Love, the primary object of the prayer of St. Paul, provides
the key for discerning the profound relation in his eyes between prayer and life.

The Apostle's Exhortation to Prayer

St. Paul wishes Christians' prayer to be like his own, i.e.
constant and persevering. He writes to the Thessalonians,
"Pray constantly. Give thanks in all circumstances, for this is
the will of God in Jesus Christ for you" (1 Th 5:17). Once
again we note here the link between prayer and thanksgiving.
The order between them may vary but they are linked. This
exhortation is to be connected with what Paul has written
above, "Our Lord Jesus Christ who died for us so that
whether we wake or sleep we might live with him" (v. 10).
Such is the foundation of prayer. To the Philippians, the
Apostle recommends, "In everything by prayer and supplication let your requests be made known to God" (4:6). For the

Ephesians, he has an exhortation even more explicit, "Pray at all times in the Spirit, with all prayer and supplication. To that end keep alert with all perseverance, making supplication for all the saints" (6:8).

We must not multiply the quotations, but let us linger for a moment at the twelfth chapter of Romans. Constant application to prayer (v. 12) is linked closely with charity which must grow within us in love of the Father, in fraternal affection, and in fervour of spirit. It is linked too with the joy kindled within us by hope, a joy that is able to come through tribulation.

In the epistles, these exhortations to pray without ceasing, continuously, with great attachment, and in perseverance are in general continued in a request by the Apostle for prayer for himself. This can take the form of striving in solidarity with Paul (Rm 15:30: also Col 4:12, where it is said that Epaphras is striving in his prayer for the Colossians that they may stand mature and fully assured). To strive together with the Apostle is, for example, to pray that he may escape the traps of the Jews on his journey to Jerusalem and that he be well received by the Christians to whom he is bringing the result of a collection (Rm 15:31). More generally however, to pray for the Apostle and to strive together with him is to ask what he himself would ask for himself, namely, that there be an opening for his preaching and that he be granted to announce boldly the mystery of the Gospel and to speak of it as he must (Ep 6:19f; Col 4:3f).

Conclusion

Prayer as St. Paul speaks of it appears as a struggle, not against God, but with him against all that opposes his plan. It is a struggle for the Gospel. But this combat is woven through with thanksgiving in which it is rooted. Thanksgiving and intercession have the same object. The first is conscious and remembers before God the salvation that is already present and acting. The second awaits the final accomplishment of this salvation.

Prayer is our own word. Yet right within the words there is

his cry and ineffable groanings addressed to Abba, the Father of our Lord Jesus Christ. For Jesus Christ is the mediator of all prayer.

Yet if prayer is a word addressed to God, a word inhabited by the Spirit and borne by the Word that is Christ, it must be added that according to Paul prayer is at all times a way of looking toward the face of Christ on which is reflected the love of the Father. The possibility and the freedom of looking at Christ and of progressively passing entirely into this looking are the work of the Holy Spirit. "Now the Lord is the Spirit, and where the Spirit of the Lord is there is freedom. And we all, with unveiled face, beholding the glory of the Lord, are being changed into his likeness from one degree of glory to another; for this comes from the Lord who is Spirit" (2 Cor 3:17ff).

"BECOME IMITATORS OF ME":
APOSTOLIC TRADITION IN PAUL

David M. Stanley, S.J.

The expression *mimētēs ginesthai* and the verb *mimeisthai* are found, in the New Testament, almost exclusively in the Pauline letters. Nor, in the Septuagint, where their appearance is late and rare, do the terms have any semantic pre-history which is significant for their meaning in Paul. In the Greek literature of the classical and postclassical periods, there are numerous instances of the use of these words, but they provide no real parallels to Pauline usage. This can be seen from a remark of Xenophon, frequently if inaccurately adduced as an illustration of the Pauline sense: *hoi didaskaloi tous mathētas mimētas heautōn apodeiknuousin*. The notion of collecting a group of disciples around his own person is so foreign to Paul's mind that the word *mathētēs* is found nowhere in his letters. It is also instructive to observe that the verb *akolouthein*, which in its derived sense might be considered a synonym of *mimeisthai*, is employed by New Testament writers only with respect to the immediate disciples of Jesus. This suggests that Paul conceives the situation in which he recommends "imitation" as quite different from that of Jesus' public ministry. In the eyes of the various New Testament authors, those who followed Jesus personally—as also the first Christians who formed the Jerusalem community—appear to have held a privileged position vis-à-vis those who in a later age, or at least in more remote parts of the world, accepted the Christian faith.

In Paul's own case, this impression—that he holds a position of privilege with respect to the communities he founded—is continually conveyed by the fact that it is always the imitation of himself which he proposes to his converts. This habit of putting himself forward as an example to be imitated, in a man as self-effacing as Paul, surely requires some explanation. It would appear to indicate that, on his view, a special relationship exists between himself and those who accepted his kerygma.

But the importance which Paul attaches to this "imitation" of himself would seem to be out of harmony with what is nowadays regarded as the characteristic note of Pauline morality. The Christian being called to liberty (Gal 5:13, 18), all extrinsic norms of conduct have been per se abolished. The Christian, ideally speaking, is guided interiorly by the "law of the Spirit" (Rm 8:2). Thus in Paul's eyes the "law of Christ" (Gal 6:2; 1 Cor 9:21) excels the Mosaic law, not as a loftier moral code excels a more primitive one, but as the living Spirit excels the "letter" which "kills" (2 Cor 3:6; Rm 7:6). Pauline realism, of course, recognizes that this is the ideal, rarely attained. Because the majority of Christians are sinners and because even the holiest of them are in constant danger of falling from grace (Gal 5:17), some external rules of Christian conduct are normally a practical necessity. Such laws, however, always remain secondary to the "law of the Spirit"; moreover, they have a reason for existing only insofar as they are somehow the expression of Christian love (Gal 5:13-14; Rm 13:8-9).

These principles of Pauline morality enable us from the start to exclude from Paul's conception of imitation any idea of a mechanical reproduction in word or gesture of the Apostle's life and conduct. Moreover, they would lead us to expect that this imitation is something pertaining to the supernatural order and is somehow an expression of Christian charity.

It must be admitted, I believe, that the Pauline letters rarely propose Jesus' earthly career as a model for Christian behavior (cf. Ph 2:5ff; Rm 15:7; Col 3:13). On the other hand, the conception of Christian life as an inchoative and graduated assimilation to the "image" of the glorified Christ is indisputably Paul's (2 Cor 3:18; Col 3:10-11). This process is foreordained by God (Rm 8:29), begun through baptism (Rm 6:5), and will be consummated by the resurrection of the just (1 Cor 15:49). Paul's celebrated use of certain verbs compounded with *syn* to describe the Christian supernatural association (through the agency of the Father) with Christ in the principal mysteries of the redemption is further evidence for this same Pauline viewpoint.

However, whether it is this doctrine which Paul attempts to express through the terms *mimētēs ginesthai* and *mimeisthai*, or whether by "imitation" he means something quite different, can only be decided by an investigation of the texts in the Pauline letters which contain these expressions.

1 THESSALONIANS 1:3-8

Paul begins his letter with a paragraph of thanksgiving in gratitude to God for the dynamic efficacy of his preaching in Thessalonica, attested by the marvelous receptiveness of the first converts and their perseverance in the Christian way of life:

> (We give thanks to God...) 3 because we retain the memory of the active quality of your faith, the labor of your love, and the persevering nature of your hope in our Lord Jesus Christ, before God our Father. 4 We are well aware, brothers whom God so loves, that you have been chosen. 5 Our gospel reached you not as a matter of mere words, but with the power of the Holy Spirit—and that in generous measure. You know, of course, what we meant to you while we were with you. 6 *You* in your turn *became imitators of us and of the Lord,* by having despite great tribulation accepted the Word with joy, a gift of the Holy Spirit. 7 As a consequence, you became an example for all the faithful in Macedonia and Achaea. 8 From your community, the Word of the Lord has re-echoed—and that, not only in Macedonia and Achaea. Everywhere, in fact, your faith in God has spread, so that we have no need to speak of it.

In v. 3, Paul gratefully recalls his converts' practice of Christianity in terms of the theological virtues. It is not a mere generalization, however, but a description of these virtues as exercised in the concrete situation in which these Christians find themselves. Their faith directs all their actions; their love undertakes painfully difficult tasks; their hope in the Lord's parousia makes them persevere despite the trials which they experience.

In vv. 4-5, Paul expresses his thanks for the divine election of the Thessalonians which has made them part of God's new "chosen people." Paul himself has evidence of this in the outpouring of those charismatic gifts bestowed on the Jerusalem community at the first Pentecost and repeatedly given to the churches founded by Paul (1 Cor 2:4-5; Gal 3:3). Moreover, as Beda Rigaux has pointed out, by the terms "gospel" or "the Word" Paul understands not his effort of preaching but rather the interior divine communication of God's mysteries, which effects through faith the salvation of the believer (Rm 1:16). Thus it is in a context which stresses the supernatural aspect of the Thessalonians' conversion and continued living of the faith that Paul speaks of "imitation."

Yet I believe it is significant that Paul speaks of "*our* gospel." While he is aware that the effective preaching of the Word of God necessarily entails Christ's operative presence through the Holy Spirit, still he never forgets (cf. Rm 10:14) that the function of the preacher is a necessary, if subordinate one. While the kerygma is primarily God's speaking to men in Christ, it is by God's design that it reaches men through the mediation of other men. Throughout his missionary career Paul always felt that there was a special bond uniting him with the communities he had evangelized—a relationship he frequently compares to that of a father towards his children (1 Th 2:11; 1 Cor 4:15; 2 Cor 6:13; Gal 4:19).

Thus, on Paul's view, if the divine truth of the gospel is unique and invariable (cf. Gal 1:6-9), yet in its transmission it appears incarnated, so to speak, in the preacher's own Christian faith. This personal character of his own manner of preaching the Word makes Paul refer to it as "our gospel." This same quality may be discerned in the various spiritualities prevalent in the Church, as also in the inspired writings of the Bible. Paul's preaching not only provides an occasion for the operation of the Spirit by faith in the hearts of his hearers; by its own characteristic modalities, which mirror Paul's own spirituality, it provides an objective norm against which the neo-Christian can measure his own experience of the Spirit of God.

"You in your turn became imitators of us—and of the Lord." The passive force of the verb (*egenēthēte*) is to be noted. The turn of expression indicates that God is the unnamed agent here, which excludes any ordinary kind of conscious imitation. Nor is any similarity with the circumstances of Paul's own conversion to be sought. This imitation of Paul lies rather in the conduct of the Thessalonian community since conversion.

The precise point of comparison is suggested by v. 6b. These Christians have imitated Paul "by having despite great tribulation accepted the Word with joy." Jesus had taught His disciples that persecution was a sign, in the Christian dispensation as in the lives of the prophets, of God's predilection, and He commanded His followers to rejoice in suffering (Mt 5:13; Lk 6:23). Joy in the face of persecution had characterized the Jerusalem community (Ac 5:41), strengthened by repetitions of the miracle of Pentecost (Ac 4:31). This same attitude is characteristic of Paul himself (Ph 1:18-20; 2:17; 2 Cor 6:10; 13:9; Col 1:24). Indeed, as is very clear from his letters, Paul conceived his apostolic vocation as a prolongation of Jesus' role as the Suffering Servant of Yahweh. There can be no doubt that in his kerygma Paul made use of this Deutero-Isaian theme in presenting the redemptive character of Christ's passion (cf. Ph 2:5ff). It is instructive to recall that, in his summary of Paul's preaching at Thessalonica, Luke suggests the prominence of this very motif: "He discussed the Scriptures with them, explaining them and showing that the Messiah had of necessity to suffer and rise from death" (Ac 17:3).

Paul's reason for asserting that the Thessalonians have become imitators of himself (and of Christ) is then clear. They have accepted his version of the gospel and proven by their own lives its efficacious force by their perseverance and fidelity "despite great tribulation, with joy." They have been given the grace of sharing in Paul's vocation as the Suffering Servant, and so have come to resemble Jesus Himself, the Suffering Servant par excellence.

One final nuance is not to be overlooked. Paul describes the Thessalonians as "imitators of us," and only as a kind of after-

thought does he call them "imitators of the Lord." This remarkable way of expressing himself is not accidental. It is "*our* gospel,"
as Paul has remarked, which the Thessalonians accepted; and by
means of it they have found faith in Christ, whose representative
as apostle and Suffering Servant Paul is.

Vv. 7-8 again reveal this Pauline concept of the gospel as a
personal living testimony to Christ. The Thessalonians add their
attestation to that of Paul, and so become "an example" to others.
"The Word of the Lord" is thus increased in volume and now "re-
echoes," because their "faith in God" has been added to the witnessing of their apostle.

1 THESSALONIANS 2:11-15a

After devoting a paragraph in chapter 2 to the attitude which
he and his co-workers displayed to their converts at Thessalonica
(2:1-12), Paul once more gives thanks for the courage these new
Christians have displayed under persecution (13-16):

> ... 11 As you know, like a father towards his children,
> each of you 12 have we exhorted, encouraged, adjured
> to live a life worthy of the God who calls you to His
> kingdom and glory. 13 That is why, on our part, we give
> thanks to God unceasingly that, in receiving the Word
> of God preached by us, you have accepted not a human
> word, but as it is in reality, God's Word. And it is
> rendered active in you who possess the faith. 14 *You
> indeed have become imitators, brothers, of the churches
> of God in Judea*, the Christian communities that is, since
> you yourselves have endured the same sufferings from
> your own countrymen as they did from the Jews, 15
> who killed the Lord Jesus and the prophets, and per-
> secuted us.

Although Paul here introduces a new point of comparison
into his description of the Thessalonians' "imitation," the passage enables us to confirm some of our notions about it and to
gain new insights into its meaning.

Paul's description of himself as a father to the Thessalonians
in v. 11 recalls the personal character of Paul's preaching, as
well as how essential in his eyes is the role of the apostle in the

conversion of others. This idea is amplified in v. 13, where Paul's kerygma is called "the Word of God preached by us." While it is "no human word," but truly "God's Word," it is Paul's own personal testimony to the gospel; hence it retains something of Paul himself, his reaction of faith to the divine message, and so he is in a real sense the father in the faith of those who accept God's gospel.

However, the Thessalonians are not called imitators of Paul here, but of those Christian Palestinian communities which constituted the primitive Church and which by their unique privilege of being the first depositaries of the Christian message are an example for all the later churches, such as those founded by Paul. Still, the "imitation" of which there is question here is not mere comparison. As in the last passage considered, it is to be explained in terms of the acceptance of "God's Word" by the Thessalonians, even under the impact of persecution. It is the working-out in them through divine grace of what constitutes the object of Paul's kerygma, their assimilation to Christ, who has attained glory through suffering.

Why does Paul express this as an "imitation" of the persecuted Palestinian churches? It seems evident, from the fact that Paul connects it with his own sufferings at the hands of the Jews of Palestine, that the persecution of which he thinks is chiefly that mentioned in Acts as following Stephen's martyrdom (Ac 8:1). This persecution was of paramount importance in Paul's eyes, leading as it did to the foundation of the Antiochian Church (Ac 11:19) of which he was a member. Luke's view that this early period in the life of the apostolic Church is to be included in Christian salvation history (and so forms an integral part of the gospel) was undoubtedly Paul's own viewpoint. In fact, he implies that these sufferings of the Palestinian communities are to be regarded as a complement to Jesus' own passion by remarking that they were persecuted by "the Jews who killed the Lord Jesus" (vv. 14-15). Accordingly, it is reasonable to assume that the experiences of these Jewish Christians and their testimony to Christ were included in Paul's version of the kerygma, and the "imitation" of which he speaks is intended to be understood in the same sense in which he already used it in the preceding passage.

2 THESSALONIANS 3:6-9

In the concluding line of his second brief note to the Thessalonian community, Paul shows concern over the immoral effects which an exaggerated anticipation of Christ's parousia has had upon some of its members. They shirk their own duties to meddle with things that are not their concern ("doing nothing but busy with everything" v. 11), with the result that they live like parasites upon the charity of other Christians.

> 6 Now we beg you brothers, in the name of our Lord Jesus Christ, to have nothing to do with any Christian whose behavior is unprincipled and contrary to the tradition they received from us. 7 For your part, you know *how you are to imitate us*. We did not while with you live an unprincipled life. 8 We did not eat anyone's food gratis. No, we worked hard and long, day and night, so as not to burden any one of you. 9 Not that we do not have the right [to support], but rather to give you an example in ourselves *for you to imitate*.

Paul interposes his apostolic authority, as the solemn formula in v. 6 ("in the name of our Lord Jesus Christ") indicates. Moreover, he appeals to the apostolic "tradition" which he has handed on to them himself as the source of those principles which must regulate Christian conduct. The acceptance of the kerygma, as we have already seen, implies much more than an intellectual assent to certain abstract doctrines; it involves a way of life in conformity with the gospel which Paul has preached and which is exemplified in his own life. The complete acceptance of the gospel demands some very practical, down-to-earth applications to Christian living (v. 10 contains a sample: "If anyone refuses to work, he must not eat").

This is also to be regarded as the "imitation" of Paul—on a less heroic scale, no doubt, than the earlier examples given in his Thessalonian correspondence, but no less necessary. In v. 7, Paul reminds the community that they know how necessary this "imitation" is and that they know how they are to carry it out. They have an example in his own life during his stay with them (vv. 8-9). His working to support himself was motivated by fraternal charity in a twofold way: "so as not to burden any of you," and "to give you an example in ourselves for you to imitate." When in the sequel (vv. 14-15) Paul prescribes a kind of "excommunication" for the recalcitrant, this principle of fraternal charity is still operative ("reprimand him as a brother").

The importance of this passage for our present study lies in Paul's presentation of himself as a concrete example of Christian tradition, which is handed on to the community which he founded. It is by "imitation" that this tradition, which comprehends the whole range of Christian faith and morality, is kept alive in the Church.

PHILIPPIANS 3:15-17

In chapter 3 of his letter to Philippi, Paul renews his exhortation to preserve unity in that church (cf. 2:3ff) by avoiding certain Jewish influences which inculcate individualism or confidence "in the flesh." Paul's own past life illustrates the necessity of repudiating such reliance upon natural merits. His Jewish ideals (vv. 4-7) were changed by his experience on the Damascus road (vv. 7-9). His new Christian life is a striving to "know" Christ, in the biblical sense of experiencing the dynamic operation of the risen Lord (vv. 8-14). Christian existence can be described as a "fellowship in His passion," the effect of "the power of His resurrection" (v. 10). God the Father is the source of this "power," operative in Jesus' resurrection and also in Paul's life and that of every Christian. God will bring them, like Jesus, through suffering and death to a future resurrection (cf. 1 Th 4:14; 2 Cor 4:10-11; Rm 14:7-9; Ep 2:4-6).

15 All of us, then, who are mature must adopt this attitude. And if on any point you have a different attitude, God will reveal this attitude to you. 16 Only no matter what we have attained, we must keep on making progress with the help of the same [ideal]. 17 *Remain united in*

> *becoming imitators of me,* brothers; and keep your eye
> on those who live according to the example you have in
> us.

Verse 15 explains that the Christian who has attained to a
spiritual maturity must adopt the attitude exhibited in the life
of Paul, as described in vv. 8-14, if unity in the Philippian Church
is to be safeguarded. This is, however, not merely a matter of
human effort, but depends primarily upon divine revelation. The
opposite viewpoint is displayed by the "enemies of the Cross of
Christ," whose perspective is limited to "the things of earth" (vv.
18-19). That the adoption of this attitude entails suffering is clear
from Paul's description of his own life as a "fellowship" in Christ's
passion (v. 10).

This method of living up to the Christian principles which
have guided Paul's own life is once again designated by the
technical term "imitation" (v. 17). By slightly varying the con-
secrated phrase (*symmimētai*), Paul suggests—it would appear—
that such "imitation" is a true source of unity, since all will live
"with the help of the same" ideal.

Earlier in this letter (Ph 2:2ff) Paul had begged the Philippians
to avoid any partisan spirit and remain united in fraternal charity
by imitating the redemptive career of Christ, reviewed by a citation from a hymn probably familiar from its use in the liturgy.
The phrase *touto phronōmen* which Paul employs (3:16) recalls
his *touto phroneite* (2:5). The parallel between these two passages
implies that the "imitation" of himself is implicitly or indirectly
imitation of Christ the Redeemer. Still, it is, I believe, significant
that Paul does not employ the word "imitation" in connection
with the earlier passage.

1 CORINTHIANS 4:14-17

This passage forms the conclusion to a rather lengthy discussion of the friction which has arisen in the Corinthian Church,
caused by exaggerated loyalty to certain leaders: Paul, Peter, or
Apollo (1 Cor 1:12). There are two causes of such division: a
false idea of Christian wisdom (1 Cor 1:18—3:4) and a miscon-

ception of the apostolic vocation (1 Cor 3:5-17). True Christian wisdom consists in realizing the oneness of the whole Church in Christ and in the Father (3:18-23). The proper view of an apostle is an essentially supernatural one, which considers him as "a servant of Christ and a steward of God's mysteries" (4:1). If one were to take a natural view of the apostle's life, it is one of obscurity, hardship, and sufferings (4:9-13).

> 4 It is not to embarrass you that I write this, but to educate you as my beloved children. 15 You may have thousands of guides in Christianity. You have not a plurality of fathers, since, as regards your union with Christ, it was I who fathered you through the gospel. 16 Consequently, I beg you, *become imitators of me.* 17 It was for this purpose I sent you Timothy, my beloved child and a faithful Christian, to help you keep in mind my Christian way of life according to my teaching everywhere in each community.

Paul claims as his paternal right the duty of educating the Corinthian Church, because it was he and no other who "fathered" them in the faith by means of his kerygma. It is this spiritual paternity which gives a unique quality to his relationship with them. No matter how many *paidagōgoi* they may have, they have only one father; and it is natural that children should resemble their father. Consequently, it is Pauline spirituality that they should adopt as their Christian way of life, since they received the faith through Paul's version of the gospel.

It is upon this line of reasoning that Paul here bases his exhortation to "become imitators" of himself (v. 16). He does not stop to explain the nature of this "imitation," because he has sent Timothy to do this. As one of Paul's own "children" in the faith, he will be quite capable of recalling to them Paul's view of the "Christian way of life."

The passage shows how the Pauline notion of "imitation" is built upon the Apostle's awareness of the personal nature of his gospel and of the close ties which bind his converts to himself. It is noteworthy that this notion of "imitation" of himself is put forward only in those letters which Paul wrote to churches of which he was the founder and apostle: Thessalonica, Philippi, Corinth, and Galatia.

Here, as in Ph 3:15-17, this "imitation" of himself is proposed by Paul as a pledge of the unity of the Church. To recognize the real nature of their relation to Paul, that of children to a father, is the one great remedy for party strife.

1 CORINTHIANS 10:31-11:1

One of the cases of conscience which Paul dealt with in this letter concerned the eating of meat that had been used in the worship of pagan idols (8:1—11:1). Paul's solution is based on three principles. The Christian is per se at perfect liberty to eat such food, since idols have no power to affect it for better or worse (8:1-6). Fraternal charity, however, can limit the Christian's freedom, as Paul's apostolic practice of earning his own living shows 8:7-9:17). Christian prudence also may modify the actions of those who seek to secure their own salvation (10:1-13). After giving his solution of the problem (10:14-30), Paul adds the following lines of exhortation:

> 31 Whether, then, you eat or drink, or whatever you do, do everything for God's glory. 32 Strive not to be an obstacle either to Jews or Greeks of God's Church, 33 just as I for my part render service to all in everything. I seek, not what benefits myself, but what benefits everyone else, so that they may be saved. 11:1 *Become imitators of me*, just as I am an *imitator of Christ.*

This passage may be regarded as a well-balanced statement of Christian liberty as Paul envisages it. Verse 31 expresses the motive that must dominate Christian living: "everything for God's glory," ultimately achieved by the winning of one's own salvation (cf. Ph 1:11; 2 Cor 4:15; Col 3:17). Verse 32 puts the same idea more concretely: the Christian must avoid in his conduct whatever might hinder the conversion of Jews or pagans, as well as anything that might scandalize his fellow Christians. The negative form which Paul's statement takes suggests the primacy of divine grace in Christian conduct.

Paul states in verse 33 that this ideal has motivated his own apostolic conduct. The phrase *panta pasin areskō* is an epitome of his whole apostolic career. His assertion that he puts the spiritual profit of others ahead of his own is simply a paradoxical way of saying that he aims at saving his own soul by saving others.

Paul resumes what he has said in verses 32-33 by saying: "Become imitators of me, just as I am an imitator of Christ." Two points in this statement are worthy of comment. In the first place, Paul does not urge the Corinthians to imitate himself *because* he imitates Christ, but "just as" he imitates Him. Secondly, he does not command them to imitate Christ, but to imitate himself. There is an essentially hierarchical structure in this Pauline conception of "imitation," which shows how important he considers his function of transmitting the apostolic faith to others. His own mediatorial role is highly necessary. He is not merely a mouthpiece through which the gospel is handed on mechanically to other men. Not only *what* he says, but *how* he says it, as well as *what he is*, have a part to play in the Christian formation of those he evangelizes. The gospel of Christ which Paul preaches is also his gospel, in a real if subordinate sense. The Corinthians are not called upon to imitate Christ *directly*, but to imitate Paul, in whom they possess a concrete realization of the imitation of Christ. By insisting upon this necessarily mediated *imitatio Christi*, Paul is simply witnessing to the necessity of apostolic tradition in the life of the Church.

GALATIANS 4:12

In chapter 4 of this letter Paul gives a sketch of true Christian liberty. By their union with Christ, the Galatians have become adoptive sons of God and heirs together with Christ of God's kingdom (vv. 1-7). To adopt the program proposed by Judaizing Christians would be tantamount to a return to a state of slavery (vv 8-11). Paul halts his development at this point to introduce a paragraph of a more personal tone, since he fears that his work in Galatia may become fruitless (v 11). He begins this passage, which recalls the specific circumstances of the Galatians' reception of his kerygma and of himself, by a plea that they imitate his own way of life.

12. *Become like me*, because I for my part have become like you.

It is true that the technical term *mimeisthai* is wanting (a sign perhaps of Paul's agitation), still, when we consider the whole context of this letter and the references immediately following to Paul's preaching in Galatia and the reception of his gospel by the Galatians, it appears that there is questioning here too of the same notion of the "imitation" of himself which we have seen in the earlier letters.

As he has stated in chapter 3, the Mosaic Law, its tradition and observances, have no longer any part to play in the divine economy of salvation. While Paul recognizes that in the gospel as preached by Peter among the Jews some concessions may legitimately be made to Mosaic legal observance (Gal 2:8), he himself in his vocation as Apostle of the Gentiles (1 Cor 9:21) has discarded the practice of the law (he is *hōs anomos*) and follows solely "the law of Christ" (*ennomos Christou*).

Since it is Paul, not Peter, who has converted the pagans of Galatia to Christianity, their Christian life must be based upon his personal version of the gospel, in which Mosaic observances have no part. The apostolic traditions, as represented by Paul's kerygma and his own life, provided the Galatian community with the necessary example for "imitation." No other type of Christian life is to be admitted among them.

CONCLUSIONS

Our inquiry has yielded the following data. (1) Paul urges this "imitation" of himself only to those communities which he has founded. (2) It is the necessary result of having accepted "his" gospel, which creates a special relationship between himself and the churches he founded personally. While Paul insists that his kerygma is essentially the same as that preached by other apostles, he is also aware that, as his personal testimony to Christ, his preaching and way of life have their own characteristic modalities, determined chiefly by his conviction that he carries on the role of Christ as the Suffering Servant of God. (3) Thus the *imitatio Christi* which Paul proposes to his communities is a mediated imitation. It springs both from Paul's apostolic authority as an authentic representative of Christian tradition, and from the recognized need of those he has fathered in the faith to have an objective, concrete norm against which they can "test" (*dokimazein*) the influence of the Spirit upon themselves. Obedience is certainly one element in this "imitation" of Paul by other Christians. It involves in addition, however, the help provided by a concrete *Vorbild*, the specific examples and lessons contained in Paul's own version of the gospel as preached and lived by him.

Consequently, this "self-imitation" proposed by the Apostle, so necessary in his eyes as a vehicle for the transmission of apostolic tradition, must not be overlooked in any systematic presentation of Pauline moral theology.

THE PAULINE THEOLOGY OF THE CHURCH

Rudolph Schnackenburg

To expound the Pauline theology of the Church would require a book. Here we can do no more than raise the question what special importance Paul had for the development of the idea of the Church in the primitive Church, that is, what his personal theological contribution consisted of, what particular ideas he sketched and what fruitful impulses he bequeathed to the period that followed. In view of our imperfect knowledge of Hellenistic Christianity before and contemporary with Paul, it will not be possible to say with certainty to what extent he had assimilated the ideas of other missionaries and theologians; nevertheless his originality is incontestable and his deeper penetration into the idea of the Church is evident.

Very probably Paul, trained in Jewish theology as he was, had reflected on the "people of God" very soon after his vocation and particularly in view of his mission to the gentiles. The relation between Israel and the gentiles in God's saving plan deeply pre-occupied him, most of all in Romans 9-11 where he presents a unique survey of sacred history. This great conception cannot, however, be taken as a starting point, for it was drawn up when he was already at the height of his missionary activity, after the conclusion of his work in the eastern half of the Roman Empire (cf. Rm 15:9), and, in view of the readiness of the gentiles to believe, it is written from a special standpoint: "Has God cast away his people?" (11:1). In order to harmonize with the divine promises to Israel the fact, so hard for him as a Jew, that the greater part of his nation was obdurate in unbelief regarding Christ, he puts very penetrating questions: Whether the word of God had become ineffectual (9:6); whether there is injustice with

God (9:14); whether perhaps God was responsible for Israel's failure (cf. c. 10), and whether God's promises for Israel will still be fulfilled after all in an unsuspected way (cf. c. 11). And with this he even warns the converted gentiles against arrogance towards Israel, which indeed in large part was faithless then, but remains nevertheless the root of the olive tree onto which the gentiles have been grafted and in regard to which God still remains faithful to his promises (cf. 11:17-24). All that is envisaged from a definite angle which is partly explained by missionary experience; it must first be asked therefore what positive judgment Paul passes on the vocation of the gentiles and what picture of the Church he draws from it.

On this, the Epistle to the Galatians is significant, the document in which Paul emphatically defends both his apostolic office, namely his legitimate right as apostle to the gentiles and his equality of rights with the original apostles, as well as his gospel without circumcision and legal observances, the foundation of his unrestricted world-wide preaching. In an allegorical exposition of Scripture he views in one passage (4:21 to 31) Abraham's two wives as types of freedom and bondage. The bond woman Agar who only bore "according to the flesh" is linked by him with the Covenant of Mount Sinai which bears children into bondage; she corresponds to the "Jerusalem which now is" and which lies in bondage as its children do. The free Sara, however, who bore her son "by reason of the promise", becomes for him the representative of the "Jerusalem above" which is "our mother"; "you, however, brethren, are like Isaac, children of the promise". It must be remembered that Paul is writing to combat the old obsolete order of bondage to the Law to which, for him, the "Jerusalem which now is" is clinging, and furthermore, that Paul saw that that empirical Israel as it in fact existed, closed against Christ, was persecuting believers in Christ (v. 29). This is a different viewpoint from that of Romans 9-11 in which, as it were, the obverse of the phenomenon "Israel" is shown. Paul is torn between the two extremes: on the one hand, Israel as the people of God of whom the promises hold good, on the other, Judaism unbelieving in regard to the heir to the promises in the absolute sense, Christ (Gal 3:16), persisting in bondage to the Law in opposition to the will of God and even persecuting the Christian believers submissive to the new order of salvation. But from this dialectic, however, there emerges, when Paul is judging calmly without regard to the empirical Israel, his positive conception of the true people of God, which equally comprises believers from Israel and the gentiles and has become "in Christ" a totally new unity: "There is neither Jew nor Greek, neither bond nor free, neither male nor female; for you are all one in Christ Jesus" (Gal 3:28). So it is clear that for Paul a new people of God has taken the place of the old, and one which, it is true, is formed on the basis of the old and more precisely on the promises of blessings made to it but for the rest stands on an entirely new foundation, that of belief in the one heir to the blessings and sole mediator of salvation, Jesus Christ.

Paul, as we have just seen, regards this new people of God as the "Jerusalem on high" (Gal 4:26), or as its earthly manifesta- tion (it is the "mother" of the Christians), and he also terms it "the Israel of God" (Gal 6:16). The attempt has been made of course to interpret this expression in another way; but the bene- diction should probably best be understood as follows: "The Galatian Christians whom Paul primarily has in mind when he speaks of those following his rule, and in addition, the Israel of God as a whole, wherever it may be, are to be blessed with peace and mercy from God. The apostle probably had the nineteenth blessing of the *Qaddish* in mind..." For here something very characteristic is occurring. The apostle is transferring the old title of honour to the new society of those who believe in Christ. In fact this must be regarded as a very deliberate theo- logical proceeding; for something similar occurs more than once in Paul: the blessing that was promised to Abraham for his physi- cal offspring is transferred to Christ and through him to all who are bound to him by faith and baptism (Gal 3:14, 16, 29), and in the Epistle to the Romans the spiritual descent from Abraham is directly ascribed to all who, like Abraham, allow themselves to be justified by faith, the uncircumcised equally with the circum- cised (Rm 4:11-17). Where it seems appropriate, Paul can also reinterpret the terms "circumcision" and "Jew" (Rm 2:25-29) or deny to some "from Israel" membership of "Israel" and of some of Abraham's offspring, that they are his children, and of his children in the flesh, that they are God's children (Rm 9:6-8).

For him the unbelieving Israel is the "Israel according to the flesh" (1 Cor 10-18) and to the unbelieving Jews and Greeks he opposes "the Church of God," that is to say, the Christian community (1 Cor 10:32). He is not alone in the primitive Church in this view; but as well as the titles of honor of Israel, he also laid full claim to its actual privileges, and presents the Church as the legitimate heir of the old people of God. Furthermore, he attempted to provide a theological basis for this inheritance by seeking to recognize the lineaments of the new people of God of believers in Jesus Christ, in the text of the Old Testament itself newly interpreted. By that he certainly heightened and developed the primitive Church's consciousness of being an independent society and even more prepared the way for the conception of the Christian believers as the "third race."

The bond between Jews and gentiles in the Church is most profoundly indicated in the Epistle to the Ephesians. It is "the mystery of Christ, which in other generations was not made known to the sons of men as it has now been revealed to his holy apostles and prophets in the Spirit" (3:4f.). Through Christ who proclaimed peace to "those afar off" (gentiles) and to "those that were near" (the Jews), both groups who formerly were separated have equal access to the Father in the one Spirit (cf. 2:16ff). It is only with the incorporation of the gentiles that the essential eschatological picture of the Church emerges and God's economy of salvation reaches its culmination and "the manifold wisdom of God" is "made known to the principalities and powers in heavenly places through the Church", that is, through her actual reality and her preaching, and so the destruction of their power is announced (cf. 1:21-23; 4:8-10). In this perspective the Church cannot be envisaged in any other way than as comprised in God's eternal salvific plan as the Church of Jews and gentiles which Christ represented in his body on the cross and made into "a new man" (3:15), and which he has redeemed (5:23) and sanctified (5:26f.); the one Body of Christ directed and built up by him, its heavenly head, whose growth is promoted and brought to the "full measure of the plenitude of Christ" (cf. 4:11-16).

That Paul also ensured the freedom of the gentiles in the Church is already sufficiently plain from what has been said. It was chiefly due to him that the settlement at the "Council of Jerusalem" which accorded the gentiles entry to the Church without circumcision or adoption of the Jewish Law was not only maintained in the ensuing period despite the intrigues of Judaizers, but was also understood. His thesis of the one way of salvation for all in faith in Jesus Christ, presented with polemic intensity in the Epistle to the Galatians and with doctrinal serenity in the Epistle to the Romans, dissipated any doubts that might have been possible: "There is no distinction; for all have sinned and have need of the glory of God, but are (all) justified by way of gift by his grace on the ground of the redemption in Christ Jesus" (Rm 3:22f). Consequently the gentiles have equal rights as brethren in Christ and there may not be any tutelage or neglect of the gentile Christians by the former Jews (cf. Gal 2:15-18). On the other hand, of course, this must again be stressed, the gentile Christians must not despise the old Israel on account of its failure (cf. Rm 9-11 *passim*) and must show loving consideration for their Jewish Christian brethren who perhaps may have a more rigid conscience in matters of food and drink (cf. Rm 14). And so Paul admonished and educated all his churches to Christian concord and also promoted harmony between the mother-church in Jerusalem and his new foundations (cf. the great collection). In that way he made an essential contribution, both theological and practical, to the formation of a common consciousness of the Church as a whole. One of the chief reasons, humanly speaking, why the Church which was quickly growing in extent, did not split up, is to be found in Paul's theology, which made all the faithful vividly conscious of the unity conferred on them by God and which imperatively called for concord: the one faith in Jesus Christ the Lord (cf. 1 Cor 8:5f), the one baptism knitting into unity in Christ (Gal 3:26ff; 1 Cor 2:13; Col 3:11; Ep

4:3-6), the common sharing in the one eucharistic bread and thereby in the Body of Christ whereby the many are themselves a single body (1 Cor 10:16f).

From this it is clear that Paul had reflected profoundly on the nature of the Church. For him it is not merely the association of those who believe in Christ, the people of God of the new Covenant, the earthly community of the exalted Lord. The metaphor of the temple of God (1 Cor 3:16; 2 Cor 6:16) which the apostle probably took over from later Judaism and early Christian views (cf. Ez 40:44; Is 28:16f; 1 [*Ethiopic*] *Enoch* 90: 28f; 91:13; *Jubilees* 1:17; 1 *QS* VIII, 5f; Mk 14:58 and parallel), gave him the opportunity of bringing out the holy nature of the Church. In this sanctuary God's Spirit dwells and anyone who destroys it, God will destroy (1 Cor 3:16). His clear and realistic conception of the Holy Spirit who fills every individual believer (1 Cor 6:19) as well as the whole edifice of the Church (cf. Ep 2:22) gave the old idea new richness and depth. His sacramental theology penetrating to the inner process of sanctification was also an enduring vital influence for the idea of the Church. "The saints", probably originally a term used by the Jerusalem Christians to designate themselves, now become "those who are sanctified in Christ Jesus" (1 Cor 1:2) in a sense understood quite realistically on the ground of baptism (cf. 1 Cor 6:11), but not only as individuals but also precisely taken as a whole (cf. Gal 3: 27f). The congregation renders actual again and again this unity in Christ (1 Cor 10:16f) which at the same time imposes the obligation of holiness and brotherly love (cf. 1 Cor 10:1-13; 11: 20-29). The whole assembly stands responsible before the Lord and is chastised by him (1 Cor 11:30-32). Even the idea, familiar from the people of God of the old Testament, that the community must watch over its purity and remove offenders from its ranks, is placed on a new plane in view of the sanctification that has taken place in Christ (cf. Cor 5:7f).

The decisive advance over previous ideas, however, was taken by Paul with his view of the Church as the Body of Christ. This conception which appears in the First Epistle to the Corinthians and is immediately richly developed (6:15-17; 10:17; 12:12-27) is also met with in the Epistle to the Romans and then under a new aspect reaches its full splendour in the Epistles to the Colossians and the Ephesians, must probably be considered a creative achievement of, and theological concept proper to St. Paul, for in this form it is not found anywhere else in the New Testament.

In the Epistles to the Colossians and to the Ephesians we enter into the light of significant statements regarding the relation of the heavenly Christ to his church—here in the sense of the church as a whole. In particular in these epistles Christ is described as the head of his body the Church (Col 1:18; Ep 1: 22; 4:15; 5:23); consequently it is possible to determine more precisely the relations between him and the Church. According to the view of the "body" which is basically implied, all life and growth, the whole building up of the body proceeds from the head (cf. Ep 4:12, 16; Col 2:19); the heavenly Christ builds himself up in the Church and through the Church itself, in love (Ep 4:16). As head, he possesses a sovereign position in relation to the Church his body (Ep 5:23f); but he only uses this to distribute his gifts to it and these are viewed concretely in Ephesians 4:11 as the charismatic offices. So Christ rules (from heaven) his Church through the organs established and directed by him, which serve the good of the whole (4:12f). But the influence of the head is even more extensive. Christ as head causes his whole nature and life, the wealth of divine blessing to pour into the Church. The Church is the "plenitude" of him who "fills all in all" (or, who is filled by all) (Ep 1:23); that means, it would seem, that "with all the forces which derive from him, Christ sovereignly governs the powers which have become subject to him (v 22a), giving life to the whole Church (v 22b)". Consequently all the Christians in the Church through him and in him are "filled" (Col 2:10), endowed with every blessing of grace. This, however, can also be expressed as a prayerful petition that they may be filled in order to attain to the whole "plenitude of God" (Ep 3:19). The previous sentences show that in this "being filled" it is a question of the riches of divine life, of "being strengthened with might in the inward man through his Spirit" (3:16), but also of fruitful knowledge and love. Once again it is ultimately the divine Spirit who, from Christ the head, flows with his vivifying power, strengthening, enlightening and impelling to good, into the body and all its members and who then is manifested in the spiritual intoxication of gladness and thanksgiving, particularly in divine worship (cf. Ep 5:18ff).

The "government" of the Church by Christ is therefore in reality a service, a perpetual care for the Church, as is clear in the "conjugal" consideration of Ephesians 5:22-23. Christ is head, yet also "saviour of the body" (v 23). He has "loved his Church and delivered himself up for it, in order to sanctify it for himself ..." (v. 25f). There the apostle is looking back at Christ's great act of redemption which was for the benefit of the Church and demonstrates its blessing in baptism; for the sanctification took place by his "cleansing it by the bath of water in the word, in order to present the Church to himself gloriously, without spot or wrinkle or any such thing, but that it should be holy and without blemish" (v. 26f). The Church, like the bride, goes through the water of baptism and becomes pure and radiant by the powers of Christ's sacrificial death (cf. Ep 5:2). Here a close connection is apparent, but is not described in more detail, between the Church and Christ's redemptive act; it is made clearer in 2:14ff. Baptism appears not only as the place where the faithful are united with Christ and (by the Spirit) are incorporated into his body (Gal 3:26f; 1 Cor 12:13), but also as Christ's solicitude for his (already existing) Church. Similarly, Christ continues to feed and cherish the Church, (v. 29), which perhaps is an allusion to the eucharist, so that here also the second "sacrament of the body of Christ" may be obliquely envisaged as well.

The "distance" between Christ and the Church disappears in this conjugal point of view, without their distinction becoming blurred, while in other passages the unity of Christ and Church is even more clearly recognizable. In Ephesians 2:5f. it is stated with evident reference to baptism (cf. Col 2:11-13) that God "when we were dead by the transgressions, has given life to us also with Christ—it is by grace you are saved—and has raised us up also and placed us also in heaven in Christ Jesus". The compound verbs with συν express in the strongest manner our link with what happened with Christ and at the same time our union with himself. We have even "in him" attained a presence in heaven. It is true that the apostle does not speak in this context of head and body; yet if the passage 1:20-22 is compared with this one, there can scarcely be any doubt that the idea is present. God has raised Christ "from the dead and set him in heaven on his right hand over every principality and power and virtue and dominion. . . has subjected all things under his feet and has given him as the head (which is set) over all things, to the Church which is his body. . ." Now if we were also raised up and also placed in heaven, that clearly took place by reason of our incorporation in the body of Christ through baptism. All the baptized, the whole Church, shares in the saving event and the heavenly sovereign position of Christ, precisely because he is its head and the Church is his body, both in indissoluble unity and solidarity. Certainly Christ in person remains the victor over the cosmic powers of perdition (cf. Col 2:14f); but as head he allows his body to share in his victory. He takes us in his body "also" up to heaven, although it is not forgotten that in our present life we are still bound fast on the earth and in this aeon must prove ourselves (Eph 2:7, 10; 4:14f) and fight against Satan and his diabolical powers (6:10-18). Consequently the Church as Body of Christ has a heavenly yet earthly appearance; it is his sphere of operation and instrument in this world and nevertheless rises with him as its head and extends up into the heavenly sphere,— a dynamic polarity which springs from the particular character of this concept and cannot be resolved.

In addition to the "vertical" point of view, however, the reference back to the redemptive action accomplished once and for all by Christ on the Cross gives rise to similar unfathomable statements regarding the Church as his "body". In Ephesians 2:14-18 the apostle is occupied with the main theme of the epistle: the unity of Jews and gentiles in the Church and precisely for this "mystery of Christ," the idea of the "body of Christ" is indispensable to him (3:4). He wishes to explain how the former gentiles who once were "far off" have become "near" in the blood of Christ (v. 13), that is to say, share in

salvation on an equal footing with Israel, and how Christ has
united both these formerly divided human groups and reconciled them with God. In order to describe this double establishment of peace, he accumulates a variety of expressions and
imagery. Among these and of particular importance for the
present purpose is the statement about Christ's purpose in his
action: "That he might make the two in his person into one new
man, making peace, and might reconcile both in one body with
God, by the cross, so killing the enmity in himself (vv. 15ff).
By this one body in the first place only the body of Christ given
up to the bloody death of the cross can be meant, his physical
body (cf. v. 14 and also Col 1:22). Nevertheless, as we read
further, precisely this body assumes a more comprehensive meaning. "Through him (Christ) we both (groups of men) have access
to the Father in one Spirit" (v. 18). The "one Spirit" corresponds
to the "one body" just as 4:4 reads "one body and one Spirit". It
is the Spirit which fills and unites the ecclesiological Body of
Christ. The apostle can therefore only be understood to be saying
that the one physical body of Christ which bled on the cross for
the two previously divided groups of mankind and which established reconciliation, then becomes after the resurrection in a new
way through the Spirit the one "Body of Christ" which is the
Church, so that v. 16 perhaps itself is deliberately intended to have
a double meaning. The same, however, follows from the previous
equivalent statement that Christ "made the two in his person into
one new man" (v. 15). This *anthropos* is nothing else than the
whole Christ with head and body—probably the strongest indication that Paul is here in fact taking up old speculations regarding
Adam and anthropos, perhaps even taking into account, and giving
a Christian interpretation to, the gnostic anthropos myth as this
can be shown to have existed in the Jewish and gentile sections
of Hellenism. That conception, which many exegetes consider is
already to be seen in the First Epistle to the Corinthians and in the
Epistle to the Romans, indubitably appears here: the body of the
crucified and risen Lord expands into the ecclesiological Body of
Christ by means of the Spirit; through the latter the Lord (the
head) builds up his Church (the body) for himself and becomes

with it a full unity. In this way the Church becomes a reality which is already present in Christ's body on the cross and which then is built up by inner and outer growth deriving from its head, Christ, and takes possession of the cosmos in order to achieve its perfect form. That may be alluded to in the pregnant statement of Ephesians 4:13 that we are all to attain "to the perfect man, to the full measure of the plenitude of Christ". At all events the Church is regarded as a cosmic and eschatological reality which in its temporal and earthly existence only unfolds and strives after what in its head, Christ, is already a reality. Viewed from Christ, the Church as his body is his instrument for bringing the cosmos more and more under the blessing of his rule, in order to make the universe (cf. 1:10) subjected to him share as far as possible in the graces of redemption. One sign of this eschatological saving event, however, is the fact that the gentiles are now "fellow-heirs and of the same body and co-partners of the promise in Christ Jesus by the gospel" (3:6). Consequently, however, it is also one of the most urgent exhortations of the apostle to preserve the unity given to the Church in Christ by the Spirit and to make it visible by brotherly love and concord and the bond of peace (Eph 4:1-7; Col 3:12-15).

For ecclesiology we may observe that it is on the heights of this theology of the Body of Christ that what is new, specific and unique in the Christian idea of the Church clearly emerges, even when the background of Old Testament thought regarding the people or community of God, the Covenant and eschatological promises is remembered or comparison is made with certain gnostic, Hellenistic conceptions. The further development of the ideas, their penetration by speculation and the Christian distinctions drawn, are guided by the revelation of Christ. The Church of Jesus Christ is only intelligible as a result of the saving event which took place in Jesus' crucifixion and resurrection and as a continuation of his activity in the Holy Spirit; its relation to the exalted Lord, however, its link with him and its dependence on him and union with him, its life deriving from him and striving directed towards him, cannot ultimately be further understood: that is the deepest mystery of the Church.

A SUMMARY LOOK AT PAUL'S GOSPEL: ROMANS, Chapters 1-8

Charles H. Giblin, S.J.

We have all heard of the lady who expressed her appreciation and understanding of Shakespeare's *Hamlet* by remarking: "It contains so many nice quotations!" Unfortunately, many Christians might express in the same way their appreciation and understanding of St. Paul's literary work, particularly his Epistle to the Romans. For many of us, perhaps, even the most carefully elaborated statement of the Apostle's gospel, Romans 1-8, is at best a thesaurus, a mine of quotable utterances. If so, we have missed the sweep of Paul's vision, the dynamic thrust of his thought, the force and coherence of his argumentation, the brilliance and originality of his oratorical presentation of the gospel as God's merciful justice and God's love for undeserving men.

If we have turned to commentaries in the hope that they would supply us with a coherent view of Paul's thought as a whole, we have probably experienced frustration. In most commentaries, relatively little attention is paid to the overall articulation of the Apostle's thought. Considerable attention is devoted to a kind of "trench warfare" exposition, verse by verse, line by line, word by word. The "old glossatorial method," as Ernst von Dobschütz called the commentary style as far back as 1909 proves to be still very much with us—and very much in the way of grasping the Apostle's argumentation as a whole. Undoubtedly, specific difficulties abound, and each of them demands attention in detail. But overall perspective would seem to merit priority. Otherwise the reader, be he layman or professional exegete, is bound to miss the whole for fragmented parts.

Accordingly, I would like to offer, if only in summary fashion, an overview of Paul's Epistle to the Romans, especially chapters 1-8. Let us begin our coverage of Romans 1-8 by considering the circumstances under which Paul wrote and the three main parts of his letter.

Circumstances For Paul's Communication

Paul reflectively composed and dictated the letter as he was waiting in Corinth during the winter of A.D. 57-58, preparing to go on to Jerusalem and Rome. Behind him lay more than ten years of intensive missionary activity in Asia Minor and Greece. Although he had directed his missionary work mainly to the Gentiles, he had regularly begun it in each city by preaching in a synagogue. For the gospel could be understood only as a message of messianic fulfillment. The event of the passion-resurrection of Jesus had to be explained in the light of God's words of promise.

A Jewish milieu provided the best initial circumstances for preaching the gospel and for gaining adherents who would themselves know the Scriptures and be able to employ them as Paul's co-workers. Well-disposed Gentiles could also best be contacted in the synagogue itself; there were always some proselytes and devout men or women, "God-fearers," in attendance. Besides Paul was "Apostle to the Gentiles" not in an exclusive sense but in an emphatic sense; he did not ignore his own people, recipients of God's norms and promises.

But experience had taught him that his own people seldom listened. They seemed to make the Law more binding than God's free, personal favor in bringing all men to justice. The Law given through Moses was exalted at the expense of understanding the creative freedom of him whose will and purpose the law helped to enunciate. Though God was freely bound to his word, he was not bound to men's understanding of it. Rather, God called for a revolutionary understanding of his divine justice. For, through the crucified and risen Jesus, his Son, he had acquitted people who had done nothing to deserve acquittal, and had thus established justice as mercy, not as judgment according to works specified by law.

Ahead of Paul lay a trip to Jerusalem, to present the collection he had gathered from the various areas of his ministry. No doubt he would have occasion to offer in Jerusalem an account of his missionary preaching and perhaps some explanation of his apparent alienation of the Jews or his attitude towards the Law. He would have to be prepared for this, even among a non-hostile audience like that of the Jewish Christians in Jerusalem.

More important, however, was the further journey he planned to make to Rome and beyond, to complete his apostolic circuit of the nations around the Mediterranean. He had not founded the community at Rome. He recognized it as a center of faith—their faith and his. But the community there seemed to include an exceptionally large number of Jewish Christians. The community was integrated in faith, but there could be occasion for misunderstanding—given reports of Paul's conflicts with Jews and Judaizers in Greece and Asia Minor—concerning the nature of his gospel. He would take care to obviate any difficulties by stating to them in advance of his coming his gospel of fulfillment for Jews and Gentiles alike. He would also try to win his Roman audience with an oratorical exposition in which the gospel would be presented as a kind of "super law" and salvific judgment. He would compose his personal testimony largely in the form of a missionary speech.

Three Principal Parts of Romans

At the outset, Paul would address himself to the Romans in terms of their shared call in faith under the same Lord (Rm 1: 1-7), then thank God for their faith and indicate his concern for them (Rm 1:8-15), and present his personal gospel in a rhetorical style that he thought would capture their interest (Rm 1:16-8:39).

This gospel, as presented in the *first principal part* of the epistle to Romans (1: 16-8:39), would deal with God's power to save all men without discrimination but in fulfillment of his promises—a fulfillment beyond men's claims or imaginings, but a fulfillment nonetheless, since it was a realization of the promises made to Israel. The message of fulfillment would take seriously God's law and judgment, but it would have to bear the stamp of the Apostle's own teachings on God's fulfillment of his promises in an entirely new dimension: a justice beyond that which could be based on law or expected from a law, a personal justice for Jew and Greek alike that reconstituted human relationships in supra-legal terms. To be true to the missionary apostolate that lay behind him and ahead of him, his Epistle to the Romans would have to be a kind of personal apologia, a presentation of his gospel of God's non-discriminatory mode of fulfillment.

This presentation would create its own problems. If the gospel of God's justice was for the Jews primarily (as recipients of the promises) but for the Gentiles as well (since the fulfillment transcended any racial or national limitations) how was it that the Jews were not converted *en masse*—or at least in proportion to the number of Gentile converts? Years of apostolic activity seemed only to have rendered disaffected most of the Jews Paul himself had contacted. Was it that "he could not care less" or that he was oblivious of the theological problem that this non-conversion of his own people posed? In effect, the theological problem was the problem of evil in terms of his apostolic work and the whole thrust of his gospel of fulfillment. What was wrong? How was it to be explained? Had God's word failed? Was it compromised even in part?

Paul would have to face these questions. He would do so in the *second principal part* of the Epistle, Romans 9-11. True to the presentation of his gospel itself (Rm 1:16-8:39), the answer to these questions would focus on the "supernatural" explanation —that God's way of fulfilling his promises lies beyond merely human claims and imaginings, and is realized in a super-justice, a new creation, hope for which is grounded in discerning faith regarding God's power and wisdom.

Paul would have to speak to the Roman community in terms of its own specific problems. He probably had only a generic knowledge of these problems, drawn from his own experience in the churches of Greece and Asia Minor and from hearsay about the situation in Rome. In the area of the community's specific problems, there was friction not between Jews and Gentiles but between those "weak" in faith and those "strong" in faith. The former seemed to be more pedestrianly dutiful and literal-minded, the latter, more discerning but perhaps overly sophisticated and somewhat inconsiderate of the consciences of other Christians.

He would begin *the third principal part* of his communication with a word on sacrifice in terms of a supernatural outlook that distinguishes Christians from the world (12:1-2). He would then stress mutual respect in the exercise of interdependent charismatic gifts, and especially the meaning of Christian love (12:3ff.). Against this background, he would address himself to the problems of the "strong" and the "weak" (14:1ff.). Christian love in the practical dimension would be rooted in a shared faith-outlook and in the hope for a shared fulfillment in Christ.

A few appendages, like Romans 13:1-7, 16:1-20, and perhaps the doxology in 16:25-27, may not have pertained to the original correspondence, but need not concern us here. Paul would conclude, as usual, with information about his personal plans (15:14-33) and summary greetings (16:21-23).

Given this general view of the three major parts of Romans, we may address ourselves in particular to chapters 1-8.

Romans 1-8.   *Introduction*

In 1:1-7, where Paul greets the Romans, he mentions his call and theirs, stressing their shared allegiance to Jesus Christ. The gospel of God to which Paul is dedicated is the fulfilled word concerning God's Son, our Lord. The Christological statement in 1:3-4 brings out the astounding mystery that enables us to call God's Son our Lord. "Our Lord" is an expression that supposes more than the divinity of the pre-existent Son. It supposes incarnation, passion, and resurrection with a fullness of sanctifying power among men. God's Son is not less or more God's Son for all this, but he is now God's Son in *power*, able to effect in a communitarian context a transformation in all men who acknowledge him in faith as their Lord. Paul then thanks God for the Romans' faith and proceeds to express his prayer and longing to impart to the Romans a richer understanding in faith according to God's expectations of him (1:8-15).

In the next few lines (1: 16-17), Paul states the basic theme of the gospel he is proud to preach and announces the thematic standpoint from which he will develop it positively in this letter. The basic theme is the gospel as a power, a word that effects salvation in everyone who receives it with faith. The thematic standpoint that clarifies this power is justice, a new positive rapport between men and God who is their judge, a relationship demanding faith as the sole condition for its realization. That realization is life in fulfillment of God's word of promise. Justice effects life in the believing man's relationship with God. It is no "legal fiction," but the basic structuring of a new personal relationship between the believing man and God.

Seven Major Sections

Seven major sections follow this enunciation of key themes. But the reader should be prepared for a jolt. The message of salvation supposes that one recognize what he is being saved *from*. The new relationship, justice, according to which salvation is effected, cannot be taken for granted. Accordingly, Paul begins his development of these themes with the negative background they require.

In the first section (1:18-32), Paul states and develops the converse of God's justice: God's wrath. This wrath is disclosed even now against men's impiety and injustice—their religious and moral perversion. Paul has in mind not just the vices of the Gentiles of his day but the aberrations of all men who have forsaken the knowledge of God and have made idols of his creatures and themselves. They have forsaken God's glory and have brought upon themselves his wrath (his "giving them over" to vice). In fact, God's wrath in the present consists in the very perversion of godless men's instincts and judgments.

Obviously, Paul is not castigating the Roman community.

Rather, he is enunciating for their benefit the theme of men's injustice and God's wrath, the state of complete alienation from God which self-centered men bring upon themselves. Men's injustice is equivalently defined as a denial of glory to the invisible but self-revealing God. Their cultic disorientation from God brings with it human self-worship and degradation to life on the level of animal existence or worse. Thus, God's wrath is existentially revealed in their becoming sinful fools by their own self-centeredness. The rhetoric may not be exaggerated in view of the pagan mores of Paul's day—or perhaps even of ours. But, exaggerated or not, the rhetoric enables Paul to enunciate the present basis and meaning of God's wrath, and to prepare the way to challenge a false sense of security on man's part.

After the blistering indictment of Romans 1:18-32, Paul turns to an imaginary hearer (again, *not* a member of the Roman Church) who would righteously dissociate himself from such people (Rm 2:1-3:20). Paul denies that any man can defend himself against God's wrath; nor can any man make a claim on God's salvific justice. The ideal of glory, to be sought through patient endurance in good work, is the reward for those who meet the standard of God's judgment. But the ideal is unattainable in practice. For man has no defense, on the score of his own works (obviously, apart from God's transformation of them), against an adverse judgment, the wrath still to come (2:1-16).

This controversy is an oratorical attack intended to show that man must be brought to his knees before he can hope for (salvific) justice instead of judgment. The man who is addressed here is a typical "unconverted" man. In the course of his controversy, Paul takes care to make his case universal in scope, though, again, universal with regard to "unconverted" men. He turns explicitly to the Jew (2:17-3:20). In effect, Paul says that the privileged man par excellence, the one who has been given God's law, is on a par with the sinful Gentile. Neither Gentile nor Jew can claim any defense against God's judgment to come.

It must be recalled that Paul is constantly making a case to bring out the nature of God's paradoxical justice; his rhetoric is in function of his stated themes (1:16-17). He is not academically concerned, for instance, with the question of whether or not God justified men prior to the preaching of the gospel, by reason of Jesus Christ who was yet to come. That God did so might be established in the light of a wider study of St. Paul and the rest of the New Testament.

In the "mission-style" approach that Paul has chosen to use here, however, such concerns would only confuse the issue and weaken the appeal to conversion. At this point in his case for God's justice, Paul must stress personal responsibility for sin and at the same time articulate the principle of universal inability on the part of men to save themselves from God's wrath. Their own works testify against them, whether they are Gentiles or Jews. They have no defense. Everyone in their position is liable to judgment.

The third section (3:21-26) is very brief, concise, and decidedly important for grasping the sweep of Paul's argument. It is an exposition of God's justice for all men. Though justice cannot be expected on the basis of law as fulfilled by men, it is attested by the Law and the prophets. It is not unannounced, but it has never been effected by the Law itself, and could not be (cf. 3:20). Jesus is the expiation-center (cf. Lv. 16:12-15) prophetically designated in connection with the rite of the Day of Atonement (Yom Kippur). God's personal favor (grace) effects justice in a new bond, the faith-relationship achieved in Jesus Christ. This new bond is open to all, without discrimination.

By Christ's death, the case against men (oriented towards judgment) has been dropped and a new rapport, justice, is effected in terms of a personal bond of faith, a bond of faith in Jesus. Justification is thus the revolutionary but promised change of men's sinful condition, provided they are associated with Jesus by faith, and it becomes the initial fulfillment of their need for God's glory (which, as subsequent sections will show, is focused on the resurrection of men in the image of God's Son). God's justice is manifested and promulgated in the crucified Jesus as the basis for faith, mercy, and forgiveness.

Having declared God's salvific justice against the background of God's right to exercise wrath (i.e., adverse judgment), Paul insists anew on the strictly divine, supra-human (and, equivalently, supernatural) nature of God's justice. He turns again to the genre of controversy (3:27-4:25). This time his target is man's unwarranted boasting. No man should think that because God's justice has been shown him, he has somehow deserved it or has become entitled to it. The salvific effectiveness in question is strictly God's alone.

The principle or "law" that excludes man's boast is the "higher" law of faith. Paul supposes that it is God's law that discloses the very nature of God: that he is *one*. But this oneness is actually disclosed as realized in the order of faith—God's being one over all men, Gentiles as well as Jews. Hence, faith is "the law" *par excellence*, realizing in actual fact the Mosaic Law's announcement of God's oneness. The law of faith stands, therefore, as the ultimate law or principle governing man's actions. Clearly, it stands over and above any reckoning on the score of man's works.

A classic example from Genesis also excludes man's boast—the example of Abraham. Even Abraham, the human father and paradigm of God's people, had no basis for boasting—and recognized this fact. He gave glory to God by admitting his own impotence as man. In effect, Abraham was justified simply as a man (not as a Jew), a man who had no human hope of life but who was enlivened simply by accepting God's creatively transforming word. He had no basis for a claim on God and made no pretense to a claim on God. Abraham's case is a type or pattern of justification as effected in those who accept the Lord who died and rose from the dead, for he exemplifies the right attitude of man before the God who gives life.

Thus far, Paul has excluded man's defense against judgment and any self-centered boast in the justice he has paradoxically been shown. In the pivotal fifth section (5:1-21), Paul presents an exposition and exhortation regarding the prospects for salvation based on the justice that God alone has effected. The messianic blessing of "peace," reconciliation with God, the initial guarantee against God's final wrath, is already a reality, thanks to justification by faith.

This reality is grounds for boasting, confident rejoicing in hope of final realization. But the boast is "in the Lord," not "in mere man." Given justification, we should boast in the hope of the glory of God, the transformation still to be realized at the resurrection. While we confidently rejoice in this prospect, we do so realistically, boasting in our trials. For trials test our hope. The hope we have will not be disappointed, for we have already the interior proof of God's love—the Holy Spirit given us as the result of God's demonstrated love in Christ's death for us. On the basis of what God has done for us men when we were alienated from him, we can fully expect him to bring justification, his own work, to fulfillment in risen life, as he did in the case of his Son who died for us.

In the second half of this section (5:12-21), Paul provides the wider historical perspective for his exhortation to boast in God (cf. 5:11). Through Adam, sin and death entered the world. The sin that affected all men through Adam ("Mr. Man," at the outset of human history as we experience it) was not a sin that was personally reckoned to his descendants. It was Adam's personal sin, but it brought about in mankind a deadly bent towards sin and universal condemnation. Law articulated the evil—simply as a matter of historical record—and there resulted not only a reign of death, but a reign of sin in death. Through the obedience of Adam's counterpart, Jesus Christ, the evolution of man was reversed, so that a reign of grace was established, through justification, leading to eternal life (the risen life of the New Adam).

In the sixth section (6:1-7:25), Paul for the third time engages in controversy with imagined opponents. In doing so, he develops the second part of the preceding chapter and continues his exhortation to those who have been justified in Christ. He points out that the reign of grace does not allow a spectator's role, but calls for a new service after death with Christ in view of baptismal commitment to Christ, who lives for God (6:1-14). The divine glory on which our hope is centered (Rm 5:2, 11) is already operative: it is the power that raised the Lord with whom the Christian is already vitally united through baptism.

Paul adds that an antinomian view, the position of one who

thinks that the overthrow of law means the overthrow of any obligation, is likewise without warrant. A new service is called for. The new service is that of one now espoused to Christ, a service in the new order of the spirit (6:15-7:6).

Lastly, in extolling the new bond in Christ, Paul refuses to condemn the law itself, for the law is God's law (7:7-25). His main concern throughout this section has been to show the practical consequences of the new reign of grace over that of sin, abetted (simply as a matter of fact) by law. The practical consequences were the wages of sin: death (not just physical death, but theological death—definitive alienation from the living God). In closing this section, he points out that law simply enunciates an ideal; it does not provide the wherewithal to meet its own demands. Given man's actual condition since the original capitulation to sin, law simply underscores man's own impotence and prompts him to look for one who will deliver him from bondage to frustration as he faces law's inexorable demands. Thanks be to God, through Jesus Christ our Lord, there is an answer to this predicament.

In the seventh and last section of the rhetorical presentation of his gospel (8:1-39), Paul offers an exposition in the first eleven verses of chapter 5. Thus, he concludes his words of exhortation to those who have been justified in Christ. The chapter begins with a direct answer to the condemned, graceless man who has presented his condition in a kind of stylized monologue in 7:7-25. The chapter then opens out into a consideration of two fundamental outlooks and tendencies that are a matter of death or life (8:1-13).

The theme of a new service (Rm. 6) is now transmuted or escalated into the theme of genuine freedom in the Spirit. Freedom from sin's tyranny unto death through the impossible demands of a law standing "outside," as it were, is now seen as freedom for a new life in the Spirit through the interior dynamism of the Spirit of God himself. The Spirit gives life in Christ, God's Son.

Paul then turns to develop the Christian experience of life in the Spirit, God's gift that not only makes men genuinely sons of God, albeit adopted sons, but helps them speak to God as sons even beyond the utterances and intentions which they themselves are able to articulate. In effect, there has been a new creation, and it is undergoing the pangs that presage manifest new life in the flesh. The new creation will be realized in hope, for it is as yet unseen, though real. It will be realized in hope not as through a desire for that which is difficult and as yet unattained, but as through that with which we have already been graced in Christ, the gift of the Spirit who works to the good with those who love God. The final stage of God's historically realized decree will be glorification, the transformation of men in the image of his risen Son.

At this point the exposition of Paul's gospel is complete. He concludes with a kind of peroration (8:31-39). Far from having to fear the verdict of God's wrath, we find ourselves in the astounding position of having no effective adversaries at all—in the whole context of creation. Trials are relatively irrelevant. The love of God in Christ Jesus our Lord proves to be the salvific power that has been shown on our behalf and that conquers every trial. "Justice," as the Christian man (converted Jew or converted Gentile) has experienced it, stands forth as nothing less than God the Father's personal love in our crucified and risen Lord, a love shown us through our present trials, a love triumphant.

Hopefully, enough has been said to indicate that Paul's Epistle to the Romans, notably its first, major part, is much more than a mine of insights and quotable statements. But nothing that can be said will substitute for reading, rereading, and prayerfully considering the words of the Apostle himself. Like all the biblical writers, channels of God's own word, he is his own best commentator and expositor. For those in need of a "conversion experience," or, like the Roman community for which Paul wrote, a deeper understanding of the conversion experience and the Christian outlook expected from Paul's apostolic preaching, the final comment can be only this: "Take and read!"

CHRIST THE COSMIC LORD
IN THE PAULINE EPISTLES

F.X. Durrwell, C.Ss.R.

In proportion as the preaching of the Apostles moved away from the Jewish center of interest, the formal title of the risen Christ lost its primitive complexion. *"Christos"* ("Messiah") became a proper name to be used without any article, suggesting the Redemption but not recalling the Hebrew messianism. *"Kyrios"* came more explicitly than before to indicate the divine being revealed in the Resurrection and the universality of his dominion. But the bond between Christ's enthronement as Lord and his resurrection remained firm: "If you confess with your mouth that Jesus is Lord, and believe in your heart that God has raised him up from the dead, you shall be saved" (Rm 10:9).

During his captivities, the Apostle had time to consider the scope of Christ's exaltation, and follow its repercussions throughout the whole cosmos.

Universal Dominion

The Epistle to the Philippians, which gives the best account of the humiliations of the Son of God in the flesh, gives a parallel account of their repercussions in glory: "He emptied himself... he humbled himself unto death.... For which cause God has also exalted him and has given him a name which is above all names: that in the name of Jesus every knee should bow, of those that are in heaven, on earth, and under the earth: and that every tongue should confess that Jesus Christ is Lord in the glory of God the Father" (2:7-11).

God has exalted Christ, giving him a name above all others,

the only sovereign name, the name proper to Yahweh himself, the "Lord-God". From the beginning Christ possessed "the condition of God": the giving of the name is no mere title of honour: for the Semites, the name and the being described by the name are one. This name, superior to all others, which compels the adoration of all creatures, can indicate none other than the sovereign majesty of God and his dominion over all things. The divine power is conferred upon this Jesus who once hung on a gibbet, and forces from us the acclaim, "Lord Jesus Christ!"

Every creature on the "three levels" of the world bends the knee at this name, paying to it the homage given to God, in heaven, on earth, and in the depths below the earth (2:10). Who are these vassals? The angels, certainly, men, and since all must be included, the demons, for these are the three categories of being who inhabit these dwellings. So say most interpreters. It may be pointed out that evil spirits also dwell in the air and the high places (Ep 2:2; 6:12), and that those who dwell under the earth seem more properly identified with the dead in Sheol, as Paul says: "To this end Christ died and rose again, that he might be Lord both of the dead and of the living" (Rm 14:9). But did he intend any such literal interpretation? Surely we must believe that he meant by this triple designation to affirm the submission to Christ of all beings, animate and inanimate, in short, of the whole universe. The man who accepted humiliation of his own free will, is established at the very summit of creation, in the power and glory of God.

Lord of the World to Come

The Epistles to the Ephesians and the Colossians are concerned with defending Christ's absolute primacy in the world and with defining its nature; for them Christ constitutes the actual principle of the cosmos: "Who is the image of the invisible God, the first-born of every creature: for in him were all things created in heaven and on earth, visible and invisible... All things were created by him and for him; and he is before all, and by him all things subsist" (Col. 1:15-17).

This Christ as principle of the cosmos is not the pre-existing Word—this would fit neither Paul's perspective nor that of John's prologue—but Christ "in whom we have redemption" (1: 14), the visible image of God (1:15), head of the Church (1:18). But he is a Christ who has passed beyond the weakness of his earthly existence: he holds the primacy over all things, "the first-born from the dead . . . in whom it has well pleased God that all fullness should dwell" (1:18-19).

Christ is "the first-born of every creature" (1:15). He holds priority both of cause and of duration over the rest of creation. The reason given by the Apostle—"for in him were all things created"— presupposes both priorities. St. Paul insists on that of duration: "He is [exists] before all" (1:17). This is, of course, a prerogative of divinity, but then the Christ of the Resurrection is wholly divine. Lifted up into the life of God, in the fullness of time (which, in the mind of St. Paul, is the fullness of reality), Christ is set before all things. While on earth, his age was measured as the world measures age, but henceforth he is wholly seen in God, at the summit and origin of creation.[1]

The title "first-born of every creature", while placing Christ above the rest of creation, does not separate him wholly from it; he becomes its principle, because of the fullness of being God has implanted in him: "He is indeed principle of them all. . . because in him it has well pleased the Father that all fullness should dwell" (Col. 1:19). The *pleroma* ("fullness") which, in biblical thought and the philosophy of the time, meant "the universe filled by the

---

1 Christ's priority of duration is not thought to be in the nature of successive time. Whatever may have been said on that score, St. Paul never seems to allow of any pre-existence of the man Christ in successive time.

Whereas Plato grants a heavenly pre-existence to the ideas of this world's realities, Judaism accorded a similar pre-existence to sacred things, to the Temple, the Torah, the Sabbath.

The Messiah was given a heavenly prehistory (cf. Mi 5:2; Dn 7:13-14; and the apocalyptic writings about the Son of Man). According to the New Testament, it was at the end of his life on earth that the Man Christ was lifted to the heights of God whence he dominates history.

creative presence of God," is primarily present, in all its being and power, in him.

It is "in him" that God calls everything into being (ἐκτίσθη) and maintains it (ἔκτίσται) (1:16). The world is based on him as upon its focal point, where all the threads, all the generating lines of the universe are knotted together and co-ordinated.

As principle, Christ is the center of cohesion and harmony; everything starts from him and returns to him (1:16-18). The world, as it were, pulls itself together in him and becomes a cosmos, an ordered universe. "In him all things stand and stand fast [συνέσιηκεν]." They are centered upon him, and depend on him for their existence, for in him dwells the whole power of God. If anyone could have an instantaneous vision of the whole universe, past, present and future, he would see all things ontologically depending from Christ, and wholly intelligible only through him.

Though he had always been Son of God, Christ did not become the center and universal bond of the cosmos until after he had saved and reunited the shattered world in his sacrifice: "It pleased the Father. . .through him to reconcile all things [by directing them] to himself, making peace through the blood of his cross, through him (I say) both the things that are on earth, and the things that are in heaven" (1:20). In Christ God does not reconcile the universe with himself, but re-establishes the harmony among things, making them all converge towards Christ. All the powers of heaven and all the creatures of earth have their culmination in him and are reunited at this pinnacle of the world's architecture, for once risen he holds the fullness of all things.

There was a time during our Lord's human existence when the various planes and lines of the universe had not yet come to culminate in him. The world remained broken apart, with a crack across the universe at the point where the upper and lower creations joined in man, until the sin that caused the crack was wiped out by the blood of the Cross. Standing in the center of the universe, because of his carnal being, Christ bore that fissure in himself during his life on earth. But by his death and resurrection he wiped out the contrasts and, lifted to the pinnacle of all things, joined the shattered pieces together again in himself. Henceforth he was to be a magnet drawing all creation, and reuniting it in himself. "He that descended is the same also that ascended above all the heavens, that he might fill all things" (Ep 4:10).

Clearly, these declarations are something of an anticipation. The world we live in is still torn apart, the submission of the angels is not yet complete, the rule of death has not been abolished. The world of harmony and peace centered wholly upon Christ, belongs to the end of time. In the Epistles of the Captivity, the eye of prophecy is being brought to bear on the world; it is being judged by a principle, by the death and resurrection of Jesus, by that cosmic revolution which took place in its entirety in Christ, but whose effects have not yet spread out over the world. The great epistles, more conscious of the delays of history, only look forward to the submission of all things to Christ and universal peace at the end (1 Cor 15:24-8).

The lordship of the universe is an eschatological attribute of Christ's, but it is a reality from the Resurrection onwards. The Lord of the next world is none other than the Christ of Easter; in his glory he is the end and fullness in which all things subsist and are consummated: "It has well pleased the Father that all fullness should dwell in him" (Col 1:19).

Because he is the end and pinnacle of all things, the action of Christ in glory goes back to the beginnings of the world; he is the first because he is the last, the goal, the *pleroma* containing all reality. One day the world will receive its perfect form from him, and will live only by him and his redemption. But the beginning is also dependent upon this goal; the whole world and the whole of time is suspended from him. "All things were created by him and for him" (Col. 1:16).

That is why carnal realities herald the spiritual ones which must of necessity follow, for they depend upon them. "If there is a psychic body, there is also a spiritual body . . . that which is psychic first, then that which is spiritual" (1 Cor 15:44, 46). The Old Testament heralded the coming of the later era as a shadow falls in front of a body: "All was a shadow of things to come, but the body [that this shadow outlined] is of Christ" (Col. 2:17).

The dead letter was the notification of the heavenly and complete reality, of the Lord who is life-giving Spirit (cf. 2 Cor 3). The Christ of glory is the prince of the past and of all lower realities, because he is lord of the world to come, possessor of all fullness, having primacy over all things by God's will (Col 1:18-19).

Lord of the Angels

There can therefore have been little understanding of the Christian mystery in those Judaizers who lessened the absolute lordship of Christ by setting angels (Col 2:18), thrones, dominations and principalities (1:16; 1:10, 15) between God and men.

Certainly, when the world was left to itself, those creatures who were the most powerful must have ruled it. Christ himself became lower than they (Heb 5:7); an evil spirit several times confronted him (Lk 4:2-13; 22:31; Jn 14:30), and a good angel came to strengthen him (Lk 22:43).

But by his resurrection, Christ "was made better than the angels" (Heb 1:4); "the almighty power worked in his resurrection" lifted him "above all principality and power, and virtue, and dominion, and every name that is named" (Ep 1:19, 21). Their dominion over the world was snatched from them. The whole angelic host was drawn into the Saviour's exaltation and fastened to his triumphal chariot: "And [God] despoiling the principalities and powers, he has exposed them confidently in open show, dragging them in triumph in Christ" (Col 2:15).

Who are these angels? Good angels or bad? St. Paul does distinguish between the two (2 Cor 11:14), but he is not concerned with the distinction here.

The angels made subject to Christ by the Father are heavenly beings appointed to govern the world, who direct the stars, who preside over the fates of nations by means of the civil authority (1 Cor 2:8; and perhaps Rom 13:1), who were mediators between God and Israel, and promulgated the Law. The Apostle shares this conception with the whole of Jewish apocalyptic writing.

Before Christ took the reins of the world, these powers held dominion over the universe; men were subject to them (Gal 4:3) and paid homage to them by obeying the laws promulgated by them. The Galatians and Colossians still thought they were subject to them, as also to Mosaic practices. The Colossians had been told that the Law had been given by angels, because they had lent their aid to promulgating it, and did not look with indifference upon disrespect to the Torah. But in Christ's death "the certificate of the debt" for which we were responsible and which placed us at the mercy of the powers' vengeance was wiped out by God: he stripped them of all hostile power by binding them to Christ's triumph (Col 2:14-15).

The Apostle is not concerned here with the goodness or badness of these angels, but with their function. His tone of hostility towards them was due to the attempts of innovators to continue to allot to them the part they had played. They were the rulers of a world which did not move in the orbit of Christ, principles of a way of life belonging to the past. They are contrasted with Christ in the same way as the Law, and the whole carnal order. Just as the flesh contradicted the spiritual economy by its weakness and often by its wickedness, so also did these powers, because they were of the order of "weak elements of the world", and because there were malevolent beings among their number. The latter, stripped of the autonomy of their power, represent disarmed adversaries in the triumph of Christ.

Christ's supremacy over the angelic powers is not, in the Apostle's mind, any mere marginal effect of the exaltation of the risen Christ; it is of its essence. Christ is the only Mediator and even the Church, since she works amid the world, can profess faith in Christ alone only if the powers that rule the world are also subject to this same head. There are now no intermediaries acting between God and man save Christ, or in Christ.

Christ's relationships with inanimate creation and with the angelic world do not follow the same pattern as his relationship with his Church. Some writers, carried away by their passion for synthesis, have thought that the whole of creation could be comprehended in the one concept of the Church with Christ at its head. "The body of Christ" would then take on fantastic dimensions, "becoming cosmic, and embracing spiritual and material creation in a vast whole". The universe of the angels, mankind rising up from the pedestal of the material creation, the whole cosmos, would thus constitute the multiform body over which Christ, as head, presides.

Several texts seem to place the angels, the Church and the world alongside each other in the same subordination to Christ. God re-establishes the whole universe under the one head (Eph 1:10); Christ is the head of the powers (Col 2:10), as of the Church (Col. 1:18); he fills all things (Ep 4:10), as well as the Church (Col 2:10).

The recapitulation of all things is certainly not limited to the establishment of the Church, but embraces the whole cosmos. But loftier than Christ's cosmic role is his role as "head of the body": "He raised him up from the dead, and set him on his right hand in the heavenly places, above all principality... He has subjected all things under his feet, and above all has made him head over the Church, which is his body" (Ep 1:20-23). To be head is a function of lordship; but in Christ's sphere of influence, one area is marked off from the rest—the Church. This role lifts him a degree above mere sovereignty over the angels; it is the highest rung in Christ's elevation. The Apostle surveys the honors of the risen Saviour (Ep 1:19-23); his seat at the right hand of God, his being lifted above the spirits, the subjection of all creatures beneath his feet—all these are, as it were, a staircase leading up to his function as head. Lordship of the cosmos is directed towards the dignity of being head of the Church.

The power of head of the faithful and the dominion over the angels derive from the same fullness of power, and the former rests upon the latter: "In him dwells all the fullness of the Godhead corporeally, and in him you are filled [function of the head of the Church], who is the head of all principality and power" (Col. 2:9-10). But the two titles, though most closely related, are not the same. The title of head, given to Christ, master of the powers, expresses supreme dignity and dominion; but the Church is the body to which Christ communicates his personality and his life.

Because the Church is identified with the Saviour's physical body the relationship between it and its head are unique and do not extend to the world of the angels. The point of identification between Christ and the Church lies in bodily human nature. In it the Saviour carried out his work of salvation, having accepted it in its carnal state that he might be numbered among a sinful race, and then having drawn it into the life of God. We are in turn made part of it and gain for our bodily being death to the flesh and divine life. Everything in St. Paul goes to show that salvation in Christ is prepared for human nature, and fitted to it. The purely spiritual creature may bathe in the influence of Christ, but does not penetrate into the focal point where the divine transformation takes place, Christ's bodily humanity.

Dominion over the powers and power over the faithful are thus on quite different levels, and this inequality is expressed in the way each is stated. The powers are subjected, put down by force, and are placed under Christ's feet by his victory. On the other hand, the Church is one with him, even if she is subjected to him. All proclaim that "Jesus Christ is Lord" (Ph 2:11), but the faithful call him familiarly and lovingly "our Lord"; they belong to him in a special sense, for he belongs to them.

REVIEW QUESTIONS
MATERIAL FOR COMMENT AND DISCUSSION

MURPHY-O'CONNOR—Christ and the presence of God. (Cf. also Stanley's "be imitators of me") Christ can be understood as God's personal presence in the world. He can also be seen as God's unique revelation and invitation to men. Discuss the thinking behind these statements. The Christ-event, a revelation about man. Comment. In the post-ascensional world how does God very often continue to communicate his presence, revelation and invitation to men? Relying so heavily on the human equation, this would seem to be a "chancy" method of divine communication. Nevertheless, speculate on the value contained in this manner of communication.

STANLEY—the last Adam. (Cf. also Giblin) What problem is Paul especially pointing to in his Christ-Adam comparison? Is it basically a problem of inheritance? Explain. What of special importance can the last Adam give that the first Adam cannot? Is it only the gift of immortality, or is it something much more? Contrast the disobedience of Adam and the obedience of Christ and the effects that flow from these different responses to God's will. Some lessons for us? How do we "identify" with the first and last Adam? To realize fully what God wants for us why is identification with the last Adam so necessary?

GRABNER-HAIDER—"Resurrection" and "Glorification". (Cf. also Cerfaux, Bruce, Audet) The New Testament is much concerned with eschatology. What generally is meant by this term and why is it so important to Christianity (and indeed to most great religions)? Are there actually two eschatologies in the New Testament? If so, comment on the role Christ plays in each. Why is the idea and event of Resurrection so religiously important? What does it say about God, about evil and death, about the human condition? Does the idea of "glorification" add much to the idea of "resurrection"? Christians believe in **bodily** resurrection. What does such a resurrection tell them about the inter-personal, community relationships and responsibilities of their present life in Christ? How do Christians know the process of personal resurrection and glorification is even begun in this life? Looking at the sad state of man and the world this seems to be saying too much. Comment.

AHERN—fellowship in his sufferings. Is suffering and God's assured power to bear it a sign of the messianic, eschatological age? Is this why we **rejoice** in it—because the "end time" has arrived and the gift to endure suffering is part of it? But wouldn't this belief about suffering be as much Jewish as Christian? Is there a new and distinctly Christian meaning Paul attaches to suffering as he matures in his understanding of the faith? Why **rejoice** in our weakness and sufferings? To many such an attitude seems quite unnatural, even masochistic. How would Paul answer this? Does Paul's theology of Baptism cast light on the theological connection between suffering and joy? Explain. Ahern talks about an "inner bond" between Christ and the Christian; does this "bond" help us to reconcile any seeming opposition between joy and suffering? In the Christian dispensation is there a social dimension to our sufferings? Comment.

DURRWELL—faith and the Christian mystery. (Cf. also Finley) Is the object of Christian faith simply that we believe in the God of the Old Testament, that he exists, that his love for men is somehow manifest in Christ? or for Paul should our faith in God be more specific than this? Explain. How especially is Christ situated in the mystery of Christian faith? Men cannot believe in God and surrender to him without the gift of faith, can they? But in a distracting, sceptical world isn't it very difficult to recognize even the offering of such a gift, and thus aren't many in danger of never finding God at all? Comment. Christian faith demands much of us, in fact that we somehow "die to self." Why must faith be this demanding? Aren't the majority of men justified in refusing (or at least hesitating) to give a faith so total? Speculate why God solicits selfless faith from people, knowing this kind of faith is hard to give and often not given.

FITZMYER—Paul and the law. (Cf. also Lyonnet) What is Paul talking about ordinarily when he uses the term law **(nomos)**? He says Christ has put an end to the law; is this idea original with Paul? But the law was **good.** It led to "life" and righteousness. Why would God want to put an end to it? What are some of the negative realities that came from the law? How could something "good" produce so many negative results and even become an **ally** of sin? Why in Paul's view do we find God's law such a difficult thing to obey? Theologically why has Christ any right or power to free us from a God-given law? Are we freed from the old law in view of taking on another, a **new** law? If so, wouldn't a new law like the old be just as difficult to obey? Comment. If in Christ we are free from the **old** law why does Paul still give us "laws" to keep?

LYONNET—gospel of freedom. (Cf. also Fitzmyer) If the old law does not justify us, what good can and did it do? If Christ frees us from the old law, are we then lawless? Comment. Why according to Lyonnet do we still need external codes even in our new freedom? What is the proper relationship between still usable external laws and the new interior law of love?

CERFAUX—Paul's eschatological message. (Cf. also Grabner-

Haider, Bruce, Audet) Again, what generally is meant by the term eschatology? Did the religion of the Jews and the pagans of Paul's time have an eschatology? Is eschatology "bad news" or "good news" or both? What kind of "news" was it for Christians and why? How did Paul express Christian eschatology in his early preaching (Thessalonica, Athens)? How did he express eschatology in his later, more mature writings? Does the mystery of the resurrection lend special substance to Christian eschatology? Comment. The dramatic images and expressions of Christian eschatology seem affected to us; why not to the ancients? Why is judgment normally associated with eschatology? If "Jesus saves" why need anyone be judged? Eternal life, the last phase of eschatology, seems an appealing concept to many, but to others it carries a connotation of endless boredom. How would Paul answer such cynicism? How does Cerfaux sum up the meaning of Christian eschatology?

BRUCE—Paul and immortality. (Cf. also Grabner-Haider, Cerfaux, Audet) Is the possibility of bodily resurrection a belief (or at least a hope) of pre-Christian Jews, including Paul? How did the Christ-event affect Jewish beliefs (or hopes) about bodily resurrection? Is there in Paul's view a necessary connection between Christ's bodily resurrection and ours? And yet isn't resurrection of the **soul** what really counts? In his early preaching when does Paul think bodily resurrection happens? What if we die before then? Paul between his epistles to the **Thessalonians** and the **Corinthians** seems to have matured in his thinking on this point and the **when** of bodily resurrection seems to change. What circumstances and what Christian belief could have led Paul to his later, more nuanced thinking on bodily resurrection? Is Paul in his later writings replacing a belief in "future" (i.e., final, Second Coming) resurrection with what is now called "realized" resurrection (i.e., resurrection-life realized somehow now before death, or at least as regards the body at the time of an individual's physical death)? Explain. Speculate about the value the mystery of bodily resurrection could have on our moral life.

AUDET—the risen spiritual body. (Cf. also Grabner-Haider, Cerfaux, Bruce) How does the term body, **sōma,** differ from the term for body, **sarx**? Why according to Paul would the body (**sōma**) **have** to be a part of the mystery of resurrection, and not **just** the soul? How can a corruptible body rise; or in Paul's (and Audet's) view is this what happens? If my corruptible body is in some way replaced, can it still be said that I am raised? Comment pro or con on Audet's conclusions drawn from this text of Paul.

SPICQ—reflections on Pauline morality. In Paul's view why is Christian morality different from other moral systems? Comment on the "new morality" as it relates to the expression "to be in

Christ." As Christians we could still describe morality in terms of "obedience to God" but the phrase would take on new and different meanings. What would they be? Does the "new morality" exclude any and all forms of servitude? Comment. Can the demanding quality of Christian behavior be understood in part at least from a theological inspection of one's baptism? Discuss. What does Spicq see as the "heart" of Pauline ethics? Christian morality is sometimes spoken of in terms of "imitation of Christ." Does this mean only that Jesus' conduct is the inspiration of our conduct or does it connote something a little more substantive than that? Explain. If Christian morality is to be understood as a vital and important part of a revolutionary gospel, such a morality must be based not only on new revelation but in a sense on a new metaphysics. Comment.

FINLEY—spirit of kenosis. (Cf. also Durrwell on faith) Why does Paul speak of Christ and Christianity in terms of an "emptying process"? Would an "attitude of surrender and giving" be another way of putting it? Discuss. Don't many reject Christianity on this general point? As they say, the Christian religion is not for them because they don't get anything out of it. How would Paul answer such a complaint in the light of the **kenosis** doctrine of his epistle to the Philippians?

GUILLET—discernment of spirits. Why is Paul worth listening to when he talks about the discernment of spirits? For the Jews could the law be considered a gift of the spirit? With it what could they discern about God and themselves? Why do Christians claim they **need** and **have** even greater gifts of the spirit, greater instruments for discernment than the law? Why are these realities called gifts? Do all Christians have these gifts; are all equally capable of spiritual discernment? Discuss. How do we recognize whether we have any of these "gifts" and whether our gifts are authentic, equipping us properly for the task of spiritual discernment? Comment on the various criteria for determining the authenticity of the Christian gifts: their fruitfulness; the edification factor; the possible "sign" aspect; the revelatory character; the elements of light and peace; the presence of fraternal love with its consequent sensitivity toward the needs of the brethren; a deepening of our relationship with Christ.

DE LA POTTERIE—the Christian and the world. In Paul's view did conversion to Christ require a spirit of detachment and separation from the world; should Christians be "worldly" or "otherworldly"? Discuss. Is Paul's "rule" on this point in a way revolutionary? Comment. Did Paul approve of slavery? Why, then, urge Christian slaves to remain slaves? Illustrate the saving implications of Paul's rule of "remaining as we are" from his words about marriage. What is de la Potterie trying to show from the "von Moltke" example? the "broken home" example?

EMERY—Paul and prayer. Does Paul in his prayer-life pray much as the prophets of the Old Testament did? Could his prayer be called unitive? Explain. Could the average Christian without benefit of Paul's conversion-experience presume to pray in like manner? Comment. Paul prays **"to God, through Jesus, in the Spirit."** Is this just another of the many "incomprehensible, enigmatic formulas" of the Christian faith, or is the phrasing meant to indicate the new, dynamic character of Christian prayer? Discuss the character of Christian prayer in light of this formula. Jesus is central to a Christian's prayer to the Father; he is our mediator. Does this mean he acts as one who stands between us and the Father; is he a go-between, or what? How does the benediction aspect of Christian prayer differ from the benediction aspect of Jewish prayer? In what sense should one presume to "ask" God for his needs according to Paul? How does Paul's thought on intercessory prayer perfect one's "moral sense"? How are love and prayer interrelated? According to Paul why is openness in prayer so important?

STANLEY—"be imitators of me." (Cf. also Murphy-O'Connor) Because of his repeated exhortation to "imitate me" many see Paul as a conceited competitor to Christ. Comment. Could this "counsel" actually be a "quasi-technical" term in Paul's gospel vocabulary? If so, what possible meanings could the phrase have, especially in the area of transmitting the gospel to others? For Paul, is **preaching** the only inspired way of "handing down" the gospel? Does Paul apparently see his personal history as being an extension or reflection of Christ, the Suffering Servant, and thus find it a legitimate subject for imitation? Comment. Who **particularly** are urged to be imitators of Paul; does this **specialized audience** throw some light on the meaning of the phrase? Does it perhaps speak to the pragmatic "needs" of this particular group of Christians? Why doesn't Paul simply urge his churches to imitate Christ and leave himself out of it? Could we possibly be dealing here with the idea contained in the Creed: "I believe in the one, holy, catholic and **apostolic** Church"? Can and should the average Christian in a sense be able to say with Paul: "imitate me"? Comment.

SCHNACKENBURG—Paul's idea of the Church. (Cf. also Durrwell on the Cosmic Christ) In Paul's view is the Church simply a more perfect form of Israel as the "people of God" or is it a radically new mystery? If the Church in a sense "replaces" the old Israel, how does Paul show this? The reconciliation of the Jews and the gentiles in the Church has an eschatological, even cosmic meaning for Paul; why so? (Cf. pp. 216-217; 223) The early Church, whose members reflected different cultural and religious backgrounds, naturally had an identity problem. Was Paul's teaching on "Christian unity" a help in solving this problem? In this connection indicate how Paul expresses the nature of the Church in contrast to

Israel's description of herself as a religious reality. What, for example, does the Pauline image of the Church as "temple" tell us about the nature and unity of the Church? the expression "the saints"? the concept of "excommunication"? With the image of the "body of Christ" Paul's theology of the Church reaches its highest point. Indicate what we learn about the nature and purpose of the Church from this image, especially what Christ does in and for his "body" as its "head" (pp. 219-220). Discuss how Christ in a mystery involving his earthly and risen bodies unites and reconciles Jews and gentiles with God (p. 222). How does this mystery of reconciliation relate to the cosmic supremacy of Christ? Speculate how Paul might answer the statement: "I accept Christ, but not the Church."

GIBLIN—ROMANS, cc. 1-8. (Cf. also Stanley's the last Adam) **Romans** sounds like a "mission-styled" letter. Why send a missionary letter to a well-established church? Why so much talk about Jewish law from an apostle appointed to preach salvation to the gentiles? Paul sometimes speaks of the gospel in terms of faith and power. Comment on the interrelation of the two terms. Paul seems very negative about pre-Christian gentile life; why? Why so much talk about God's **wrath**? What is it? Could the term be understood in a mythical sense? Speculate on possible mythical meanings. Paul seems equally negative about pre-Christian (and perhaps anti-Christian) Jewish life. What is he up to? Why so much effort to destroy a spirit of boasting? How does the example of Abraham show faith to be more important in God's sight than works? Christians, however, once converted, can boast in a different way. Why? Why speak of Jesus in relation to Adam? Why can "works" be said to be salutary **now** and not **before** our conversion? Why, though weak and beset with temptations, can Christians be confident in the hope of ultimate salvation?

DURRWELL—Christ, the cosmic Lord. (Cf. also Schnackenburg) Why is it not enough to say Jesus' death, resurrection and exaltation make him universal Lord of all men? How could the human Jesus be pre-existent, involved in the creation of all being, or is he? Does the mystery described as the "fullness of being" which Jesus gained as our exalted savior provide a clue to his pre-eminence even over the "cosmos"? How can a human savior be the reconciler and unifier of all being, even being which is superior to man? Certainly world history, marked by so much indifference or outright hostility to Christ, with men frequently allying themselves with supposed "higher powers" seems to contradict any possible lordly influence of Christ over the cosmos. Comment. Why would angels constitute a problem for the Christian audiences of the captivity epistles? How do the epistles "solve" the problem? "Cosmic Lord" and "Head of the Church"—which Christian title according to Durrwell seems more important and significant to Paul? and why?